GET YOUR MONEY!

GET YOUR MONEY!

How to Protect Your Business
Without Losing Your Customers

Eliot M. Wagonheim

HarperBusiness
A Division of HarperCollinsPublishers

HarperCollins books may be purchased for educational, business, or sales promotional use. For information please write: Special Markets Department, HarperCollins Publishers Inc., 10 East 53rd Street, New York, NY 10022.

FIRST EDITION

Designed by Nancy Singer Olaguera

Printed on acid-free paper.

ISBN 0-06-273716-3

00 01 02 03 04 ❖/RRD 10 9 8 7 6 5 4 3 2 1

► *For Nikki, without whom I would simply wither and die on the vine, and for David, who, while only three months old at the time of this writing, has shown me that toothless grins, all by their lonesome, can be things to live for. Like myself, this book is dedicated in its entirety to both of you.*

Contents

Acknowledgments

A small group of talented individuals deserve mention where "thank you" simply is not enough. Through the filter of their patience, skill, and commitment has been distilled whatever quality may be found in these pages.

As an adviser, critic, and sounding board, my friend and accountant, Allan Alperstein, gave of his time, experience, and considerable expertise. Our frequent project meetings and consultations provided me with much needed bright spots during some of the more tedious stretches in writing this book.

To Paula Smith, I present my sincere gratitude for her invaluable suggestions, for keeping me mindful of my true audience, and for demonstrating that it is actually possible to run a successful business in a competitive field and still be a wonderful person.

The words *thank you* are also not enough to express my appreciation for the contributions of Joan Denisch and Rebecca Sigler in compiling and formatting some of the more technical aspects of this book. Without their hours on phone and fax, this book would still be nothing more than a glimmer in my eye.

Finally, no acknowledgment would be complete without mention of my agents, Lynn Chu and Glen Hartley. For making this unknown, first-time author feel like their most important client and for teaching with patience and without condescension, they earned much more than could ever be realized by this work.

Introduction

If there is one guiding principle of this book, it is this: Businesses should not feel helpless when clients refuse to pay. They shouldn't have to choose between giving their money to a deadbeat customer or paying it to their lawyer. This book gives business owners the tools to fight for the money they're owed.

After all, the question is not whether your business has a debt collection problem. It does. Rather, the questions you should be asking concern the size of that problem and, more important, what you plan to do about it.

When you do work, you deserve to be paid everything you're owed . . . on time . . . every time. How far short your company falls from this standard constitutes the measure of your receivables problem. What you do to make up the difference measures your determination to benefit from the fruits of your own labor.

This guide to the art of getting paid is intended for those companies who refuse to give away any of their hard-earned money without a fight. Every time you write off a debt, or neglect to pursue one, whether it be from a bad check, an old account, or a deadbeat client, you give away your money. And these people—the ones you have given it to—are the ones who least deserve it because they took it without asking. **GET IT BACK!**

How to Make Your Business (Virtually) Deadbeat Proof

1
Preparing to Get Paid

Overview

Good business is an act in three parts: (1) Getting customers in the door, (2) doing the work or providing the merchandise once they're there, and (3) getting paid. Too many companies spend so much of their time and resources concentrating on 1 and 2 that they forget to pay attention to the very reason they are in business in the first place—to earn money. These companies—the ones that don't prepare to get paid—either survive on dumb luck or fail.

Preparing to get paid requires attention to five simple questions:

1. What do you have to do to get paid?

2. How are you going to get paid?

3. When are you going to get paid?

4. By whom are you going to get paid?

5. What happens if you don't get paid?

As a business owner, you should be able to answer these questions for each and every transaction. What's more, you should be able to confirm your answers without relying on the integrity and cooperation of the customer. If you can't . . . if you are unable to pick up any file or job folder and pull out documentation that would answer all five of these questions . . . you have work to do.

Deadbeat clients can damage or even destroy your company. This is true whether you are starting a new venture from scratch or working to improve an existing business. While it may be impossible to collect every penny from every customer every time, there are a number of steps you can and should take *now* to safeguard your hard-earned profits. This chapter focuses on how you can design (or redesign) your business to maximize your profits by protecting your bottom line from deadbeat clients.

▶ LEGAL ADVICE VS. THE REAL WORLD

Legal advice and real-world business are two separate roads that intersect only at odd and random points. Very often, a decision to travel one road exclusively requires abandonment of the other. Your goal as a business owner is to figure out a way to straddle both paths.

As an attorney, I can tell you that your company will best be protected from nonpaying clients by a fifteen-page single-spaced contract, written in Latin, by a team of attorneys for $25,000. Of course, the main thing this kind of contract will protect you from is having any clients to worry about in the first place. This is an illustration of where legal advice parts company with the real world.

In the real world, *you* must decide what will and what will not work for your business. Always keep in mind that all suggestions will not work for all businesses. Adapt the tips and comments below to your purposes. Keep the ones you like and discard the ones that don't apply. That way, you can ensure that you'll have the best of both worlds—effective legal protection *and* real-world solutions.

Conducting a ~~Legal Audit~~ Fire Drill

After years of advising clients to conduct a "legal audit," I finally realized that what I was really recommending was a fire drill. From our first days in school, we learn to plan for emergencies in order to survive them. Somehow, this insight gets lost as soon as we stop lining up in single file. It's time to relearn the lesson.

If you perform work or provide goods to your customers prior to receiving full payment in cash, you are, by definition, putting your company at risk. That's OK; such risk is often inevitable. Customers frequently insist on such accommodations as paying on account, seeing the work before making final payment, or writing personal and/or company checks to pay for goods and services. If you cannot eliminate risk by doing a 100 percent cash business or insisting on full payment in advance (and few businesses have this luxury), you can limit your risk by adopting some sound business policies. Your first step is to conduct a fire drill.

Try this exercise: Choose any of your customer files at random. Now with the five questions in mind, assume that your customer will lie.

- "We never agreed to pay that amount."

- "We agreed to pay only if you completed the work by January 1, and you were late."

- "You never finished the job. You were supposed to do five other things that you never did. Consequently, we don't owe you a thing."

- "We're not the one that has to pay. You have to get it from John Smith Limited Partnership West. We're John Smith, Inc."

Assume you will hear any or all of these things or make up your own. Either way, with these assumptions in mind, look at your file. Does your file back up your claim? If you're like most companies, your paperwork leaves holes you could drive a truck through. And trust me, when it comes to loopholes, nonpaying customers and their lawyers are great truck drivers.

The lack of paperwork does not necessarily mean that you won't get paid. Even if you have to go to court, poor documentation does not always result in an adverse verdict. What it does mean, however, is that it's your word against your customer's. At that point, it's a toss-up whom the judge will believe.

From where I'm sitting, when you've done the work or supplied the materials, a toss-up is unacceptable. Your job as a business owner is to push the odds of winning in your favor. In other words, to stack the deck.

▶ **TRUST IN GOD BUT LOCK YOUR CAR**

"Assume that my customers will lie to me?" Believe me, having given my "fire drill" lecture before enough audiences, I know how foreign and even offensive that notion can be. So let me state here for the record (do you know any nonlawyers who actually say "for the record"?) that I believe most people to be honest. Unless shown otherwise, I assume that each new person I meet is a person of integrity. That assumption should not, however, prevent one from preparing for the occasional cheat.

There is an old saying that any ounce of dishonesty in a person's heart will make its appearance while playing golf. I think it's more true in business. There is no more desperate creature than a businessperson with poor cash flow. When pushed to the wall, even honest people will sometimes seek refuge in the gray areas of a transaction. That is why I embrace the philosophy best summed up by the saying "Trust in God, but lock your car." Believe the best of people, but prepare for the worst.

The exercise you just completed is the first step in a legal audit. A legal audit is a tip-to-tail review of the way your company conducts business. In the sections below, we will review and discuss the areas you should consider in your own legal audit.

Creating a Payment Policy

A payment policy is not a wish list. Every business owner would like to receive 100 percent cash on the barrelhead as soon as the customer places the order. Unless you're running a grocery store, this simply is not going to happen. What's more, if you draft a payment policy containing this requirement, either you will lose more customers than you keep or your payment policy will be honored only in the breach.

Instead, when you create a payment policy, your first priority is to ensure that the terms you have settled upon are realistic for your type of business. By that I mean you should consider what your customers will and will not find acceptable. Many businesses require a deposit prior to beginning work, with final payment due upon delivery. In others, customers may need (or simply insist upon) a little time to look over the merchandise or use the services before payment is due. Either way, the keys are, first, to get it in writing and, second, to show that you mean it.

Get It in Writing . . . Without Offending Your Customers

Whether your business works best by preparing estimates, purchase orders, account agreements, or simply letters of confirmation, you should *always* do your best to get something in writing from your customer that spells out the terms of your agreement. Now, as I said earlier, I am not urging you to hand your customer a fifteen-page single-spaced contract written in Latin and drafted by an high-priced lawyer. Instead, you should simply have something in writing that specifies:

1. What you are promising to do.

2. When you are promising to do it.

3. What your customer agrees to pay.

4. Who will be responsible for paying you.

5. When your customer will pay.

6. What your rights are if your customer doesn't pay.

New Customers

If your new customer plans to make purchases on account or is asking you to extend credit by providing services or merchandise before receiving full payment, he or she should be required to sign an agreement acknowledging your payment policies. As will be shown a bit later on, this acknowledgment can be combined with an account application, estimate, purchase order, or questionnaire in which the customer is asked to provide you with certain basic information.

How do you explain this information-gathering exercise to a customer who finds it intrusive? One word—"policy." You'd be surprised to find how many sophisticated, even argumentative people back down in the face of "policy."

You can almost hear them thinking, "Well, I think it's unreasonable, but if it's POLICY, I guess there's nothing I can do." OK, so it's a herd mentality, but take advantage of it. After all, it's your money.

Existing Customers

Existing customers are another story. Customers who have been with you for a while know that the execution of commercial account agreements is not "policy." And as we all know, a repeat customer is a very precious commodity. These are the customers that have been doing business with you long enough to simply call you with a new order or request and have it honored without the hassle of completing all that paperwork. It would not do to offend these people.

So how do you do it? Once you've decided to make changes in the way you do business, how do you approach your current customers and ask them to sign something without telling them you no longer trust them?

My clients ask this question all the time. Not a week goes by when a client going through this process doesn't tell me how risky it would be to approach these customers with a sudden request that they sign a contract after all this time of handshake deals.

Certainly a valid point, but by no means the determinative one. There are a number of ways to explain the new policy to these customers. They fall into two broad categories: (1) adding convenience and (2) shifting the blame. We'll take the fun one first—shifting the blame:

1. *Blame it on the lawyer.* ("I'm sorry, Jack, but my lawyer's insisting that I get agreements signed by everyone.")

2. *Blame it on your banker or accountant.* Discuss how your banker and/or accountant are now requiring that you pay more attention to documenting your business relationships in order to properly value your business and/or obtain needed financing.

If neither of these works for you, try this:

1. *Explain that you are streamlining procedures.* After all, this one agreement in the customer's file will enable anyone in your

company to approve a telephone or fax order without having to run it by you first. This is especially true if you're getting bigger and you can no longer ensure that your customer will reach the same person every time he or she places an order. Rather than relying upon being able to recognize the customer by voice, your representatives can look in the file and see that the customer is cleared to place orders by phone.

Of course, there's always a fourth option: Give them my phone number. I'll explain it to them.

Policy Options

Your payment policy should be designed with two goals in mind: (1) to force the customer to make a commitment to the order and (2) to protect your bottom line.

Advance Deposits (or "Getting Them to Put Their Money Where Their Mouth Is")

Although it would be nice to get full payment in advance, it is frequently impractical even to request it. Instead, the utility of an advance deposit is often more psychological than financial in that it makes the customer commit to the project. You see, no matter how interested or excited your customer may seem at the outset, his or her enthusiasm may wane somewhere down the road for reasons unrelated to you or your performance. Nothing binds people . . . nothing commits businesses . . . like money.

A second reason behind advance deposits is that they become the customer's ratification of the agreement. As we will discuss later, should a dispute arise, a piece of paper that shows the full price for the project and documents the customer's down payment is an invaluable tool in proving that the customer accepted the terms of the contract.

Final Payment Due upon Receipt

This is a wonderful policy, and I can count on one hand the number of business that successfully and consistently implement it. Most of the time, customers require some time to review the product or simply insist on the courtesy of a thirty-day float. That's fine; extending these accommodations is often the cost of doing business. But remember, if you know deep down that you will never be able to obtain final payment upon delivery, don't express it as a policy. Creating a policy that you know will be violated on a daily basis undermines your credibility with both your customers and your staff.

Payment Due in X Days

By far the most prevalent way of doing business, this arrangement places several burdens upon the business offering it:

1. Make the customer understand when payment is due.

2. Present the customer with a written invoice or statement upon completion of your work or delivery of your product clearly stating the payment due date and amount.

3. If payment is not due for more than thirty days (some businesses allow their customers to stretch payments out to ninety days and beyond), send the customer a reminder no less than ten days before the due date.

4. Send an invoice to the customer if payment is not received on time.

5. Track accounts receivable as detailed in the following chapters.

Interest Charges

If you don't charge interest, you are doing nothing more than giving your late-paying customers an interest-free loan. Conversely, charging interest on overdue balances is a fundamental way many businesses convince their customers that making timely payments is in their best interest (no pun intended). Equally as important, it enables companies to control the financial risk of extending credit. I wholeheartedly recommend it.

Most businesses charge 18 percent per year (or $1\frac{1}{2}$ percent per month) on all outstanding balances.

Building Your File

The purpose of the exercise we discussed in the legal audit/fire drill section was to emphasize the absolute need for documentation. If, in completing that exercise, you found that you did not have the paperwork to prove the terms of your agreement with the customer to an objective third party (such as a judge), you should make some changes. Your first step should be the creation of an informational form to be completed before you begin work or fill an order for *any* customer who's not paying in full at the time of the transaction. Whether you call it an account application, Section 1 of a contract, or simply a questionnaire, you should always know who you are dealing with . . . and get it in writing.

▶ IT'S ELEVEN O'CLOCK. DO YOU KNOW WHO YOUR CLIENT IS?

More times than I care to count, a business owner or manager will walk into my office and ask me to file suit to collect a substantial amount of money owed the company, only to be caught up short by my first question: "Who owes you the money?" Amazingly, even successful and well-established businesses forget to ask who the customer is.

It sounds so simple, but it's not. The same person may do business with you under several different corporate names. You think you're dealing with one person, but really, when it comes to getting paid, you may be dealing with several different companies with similar names like American Development, Inc., American Development West, Inc., American Development, Limited, and American Development Corporation.[1] Now who do you look to for payment?

Bottom line: You should be the one deciding who you are doing business with. Take control by insisting that your customers identify themselves in writing.

---

[1] Please note that these names are fictional and are not intended to portray any actual corporate or business entities. Any resemblance between one or more of these names and that of an existing business is purely coincidental.

How to Create an Account Application

Explanation and Overview

Before extending credit, have the prospective customer fill out an account application. Once you have this, you can decide if you trust the customer enough to extend the credit he is requesting. After all, buying on credit is a privilege you extend to your customers. It is not their God-given right. The following sections review the information you should require.

Account applications serve two purposes: First, they provide you with information on your customer. Second, by signing at the bottom, the customer acknowledges the terms and conditions that will govern the account should the two of you do business.

We will discuss the terms and conditions of a well-drafted account agreement a bit later on. For now, we will review the information your business should have on *every* customer you deal with.

Basic Information

The account information sheet can be as long or as brief as you choose, but remember the more information you obtain, the better. I do recognize, however, that many clients would balk at filling out a seven-page form and that you might lose business if you insisted on it.

Consequently, to help create a form that is right for your business and your clientele, I have listed below the types of information that would be most helpful to you, both in sizing up the customer and in collections, should you ever have to go to court to collect on the bill.

Name of Customer

Who can you hold responsible for paying you? This does not necessarily mean the person filling out the application. Rather, the name in this blank is the person or company you will have to file suit against if push comes to shove and you have to go to court.

Individual

The differences between relying on a company for payment and looking to an individual are substantial. While we will review those differences in other chapters, you should take this opportunity at the very outset of the relationship to make a note of the type of customer with whom you are now considering conducting business.

Required Information

I recommend you obtain the following information from an individual customer:

- Address (current and former if customer has lived there less than three years).

- Does the customer own or rent?

- Date of birth.

- Spouse's full name (if applicable).

- Occupation.

- Employer's name and address (current and former if with current employer less than three years).

- Social Security number.

- Driver's license information—number and state of issuance.

- Name, address, and telephone number of closest relative not living with the customer.

- Home and work telephone numbers.

If the Customer Wants to Pay by Personal Check

In addition to the information listed above, if the customer wants to be able to pay you by personal check, have him provide you with the following:

- Name and address of the customer's financial institution.

- Checking and savings account numbers.

- Optional: a voided check for attachment to the account application.

Business

A company is an artificial being. It can't be placed in custody. On its own, it has no conscience, morals, or sense of honor, yet corporations are often your best (even your only) customers. Consequently, it is imperative that you get some information before adding another one to your customer list.

Years in Business

How long has the applicant been in business *under the same name?* Longevity means something. It may not be determinative of good character, but there is a certain comfort in knowing that your customer has a history and is unlikely to disappear in the next five minutes.

Type of Business

Often corporate names are generic or nondescriptive. Find out what the applicant does. There are a number of good reasons to ask this question. First, knowing your customer's business could give you valuable cross-selling opportunities. Second, should you ever have to locate a wayward customer, knowing his business could give you some leads through trade organizations or professional groups. Finally, it is always a good idea to get a handle on the direction your customer base is heading. That way, you can adapt your business to its needs and continue expanding your customer base in the areas you find most profitable.

Structure

Is the applicant a partnership, corporation, limited liability company, or perhaps a sole proprietor? Your decision to extend credit could depend on the answer. Why? Because the answer will determine who you can look to for payment. If the customer is a sole proprietor or partnership, the individuals behind the business are personally responsible for its debts. If the customer is a corporation, LLC, or similar entity, you may wish to consider requiring a personal guarantee from one or more of the principals depending on how long the company has been in business, how well financed the company is, and your level of familiarity with the company.

Officers/Directors/Owners

These are the people behind the company name. Remember how I said that a company, in and of itself, has no conscience or sense of honor? It is the management of the company that endows it with these qualities . . . or not. Make it a point to know the people with whom you are doing business.

On those occasions when you are doing business with a national or international company, at least make sure to obtain the names of local management. There should always be a person you have identified as someone you can call should a problem arise with the account.

Primary Contact

Get the name of a real, live person. Never allow yourself to be placed in the position of having to call "accounts payable" or having to ask for "the office manager." You should send all invoices and direct all inquiries to a primary contact in the applicant's organization. Not only will you get faster action, but you will also have a real person to talk to if things go awry.

Address—Principal and Branch Office

While it's always important to know the location of your applicant's headquarters as well as where it conducts business in your area, the information is especially significant when dealing with out-of-state businesses.

Telephone and Fax Numbers

I'm not just talking about the numbers to the main switchboard and the central fax machine. Make sure you ask for the telephone and fax numbers used by your primary contact. This includes extensions and direct numbers.

E-mail Address

Combining the utility of phone and fax, an E-mail address allows you to instantly transmit a message or inquiry directly to your contact. Even if your company is not currently using E-mail, get the information. The time is coming.

Trade References

Whenever I recommend that my clients ask prospective customers for trade references, they inevitably question the usefulness of the information. After all, applicants will always provide the names of people who view them favorably. In other words, you'll never call an applicant's reference only to hear, "That guy'll stiff you every time. You have to be nuts to do business with him!"

What you will hear, however, is how long your applicant has been doing business with them and how much credit they've extended. Just as important is the fact that your applicant is able to supply trade references—not his uncle, grandfather, cousin, or best friend, but real, honest-to-goodness trade references. (The normal number is three.) Besides, if you ever have to come looking for him down the road, those references are the first people you should call.

Requested Credit Limit

How much credit is your new customer requesting? While it is your job, not your customer's, to determine the appropriate credit limit, this question does serve a purpose. Having your applicant state the amount will not only provide you with a guide as to his expectations but will also allow you to limit your exposure to loss when your new customer approaches its self-imposed limit.

Update Your Paperwork

The benefits of the account application do not end once the applicant has been accepted as a customer. The application is the first place you'll turn once a problem develops and you need information on your customer. It has contact names, phone and fax numbers, and addresses for your use. Keep them up to date. Look over your customer files annually and call to update the information. What's more, if a customer comes back to you after an absence of more than a year, have him review the existing application to check for inaccurate information, even if you have already approved him as a customer.

How to Create a Commercial Account Agreement

Purpose of Agreement

The account application and the account agreement are two sides of the same coin. Through the application, the applicant tells you why you should accept him as a customer. In the agreement, usually printed on the reverse of the application or, at the very least, attached as part of the same document, you advise the applicant of the terms and conditions that will govern the relationship.

Obviously, you are the judge of whether you need to draft an account agreement. After all, these agreements are not necessary for all businesses. Use your average invoice as a guidepost. If you sell low-cost items and your average invoice is $50 to $100, an account agreement may be more trouble than it's worth. In this case, you may want to require an agreement only for unusually high purchases. Conversely, the more money involved in each transaction, the more necessary an account agreement is, even for one-time customers.

Provide Terms of Repeat Jobs

Repeat customers are the bread and butter of many businesses. These customers will not look kindly upon the delay and inconvenience of having to sign a new contract for each new transaction. Frequently, a repeat customer just wants to call, request action, and wait for results. While you understandably have an interest in providing this kind of service, you must also ensure that your business is protected. A commercial account agreement allows your customers to sign one agreement that will govern all transactions. You will not have to restate your rates, billing policies, and so forth every time you're given a new assignment. All you have to do is confirm the goods or services particular to the new request and you're off and running.

Provide Terms of One Transaction

Even one-time customers should sign an account agreement for two reasons. First, you never know when a one-time customer will come back. Second, just because the customer may not be coming back doesn't mean that you shouldn't have all the protection you can get on this one transaction.

Recommended Elements

As is shown on the model account agreement in the appendix, I recommend you include the following elements in your account agreements.

Account Number

Every customer should have its own account number. Why? Let's go back to the example of American Development Corporation discussed in the box on page 11. If your contact has signed your account agreement and has been given an account number, it doesn't matter how many difference corporations he may have. Whenever you are requested by that customer to perform additional services or fill another order, you simply send your letter of confirmation as shown in the appendix, confirming: (1) what you are supposed to do; and, (2) that the terms of account #XXXXX will apply.

Personal Guarantee

This is number one on my wish list. What's more, if you are unfamiliar with the customer, a personal guarantee should also be number one on *your* list of requirements. The reason is simple: It takes a filing fee of less than $100 plus completion of a form you can find in any good office-supply store to create a corporation. It doesn't take a large bank account, a good credit history, or even a steady stream of income.

For example, if Eliot M. Wagonheim, Inc., applies for credit from your business, you may have no idea how much money or income Eliot M. Wagonheim, Inc., has available to pay you. It may turn out that when payment is due, Eliot M. Wagonheim, Inc., simply folds up shop and disappears, leaving you holding the bag for $200, $500, even several thousand dollars. And make no mistake about it, despite the fact that the company bears the name of a person, that "Inc." means that you won't be able to look to the individual to pay a corporate debt absent a personal guarantee. Bottom line: You want that personal guarantee to be able to look to a person for payment, not just a company.

A request for a personal guarantee is not going to be heeded in every (or possibly even in most) situations. You won't get the CEO of Wal-Mart Stores, Inc. or Sony to sign a guarantee, but if you want to do business with them (or more commonly, if they want to business with you), you'll accept the business without the guarantee.

The decision to insist on a guarantee as a prerequisite to working with a customer is a business judgment call that only you can make. Nevertheless, I recommend seeking a guarantee from an unfamiliar customer or a customer who, through slow payments or missed payments, has caused you some reason to be concerned.

▶ "IF YOU DON'T HAVE FAITH IN YOUR COMPANY, WHY SHOULD I?"

Brian Green runs his own commercial insurance agency. He provides insurance for businesses of every shape and size from accounting firms to cleaning services.

One of Brian's largest customers is a construction company. Over the years, Brian had become friends with the president of the company, and he had come to rely upon the fact that the company would always make good on its payments, even if it tended to run a little behind from time to time.

Not too long ago, the company had begun to drop even further behind in its payments. The president called Brian and explained that certain projects had been delayed. The president asked if Brian could extend him a few months' worth of credit so that the company could straighten out its cash flow.

The company had always been a solid customer and Brian valued the relationship, but honoring the request meant over $10,000 of additional exposure to Brian's company if his client went under. The question was: "How could Brian honor the relationship while protecting his company?"

Brian decided to agree to extend the extra credit *IF* the president of the company would sign a personal guarantee. He told the president that his agency could stand behind the company only as long as the president, personally, was willing to do so. Brian reasoned that, if the risk was too great for the company's president to take, it was, by definition, too great for Brian.

Bottom line: The president agreed, the company did make good on payment after three months, and the relationship between the construction company and Brian's agency continued to prosper.

Permission to Contact Debtor

There is an alarming trend in state legislatures throughout the country to endow debtors with the capacity to file suit against creditors for "emotional distress" with frighteningly little proof of actual harassment or real distress. Many state laws prevent creditors from contacting a debtor at work without the debtor's express permission. (Obviously, this relates to personal debts. If the customer *is* the business, you can always contact it to request payment.)

As you might expect, once the customer falls behind, there is little hope that he will grant permission to contact him at work or that he will accept the call at home. Although the dust hasn't settled on the effect of these new laws, I have advised all of my clients to add a provision to their account agreements in which the customer consents, in advance, to allow contact at work. This is especially important to companies whose customers are individuals rather than other businesses.

Waiver of Harassment Countersuit

The judge may not allow you to enforce the waiver, but hey . . . it's worth a shot.

Waiver of Jury Trial

Jury trials are expensive and time-consuming. Worse, once one side requests a trial by jury, there is precious little the other side can do to avoid it. That's why debtors find the filing of jury trial requests to be such a popular and successful tactic. Once the creditor sees what an ordeal collecting on the account is going to be, he often gives up or settles for pennies on the dollar. A waiver of a jury trial built into your account agreements can take this kind of legal blackmail away from the debtor.

Jurisdiction

The debtor should always agree that the courts in your home state and possibly even your home county will have jurisdiction in the event of a dispute. This is especially crucial for those companies conducting business across state lines. In essence, this is one more provision designed to make collection as convenient for you as possible.

Payment Terms

When is payment due? Ten days? Thirty days? Upon receipt of the invoice? Stating your terms once in the account agreement will save you the trouble of repeating them every time your customer places an order.

Interest

If you fail to charge interest on overdue accounts, you are providing interest-free loans to your late-paying and nonpaying clients. I've said it before and I'll say it again: You *must* provide your customers with an incentive to pay you. Finance charges *are* that incentive. You can always decide to waive the charges, perhaps as part of a settlement, but you should use the account agreement to reserve the option of assessing the charges.

▶ HOW ABOUT IF WE LOAN YOU THE MONEY AT 3 PERCENT BELOW PRIME?

I wouldn't have thought it necessary to mention this if I didn't see it on a client's account agreement. "Interest at the rate of 6%

per annum will be assessed on all balances unpaid after 30 days."
Six Percent!?! What a deal! Any customer with limited resources
and a command of math would use his money to pay almost anybody—banks, credit cards, department stores—before paying my
client. Why? Because my client is giving him a loan at 6 percent
interest. Needless to say, we changed that to 18 percent rather
quickly, but the appearance of 6 percent in my client's agreement
warrants its appearance here.

*Bottom line: If you are going to charge interest, make it a penalty
your customers would just as soon avoid. I recommend the standard
18 percent per annum (or 1½ percent per month).*

Attorney's Fees

Certainly the most expensive aspect of litigation, helping people
avoid attorney's fees is my primary motivation for writing this book
(and most people's motivation for buying it). Nevertheless, sometimes a debt is too large to be considered a small claim in which a
company can represent itself without an attorney. Your best protection in such a situation is a provision in your account agreement
that will allow you to collect reimbursement for reasonable attorney's fees from the debtor if you prevail.

Limit of Liability

No matter how important the project, you should never put your
entire business at risk. Sometimes the damages resulting from poor
performance can dwarf the amount the customer originally paid.

If the photographer works the entire wedding with the lens cap
on; if the advertisements for a major promotion are sent out with
the wrong date or phone number; or even if a skier hits an unexpected hazard that costs him his whole vacation after losing an
argument with a tree, the resultant damages can do a lot more than
ruin your whole day. This is where a limit of liability comes in.

Your account agreement should provide that the most a customer may recover from you due to poor or incomplete performance

is a refund. Period. End of story. Think that's unusually harsh? Check the contract for any commercial photographer. Chances are you'll find that the damages that can be recovered are limited to either the cost of the film or, perhaps, the amount of money already paid to the photographer—not the cost of the wedding.

Check the back of the lift ticket next time you go skiing. I'll bet you'll find a limit-of-liability provision that explains that skiing is an inherently dangerous activity and that the damages that may be recovered in a lawsuit are limited to a refund of the lift ticket price.

A limit of liability is perhaps the most important provision you can have in your agreement. Its purpose is to place a limit on your exposure to a suit by your customer. Many agreements provide that the most a disgruntled customer can recover is a refund of money already paid. No matter what limit you set, if a judge allows the provision to be enforced, you may wind up saving yourself tens of thousands of dollars with this one paragraph.

Nondischargeability

Sophisticated, world-weary businesspeople know: If the customer goes into bankruptcy, kiss your money good-bye. Well, not necessarily. Allow me to explain.

Bankruptcy is a system that affords a qualifying business or person protection from creditors. In most cases general, unsecured creditors (e.g., those without the security of collateral) wind up being paid either a small percentage of the debt or nothing at all. Either way, the debt in question will be considered "discharged" and the creditor will not be able to pursue the debtor for the remaining unpaid balance.

What most people don't realize is that businesses, with few exceptions, can select certain debts that are not dischargeable in bankruptcy. In effect, the businesses agree in advance that they will not request protection from or discharge of the selected debts even if they file for bankruptcy.

Sure, your debt may still wind up in second place to tax liens and the like, but you'd certainly be well ahead of all those other creditors without this provision in their back pockets. Note, however, that this will be enforceable only for business debts. If your customer is a consumer and the transaction is for personal rather than business purposes, such as the purchase of a television or car repair services, you will not be able to use this provision.

For a more detailed explanation of consumer versus commercial debts, see pages 135–139.

No Modification

When backed up against a wall, a debtor will often claim that he was promised extended payment terms, a waiver of interest, additional services or merchandise, or some other change from the agreement you presented in court. That's where a "no modification" provision comes in. As long as you can point to a provision in your agreement that invalidates any modifications of your agreement except those made in writing signed by both parties, the debtor's argument should fall on deaf ears.

Say What You Mean . . . Mean What You Say

All successful relationships operate within certain defined rules. Nowhere is this more true than in business. Creating the right payment policies—even getting your customer's signature on the bottom line—gets you only halfway there. You must enforce the rules you make. In this respect, running a business is no different than raising children (or so I'm told). If your customers learn that you will not enforce your policies, you may as well not have created policies at all.

If You Can't/Don't Have an Account Agreement

A signed account agreement (with a personal guarantee) tops my list of recommendations. Unfortunately, it is sometimes either not possible or, at the very best, impractical to insist on one. You should still document your file with the terms of the deal.

In General

The way to win a court case is to convince the judge to decide the dispute on your terms. So, if you don't want or don't have an account agreement, write down what you consider the terms of the agreement to be, send the document to the customer, and put the burden on him to object. Anything you send to the customer can serve this purpose.

In essence, if you show the judge that you advised the customer of the terms you considered applicable, and the customer failed to object until he found himself on the wrong side of a lawsuit, you'll have won most of the battle before the customer even gets a chance to present a defense.

The sections below demonstrate the various types of confirmatory documentation you can use to memorialize the terms of the deal, even without the customer's signature.

Invoices

"Payment is due within thirty (30) days of receipt. Interest at the rate of 18 percent per annum ($1\frac{1}{2}$% per month) will be assessed on all overdue balances." This statement at the bottom of your invoices will entitle you to claim finance charges on overdue balances in most states, even without an agreement to this term signed by the customer.

One note of caution: You cannot print two pages of terms at the bottom of the invoice and expect the judge to enforce all of the terms in your favor just because the customer failed to protest. Many states, for example, require the customer's signature on an agreement before assessing attorney's fees and the costs of collection against the customer. You can try to get your attorney's fees back or enforce a limitation of liability without the customer's signature on the bottom line, but you'll probably lose.

Estimates

Estimates differ from invoices in that they are delivered to the customer ahead of time rather than after the fact. Consequently, with the words "this estimate is subject to the following terms," you can establish the same provisions that would be present had the customer signed your account agreement. Of course, I recommend having the customer sign the estimate in the first place if he or she is actually placing the order, but in the absence of a signature, you will still be allowed to enforce most, if not all, of the terms.

Letter of Confirmation

By far the most basic, and most overlooked, of all business tools, the letter of confirmation can and should play a vital role in the way you do business. In short, it is the last word, and in business, just as in sibling rivalry, getting the last word is key.

Once you receive a purchase order, even if the products and the prices are stated exactly right, it is doubtful that the customer would include a statement reflecting your payment terms. Accordingly, send a letter of confirmation like that shown in the appendix at the end of this chapter.

A letter of confirmation not only restates the deal in your terms but serves as a reminder to you of exactly what the deal *is*. Most important, it is the last piece of paper in the file that documents the agreement. Thus, it is the first piece of paper a judge will look at in deciding the outcome of a case. I've included a model letter of confirmation at the end of this chapter just in case you would like to adapt it to your business practices.

What to Look for in the Other Guy's Contract

If you stay in business long enough, you will have to sign (or consider signing) someone else's contract. In fact, signing someone else's contract is a way of life for many businesses, such as construction subcontractors. As I always tell my clients, the key to making a good decision about signing someone else's contract is to S.T.O.P.

*S*cope of Work

What are you being asked to do? Make sure that the scope of work or list of materials spelled out in the contract matches *exactly* your understanding of the agreement. Do not rely upon what you and the customer may have orally agreed. The written word *always* controls in the event of a dispute. If you think you'll regret obligating yourself to the terms in that agreement, or if you doubt whether you can live up to it, don't sign.

As a small aside, every time I hear that a client of mine signed an objectionable contract after hearing the other person say, "Aw, hell, we never enforce *that*," I increase my hourly rate. (My partner, Mitch Kearney, describes this as a "stupid tax.")

*T*ime of Performance

When will you have to perform? What are the deadlines? Will you be penalized if you're late? Don't sign unless these terms are spelled out to your satisfaction in the contract.

*O*ther Obligations

Is your contract being held subject to the terms of any other documents? "All work to be performed in accordance with the plans and specifications." "This contract is subject to the terms of the agreement between 'X' and 'Y.'" These are by far the most dangerous statements in any agreement, yet they appear every day, particularly in construction contracts. If your contract is going to be subject to the terms of any other documents or agreements, check them out. You may not like what you see. Bottom line: Make sure you understand the entire deal before agreeing to become part of it.

*P*ayment

How much are you going to get paid and when? What rights does the customer have to delay or limit payment? These questions must be addressed and resolved to your satisfaction before any contract passes muster.

Sizing up a New Customer

Determine in advance what aspects of a prospective customer would satisfy your comfort level. Is a steady pulse your only requirement (reminiscent of my dating history), or will you require that the customer demonstrate that he or she has been a resident of your state for at least one year before you extend credit? Must he or she have an in-state driver's license and/or be employed? These are decisions you *can* make. My advice: Whatever your decision, explain your policies and the reasoning behind them to all applicants *before* they fill out the account application. This will not only save them some embarrassment, but it might save you a lawsuit as well.

Performing Your Due Diligence

In addition to reviewing the account application and taking the information at face value, you may want to dig a bit deeper, depending upon the amount of credit you will be extending. In other words, you may want to perform what is known as your "due diligence."

What Can You Look At?

You can look at anything the applicant gives you permission to examine. References, credit history, financial statements, and other financial and historical records are all fair game. Now, it is the rare applicant who will provide you with carte blanche to contact bankers and accountants and examine private financial records for an average transaction. Moreover, you may lose a customer if you insist on seeing material you know is far more detailed than is justified by your particular transaction.

At the very least, however, your account application should contain an acknowledgment from the applicant that you have permission to contact references and run a credit check. For information on how this section should be phrased, please refer to the model account application in the appendix on page 32.

State Agencies

To conduct business, companies (corporations, LLCs, LLPs, etc.) must register with the appropriate state agency. Consequently, these agencies are great sources of information. With one phone call, you can find out how long your applicant has been in business, whether it is even registered to conduct business in the first place, and the location of its principal office.

We have included a chart of state agencies and phone numbers in the appendix to this chapter. Make the call.

Credit-Reporting Agencies

Dun & Bradstreet, Moody's, and Standard & Poor's report and provide ratings on creditworthiness for businesses and corporations. These services provide ratings on demand to subscribing members. If your business routinely extends credit to commercial purchasers, or if you have a small number of large accounts, you may want to seriously consider subscribing to these services.

On the other hand, if your business does not warrant the cost of subscribing to these services, check with your public library. Many libraries offer access to these services at no cost. Although going to the library may be somewhat inconvenient, it is much more convenient than losing a lot of money to a company with a lousy payment record.

You Must Apply Your Policies Across the Board

When considering extending credit to a customer, you *may* use financial information, but you *may not* use a person's religion, gender, creed, color, or national origin as a factor in your decision. While it is reasonable that you require the customer to be employed or to have established local residency for a certain period of time before you allow that person to open up an account, you *MUST* apply these policies to everyone.

This sentiment not only represents the views of the author (although it most assuredly does), but it is also the law. Should you apply your policies in a discriminatory manner, you may become liable for stiff penalties, a discussion of which is well beyond the scope of this book. If you are not sure whether your policies are discriminatory, I strongly urge you to consult with your attorney immediately.

If the Applicant Doesn't Meet Your Requirements

Yes, you can simply insist on cash up front if the applicant does not meet your requirements, but my advice would be to allow the customer to prove his or her creditworthiness. You may want to consider establishing a "starter account" with more limited credit than your general accounts. For example, a starter account may allow the customer to charge up to $200 on account. After a certain amount of time, if you find the customer to be worth the risk, turn the starter account into a general account.

Another possibility is asking the customer for a blank charge slip. You've undoubtedly seen this practice in action at rental car companies and video stores. There is no reason why you can't enact the same policy in your business for that extra measure of security.

Whatever your decision, insist that your staff be courteous and treat all prospective customers with the respect with which you would like to be treated. It's the right thing to do, and it's just good business.

Never Underestimate the Importance of Good Office Staff

Many businesses lose at least as much to poor office procedures as to nonpaying clients. Remember that you are trusting your livelihood to your office staff and that you should treat them accordingly. It is vital that they be motivated to collect your money. Although monetary rewards are nice—and sometimes there's no substitute—never underestimate the importance of a simple thank-you. Recognizing that someone has really been doing a lot of work and letting them know that you appreciate their efforts is often more important than money . . . or so my wife keeps telling me.

As good as your office staff may be, however, you should never rely on them completely. After all, it's your business. As soon as you get "successful" enough not to have to concern yourself with such mundane things as the checkbook and accounts receivable reports, you have begun to guarantee the failure of your company. You must always maintain an interest in the billing and filing procedures and check up on them.

▶ **YOU GET WHAT YOU PAY FOR**

When my partners and I first started our law firm, money was very tight. We did not have the luxury of several hundred thousand dollars in seed money and we had a lot of expenses right off the bat. There were computers to buy, space to rent and build out, expenses for furniture, books, and office supplies, not to mention the computer consultants who were seemingly being shipped in by the carload in order to hook up a simple network with Internet capacity. When it came to personnel, what we really needed were people who would work for . . . shall we say . . . a bit less than the going rate. (The word "peanuts" seems a bit harsh.)

"We'll train them," we rationalized. "Why pay for an experienced office staff when you can get great raw material and mold it into the perfect team?" Why? Here's why. My partners and I are very good at what we do. When it comes to representing businesses in transactional work or litigation, there's no one better. When it comes to training personnel . . . we suck. (Sorry to use technical legal jargon, but we do.)

Consequently, our personnel was often left floundering, without any clear direction and no training program in sight. When we were able to take some time away from practicing law to dabble in personnel training, our efforts were . . . inefficient at best. (Some would say "laughable" but I prefer "inefficient.") What we finally learned after fits and starts in productivity, low morale, and turnover was that you would never be sorry for hiring top-flight people and paying them what they're worth. If you must cut corners, do it elsewhere, but your personnel can make or break your company.

Model Letter of Confirmation

[Date]

VIA FACSIMILE (410) 555–1212
AND FIRST CLASS MAIL
Cindy Diamond, President
Bradley Industries
1223 Maple Lane
Baltimore, MD 21208

Re: Order Number 44–8990

Dear Ms. Diamond:

The purpose of this letter is to confirm the placement of an order by Bradley Industries for 2,500 sheets of letterhead and 5,000 business cards in the design we currently have on file. The total price, excluding tax and shipping charges, will be $450.00, payment of which will be due upon receipt. We will begin processing this order on Monday, July 17 and deliver the finished product to you by Thursday, July 20.

If these terms do not reflect our understanding, please contact me immediately. Should we not hear from you, we shall proceed with this work on the understanding that you are in agreement with each of these terms.

Thank you once again for your order.

Very truly yours,

Andrew Hartman, President

AJH/bfl

CREDIT APPLICATION

We wish to open an account with [Company, Inc.] and desire that credit be extended to us for this purpose. By providing this information, we agree that all work performed and materials supplied by [Company] shall be subject to the Terms and Conditions set forth below. By our signature below, we expressly authorize [Company] to verify all credit information provided and to obtain credit reports on each applicant and guarantor indicated below.

Applicant Name: _____

Mailing Address: _____

Street Address (if the above is a P.O. Box):_____

☐ Sole Proprietorship ☐ Partnership ☐ Corporation ☐ Other _____

List Owner, Partners, or Corporate Officers, as appropriate:

_____ Title: _____

Name & Address

_____ Title: _____

Name & Address

Credit Limit Requested:_____ Terms: ☐ COD   ☐ Net 10

Rush Orders via Phone? ☐   Authorized Personnel: _____

Person to Contact regarding Payment: _____

Bank:_____ Address: _____

Account Number: _____ Type of Account: _____

Active Trade References:

Name and Account Number: _____ Phone: _____

Name and Account Number: _____ Phone: _____

Name and Account Number: _____ Phone: _____

Applicant acknowledges that all of the TERMS & CONDITIONS printed on the reverse hereof shall constitute the account agreement in the event [Company] accepts this application.

_____   _____(SEAL)

Printed Name of Applicant   Signature

_____   _____(SEAL)

Printed Name of Guarantor   Signature

_____

Social Security Number of Guarantor

_____

For Office Use Only:

☐ Approved: _____ Credit Limit: _____ Terms: _____

Model Terms and Conditions (on Reverse of Account Application)

(Now, I realize that these terms and conditions take up more than one page. But that's here—with this type size and on this size page. A good printer can convert these terms and conditions, keeping them legible, into a two-column, one-page layout appearing on the back of your account applications. Trust me.)

TERMS AND CONDITIONS

1. All goods and/or services sold by Company, Inc. ("Company") to Buyer and all purchase orders placed by Buyer for such goods and/or services are subject to these Terms & Conditions. Buyer agrees that the terms & conditions of any purchase order which are in any way inconsistent or in addition to these Terms & Conditions shall not be binding upon COMPANY and shall be inapplicable to this sale unless expressly agreed to in writing by an authorized officer of Customer.

2. Unless otherwise specified on the reverse hereof, payment is due upon COMPANY's completion of each order. Late payment shall constitute a default of this Agreement and shall be subject a late charge at a rate equal to one and one half percent ($1\frac{1}{2}$) per month multiplied by the amount which is in arrears. If collection efforts are commenced to enforce Buyer's performance, Buyer shall reimburse COMPANY for all costs and expenses associated with said enforcement, including attorneys' fees.

3. In the event Buyer defaults on this Agreement, either by failing to pay in accordance with the terms of any agreements with COMPANY or through its failure to honor any other obligations recited herein, **ALL** monies which are or which shall become due to COMPANY arising out of any agreements, or purchase orders existing between the Buyer and COMPANY shall be immediately due and owing irrespective of the payment terms recited on individual agreements or purchase orders.

4. All materials must be inspected by the Buyer upon receipt. Any claim of shortage, damage, or other deficiencies must be made

at delivery or, if not delivered, at pick-up or are waived by Buyer. Buyer acknowledges that all decisions concerning credits for the return of materials are made at the sole discretion of COMPANY and that said return policies may be modified or revoked at any time without notice.

5. The **RISK OF LOSS** of any goods purchased hereunder shall pass to the Buyer upon delivery to Buyer at the designated and agreed location. If the Buyer is to pick up the goods at COMPANY's facility, the Risk of Loss passes to Buyer at pickup or 24 hours after Buyer is notified that the goods are ready, whichever is sooner.

6. A fifty percent (50%) deposit is required for all first orders at the time of order, with the balance due at the time of pickup or delivery.

7. Buyer's sole remedy for any claim arising out of any sale, order, or installation hereunder, shall be a refund of monies paid by Buyer to COMPANY for said materials and/or installation. Buyer expressly waives its right to claim consequential or incidental damages.

8. With the exception of any warranties specifically granted herein, COMPANY expressly disclaims all warranties, express and/or implied, including the implied warranties of merchantability and fitness for a particular purpose.

9. If Buyer is a corporation or other legal entity, the individual(s) whose signature appears hereon hereby personally guarantee Buyer's compliance with this Agreement, including payment of all charges and costs.

10. This Agreement shall be binding upon and inure to the benefit of COMPANY and Buyer, and their respective successors and assigns. This Agreement shall be governed by the laws of the State of _____. Jurisdiction and venue for any legal action arising out of or relating to this Agreement shall reside exclusively in a court of competent jurisdiction in _____ County.

11. Buyer and Guarantor agree that the obligations listed in this Agreement shall not be impaired, modified, changed, released, or limited in any manner whatsoever by any impairment, modification, change, release or limitation of liability of the Guarantor or the Company or their respective estates by reason of the commencement of any case, proceeding, or other action seeking reorganization, arrangement, adjustment, liquidation, dissolution, or composition of it or its debts under any law relating to bankruptcy, insolvency, reorganization, relief of debtors or seeking appointment of a receiver, trustee, custodian, or similar official for it or all or part of its property.

12. The waiver or acquiescence by COMPANY of strict compliance with any term or condition shall not constitute a waiver of any subsequent default or failure.

US STATE CORPORATE FILING CHART

State Name	Provides	Attention	Mailing Address	Courier Address	Telephones	Fax	Hours	URL (St. Main, Sec of State, or Other)
Alabama	Corporation Records, Limited Partnership Records, Limited Liability Company Records, Limited Liability Partnerships, Trade Names, Trademarks/ Servicemarks	Secretary of State, Corporations Division,	PO Box 5616, Montgomery, AL 36103–5616	11 S Union St, Ste 207, Montgomery, AL 36104	334-242-5324, 334-242-5325 (Trademarks)	334-240-3138	8AM–5PM	www.alalinc.net/alsecst
Alaska	Corporation Records, Trademarks/ Servicemarks, Fictitious Name, Assumed Name, Limited Partnership Records, Limited Liability Company Records	Department of Commerce, Division of Banking, Securities & Corporations	PO Box 110808, Juneau, AK 99811	333 Willoughby Ave, 9th Floor of the State Office Bldg, Juneau, AK 99811	907-465-2530	907-465-3257	8AM–5PM	commerce.state.ak.us/dced/ bsc/search.htm
Arizona	Corporation Records, Limited Liability Company Records	Corporation Commission	1300 W Washington, Phoenix, AZ 85007		602-542-3026 (Status), 602-542-3285 (Annual Reports)	602-542-3414	8AM–5PM	www.cc.state.az.us

Data provided by BRB Publications. A leader in the research of public record sources.

BRB Publications, 1971 E Fifth St, Tempe AZ 85281, 480–829–7475, 800–929–3811, 800 929–3810 (Fax)

State Name	Provides	Attention	Mailing Address	Courier Address	Telephones	Fax	Hours	URL (St. Main, Sec of State, or Other)
Arkansas	Corporation Records, Fictitious Name, Limited Liability Company Records, Limited Partnerships	Secretary of State, Corporation Department- Aegon Bldg	501 Woodlane, Rm 310, Little Rock, AR 72201–1094		501–682–3409	501–682–3437	8AM–4:30PM	sosweb.state.ar.us/corps/ incorp/
California	Corporation Records, Limited Liability Company Records, Limited Partnerships	Secretary of State, Information Retrieval Unit	1500 11th Street, Sacramento, CA 95814		916–657–5448, 916–653–3794 (LLCs), 916–653–3365 (LPs)		8AM–4:30PM	
Colorado	Corporation Records, Trademarks/ Servicemarks, Fictitious Name, Limited Liability Company Records, Assumed Name	Secretary of State, Corporation Division	1560 Broadway, Suite 200, Denver, CO 80202		303–894–2251 (Corporations), 900–555–1717 (Status-Name)	303–894–2242	8:30AM–5PM	
Connecticut	Corporation Records, Limited Partnership Records, Trademarks/ Servicemarks, Limited Liability Company Records	Secretary of State, Commercial Recording Division	30 Trinity St, Hartford, CT 06106		860–509–6003	860–509–6068	8:45AM–3PM	www.state.ct.us/sots
Delaware	Corporation Records, Limited Partnership Records, Trademarks/ Servicemarks, Limited Liability Company Records, Assumed Name	Secretary of State, Division of Corporations	PO Box 898, Dover, DE 19903	John G Townsend Bldg, Dover, DE 19901	302–739–3073	302–739–3812	8AM–4:30PM	www.state.de.us/corp/ index.htm

State	Agency	Address	Phone	Hours	Website
District of Columbia	Department of Consumer & Regulatory Affairs	614 H St, NW, Room 407, Washington, DC 20001	202-727-7283	9AM-3PM	www.dcra.org/Bracorp.htm,
	Corporation Records, Limited Partnership Records, Limited Liability Company Records				
Florida	Division of Corporations, Department of State	PO Box 6327, Tallahassee, FL 32314	850-488-9000 (Telephone Inquires) 850-487-6053 (Copy Requests), 850-487-6056 (Annual Reports)		www.dos.state.fl.us
	Corporation Records, Limited Partnership Records, Trademarks/ Servicemarks, Assumed Name, Fictitious Names	409 E Gaines St, Tallahassee, FL 32399		8:30AM-4:30PM	
Georgia	Secretary of State, Corporation Division	2 M L King Dr, Suite 315, W Tower, Atlanta, GA 30334-1530	404-656-2817, 404-656-2817 (Filing Questions)	8AM-5PM	www.sos.state.ga.us/corporations/
	Corporation Records, Limited Partnership Records, Limited Liability Company Records		404-651-9059		
Hawaii	Business Registration Division	PO Box 40, Honolulu, HI 96810	808-586-2727	7:45AM-4:30PM	www.state.hi.us/dbedt/start.html
	Corporation Records, Fictitious Name, Limited Partnership Records, Assumed Name, Trademarks/ Servicemarks	1010 Richard St, 1st Floor, Honolulu, HI 96813	808-586-2733		
Idaho	Secretary of State, Corporation Division	PO Box 83720, Boise, ID 83720-0080	208-334-2301	8AM-5PM	idsos.state.id.us
	Corporation Records, Limited Partnerships, Trademarks/ Servicemarks, Limited Liability Company Records, Fictitious Names, Trade Names	700 W Jefferson, Boise, ID 83720	208-334-2847		

Data provided by BRB Publications. A leader in the research of public record sources.

BRB Publications, 1971 E Fifth St, Tempe AZ 85281, 480-829-7475, 800-929-3811, 800 929-3810 (Fax)

State Name	Provides	Attention	Mailing Address	Courier Address	Telephones	Fax	Hours	URL (St. Main, Sec of State, or Other)
Illinois	Corporation Records, Limited Partnership Records, Trade Names, Assumed Name, Limited Liability Company Records	Department of Business Services, Corporate Department	Howlett Bldg, 3rd Floor, Copy Section, Springfield, IL 62756	Corner of 2nd & Edwards Sts, Springfield, IL 62756	217–782–7880	212–782–4528	8AM–4:30PM	
Indiana	Corporation Records, Limited Partnerships, Fictitious Name, Assumed Name, Limited Liability Company Records, Limited Liability Partnerships	Corporation Division, Secretary of State	302 W Washington St, Room E018, Indianapolis, IN 46204		317–232–6576	317–233–3387	8AM–5:30PM M-F	www.state.in.us/sos
Iowa	Corporation Records, Limited Liability Company Records, Fictitious Name, Limited Partnership Records, Assumed Name, Trademarks/ Servicemarks	Secretary of State, Corporation Division	2nd Floor, Hoover Bldg, Des Moines, IA 50319		515–281–5204	515–242–6556 (Other Fax Line), 515–242–5953	8AM–4:30PM	sos.state.ia.us
Kansas	Corporation Records, Limited Partnerships, Limited Liability Company Records	Secretary of State, Corporation Division	300 SW 10th St, 2nd Floor, Topeka, KS 66612–1594		785–296–4564	785–296–4570	8AM – 5PM	www.ink.org/public/sos
Kentucky	Corporation Records, Limited Partnerships, Assumed Name, Limited Liability Company Records	Secretary of State, Corporate Records	PO Box 718, Frankfort, KY 40602–0718	700 Capitol Ave, Room 156, Frankfort, KY 40601	502–564–7330	502–564–4075	8AM–4PM	www.sos.state.ky.us

State	Records	Division	Address (Mailing)	Address (Physical)	Phone	Phone	Hours	Website
Louisiana	Corporation Records, Limited Partnership Records, Limited Liability Company Records, Trademarks/Servicemarks	Commercial Division, Corporation Department	PO Box 94125, Baton Rouge, LA 70804–9125	3851 Essen Lane, Baton Rouge, LA 70809	225–925–4704	225–925–4726	8AM–4:30PM	sec.state.la.us
Maine	Corporation Records, Limited Partnerships, Trademarks/Servicemarks, Assumed Name, Limited Liability Company Records	Secretary of State, Reports & Information Division	101 State House Station, Augusta, ME 04333–0101	Room 221, State Office Bldg, Corner Capitol & Seward Sts, Augusta, ME 04333	207–287–4190, 207–287–4195 (Main Number)	207–287–5874	8AM – 5PM	www.state.me.us/sos/corpinfo.htm
Maryland	Corporation Records, Limited Partnerships, Trade Names, Limited Liability Company Records, Fictitious Name	Department of Assessments & Taxation, Corporations Division	301 W Preston St, Room 809, Baltimore, MD 21201		410–767–1340, 410–767–1330 (Charter Information)	410–333–7097	8AM–4:30PM	www.dat.state.md.us/sdatweb/services.html
Massachusetts	Corporation Records, Trademarks/Servicemarks, Limited Liability Partnerships, Limited Partnership Records	Secretary of the Commonwealth, Corporation Division	One Ashburton Pl, 17th Floor, Boston, MA 02108		617–727–9640 (Corporations), 617–727–2850 (Records), 617–727–8329 (Trademarks), 617–727–9440 (Forms request line)	617–742–4538	8:45AM–5PM	state.ma.us/sec/cor/coridx.htm

Data provided by BRB Publications. A leader in the research of public record sources.

BRB Publications, 1971 E Fifth St, Tempe AZ 85281, 480–829–7475, 800–929–3811, 800 929–3810 (Fax)

State Name	Provides	Attention	Mailing Address	Courier Address	Telephones	Fax	Hours	URL (St. Main, Sec of State, or Other)
Michigan	Corporation Records, Limited Liability Company Records, Fictitious Name, Limited Partnership Records, Assumed Name	Department of Consumer & Industrial Srvs, Corporation Division	PO Box 30054, Lansing, MI 48909-7554	6546 Mercantile Way, Lansing, MI 48910	517-334-7561 (Information Unit), 900-555-0031 (Copies), 517-373-1408 (Archived Records)	517-334-8329 517-334-7145 (Fax for Copies)	8AM-5PM	www.cis.state.mi.us/corp/
Minnesota	Corporation Records, Limited Liability Company Records, Assumed Name, Trademarks/Servicemarks, Limited Partnerships	Business Records Services, Secretary of State	180 State Office Bldg, 100 Constitution Ave, St Paul, MN 55155-1299		651-296-2803 (Information), 651-297-9102 (Copies)	651-215-0683	8AM-4:30PM	www.sos.state.mn.us
Mississippi	Corporation Records, Limited Partnership Records, Limited Liability Company Records, Trademarks/Servicemarks	Corporation Commission, Secretary of State	PO Box 136, Jackson, MS 39205-0136	202 N Congress, Suite 601, Jackson, MS 39201	601-359-1633, 800-256-3494 (Alternate Telephone)	601-359-1607	8AM-5PM	www.sos.state.ms.us/
Missouri	Corporation Records, Fictitious Name, Limited Partnership Records, Assumed Name, Trademarks/Servicemarks, Limited Liability Company Records	Secretary of State, Corporation Services	PO Box 778, Jefferson City, MO 65102	600 W Main, Jefferson City, MO 65101	573-751-4153	573-751-5841	8AM-5PM	http://mosl.sos.state.mo.us/

State	Records	Office	Address	Phone	Phone	Hours	Website
Montana	Corporation Records, Limited Liability Company Records, Fictitious Name, Limited Partnerships, Assumed Name, Trademarks/Servicemarks	Business Services Bureau, Secretary of State	PO Box 202801, Helena, MT 59620–2801	State Capitol, Room 225, Helena, MT 59620)	406-444-3665	406-444-3976	8AM–5PM	www.mt/gov/sos/
Nebraska	Corporation Records, Limited Liability Company Records, Limited Partnerships, Trade Names, Trademarks/Servicemarks	Secretary of State, Corporation Commission	1301 State Capitol Bldg, Lincoln, NE 68509		402-471-4079	402-471-3666	8AM – PM	www.nol.org.home/SOS/
Nevada	Corporation Records, Limited Partnerships, Limited Liability Company Records, Limited Partnership Records	Secretary of State, Status Division	101 N Carson, #3, Carson City, NV 89701–4786		775-684-5708, 900-535-3355 (Status Line)	775-685-5725	8AM–5PM	http://sos.state.nv.us
New Hampshire	Corporation Records, Limited Partnership Records, Limited Liability Company Records, Trademarks/Servicemarks, Trade Names, Limited Liability Partnerships	Secretary of State, Corporation Division	State House, Room 204, Concord, NH 03301		603-271-3246, 603-271-3244 (Alternate Telephone)	603-271-3247	8AM-4:30PM	www.state.nh.us/sos

Data provided by BRB Publications. A leader in the research of public record sources.

BRB Publications, 1971 E Fifth St, Tempe AZ 85281, 480–829–7475, 800–929–3811, 800 929–3810 (Fax)

State Name	Provides	Attention	Mailing Address	Courier Address	Telephones	Fax	Hours	URL (St. Main, Sec of State, or Other)
New Jersey	Corporation Records, Limited Liability Company Records, Fictitious Name, Limited Partnerships	Department of Treasury, Division of Commercial Recording	PO 450, Trenton, NJ 08625	820 Bear Tavern Rd, West Trenton, NJ 08628	609–530–6400, 609–530–6432 (Copies)	609–530–8290	8:30AM–5:00PM	accessnet.state.nj.us/index
New Mexico	Corporation Records, Limited Liability Company Records	State Corporation Commission, Corporate Department	PO Box 1269, Santa Fe, NM 87504–1269	1120 Paseo de Peralta, Pera Bldg 4th Fl, Rm 418, Santa Fe, NM 87501	505–827–4502 (Main Number), 800–947–4722 (In-state Only), 505–827–4510 (Good Standing), 505–827–4513 (Copy Request)	505–827–4387	8AM–12:00: 1PM–5PM	www.state.nm.us/scc/sccfind.htm
New York	Corporation Records, Limited Partnership Records, Limited Liability Company Records, Limited Liability Partnerships	Division of Corporations, Department of State	41 State St, Albany, NY 12231		518–473–2492 (General Information), 900–835–2677 (Corporate Searches)		8AM–4:30PM	www.dos.state.ny.us
North Carolina	Corporation Records, Limited Partnerships, Limited Liability Company Records, Trademarks/Servicemarks	Secretary of State, Corporations Section	300 N Salisbury St, Raleigh, NC 27603–5909		919–733–4201 (Corporations), 919–733–4129 (Trademarks)	919–733–1837	8AM–5PM	www.state.nc.us/secstate
North Dakota	Corporation Records, Limited Liability Company Records, Limited Partnership Records, Trademarks/Servicemarks, Fictitious Name, Assumed Name	Secretary of State, Business Information/Registration	600 E Boulevard Ave, Dept 108, Bismarck, ND 58505–0500		701–328–4284	701–328–2992	8AM–5PM	www.state.nd.us/sec

State	Office	Address	Phone	Hours	Website
Ohio	Secretary of State, Attn: Certification Desk	30 E Broad St, 14th Floor, Columbus, OH 43266-0418	614-466-3910, 614-466-1776 (Forms and Copies), 614-466-0590 (Name Availability)	614-466-2892	8AM-5PM	www.state.oh.us/sos/info.html
	Corporation Records, Fictitious Name, Limited Partnership Records, Assumed Name, Trademarks/ Servicemarks, Limited Liability Company Records				
Oklahoma	Secretary of State	2300 N Lincoln Blvd, Rm 101, Oklahoma City, OK 73105-4897	405-521-3911, 900-825-2424 (Corporate Records)	405-521-3771	8AM-5PM	www.oklaosf.state.ok.us/~sos/
	Corporation Records, Limited Liability Company Records, Limited Partnerships, Trademarks/ Servicemarks, Limited Liability Partnerships				
Oregon	Corporation Division, Public Service Building	255 Capital St NE, #151, Salem, OR 97310-1327	503-986-2200	503-378-4381	8AM-5PM	www.sos.state.or.us/corporation/corphp.htm
	Corporation Records, Limited Partnership Records, Trademarks/ Servicemarks, Fictitious Name, Assumed Name, Limited Liability Company Records				
Pennsylvania	Corporation Bureau, Department of State	308 North Office Bldg, Harrisburg, PA 17120	717-787-1057	717-783-2244	8AM – 5PM	www.dos.state.pa.us/corp.htm
	PO Box 8722, Harrisburg, PA 17105-8722				
	Corporation Records, Limited Partnership Records, Trademarks/ Servicemarks, Fictitious Name, Assumed Name, Limited Liability Company Records				

Data provided by BRB Publications. A leader in the research of public record sources.

BRB Publications, 1971 E Fifth St, Tempe AZ 85281, 480-829-7475, 800-929-3811, 800 929-3810 (Fax)

State Name	Provides	Attention	Mailing Address	Courier Address	Telephones	Fax	Hours	URL (St. Main, Sec of State, or Other)
Rhode Island	Corporation Records, Fictitious Name, Limited Partnerships, Limited Liability Company Records, Limited Liability Partnerships	Secretary of State, Corporations Division	100 N Main St, Providence, RI 02903		401-222-3040	401-222-1309	8:30AM–4:30PM	
South Carolina	Corporation Records, Trademarks/Servicemarks, Limited Partnerships, Limited Liability Company Records	Corporation Division, Capitol Complex	PO Box 11350, Columbia, SC 29211	Edgar A. Brown Bldg, Room 525, Columbia, SC 29201	803-734-2158	803-734-2164	8:30PM–5PM	
South Dakota	Corporation Records, Limited Partnerships, Limited Liability Company Records, Trademarks/Servicemarks	Corporation Division, Secretary of State	500 E Capitol Ave, Suite B-05, Pierre, SD 57501-5070		605-773-4845	605-773-4550	8AM–5PM	
Tennessee	Corporation Records, Limited Partnership Records, Fictitious Name, Assumed Name, Limited Liability Company Records	Corporation Section. Secretary of State, Polk Bldg.	500 Deaderick St, #1800, Nashville, TN 37243-0306		615-741-0537	615-741-7310	8AM–4:30PM	www.state.tn.us/sos/
Texas	Corporation Records, Fictitious Name, Limited Partnership Records, Limited Liability Company Records, Assumed Name, Trademarks/Servicemarks	Secretary of State, Corporation Section	PO Box 13697, Austin, TX 78711-3697	J Earl Rudder Bldg, 1019 Brazos, B-13, Austin, TX 78701	512-463-5555 (Information), 5 12-463-5578 (Copies), 512-463-5576 (Trademarks)	512-463-5709	8AM–5PM	www.sos.state.tx.us

State	Agency	Mailing Address	Physical Address	Phone	Phone	Hours	Website	Records
Utah	Commerce Department, Corporate Division	PO Box 146705, Salt Lake City, UT 84114-6705	160 E 300 S, 2nd fl, Salt Lake City, UT 84111	801-530-4849 (Administration) 801-530-6205 (Certified Records), 801-530-6034 (Non-Certified), 801-530-6363 (Good Standing)	801-530-6111	8AM-5PM		Corporation Records, Limited Liability Company Records, Fictitious Name, Limited Partnership Records, Assumed Name, Trademarks/Servicemarks
Vermont	Secretary of State, Corporation Division	109 State St, Montpelier, VT 05609-1101	81 River St, Heritage Bldg, Montpelier, VT 05602	802-828-2386	802-828-2853	7:45AM-4:30PM	sec.state.vt.us/soshome.htm	Corporation Records, Limited Liability Company Records, Limited Liability Partnerships, Limited Partnerships, Trademarks/Servicemarks
Virginia	State Corporation Commission, Clerks Office	PO Box 1197, Richmond, VA 23218-1197	Tyler Bldg, 1st Floor, 1300 E Main St, Richmond, VA 23219	804-371-9733	804-371-9133 (Other fax), 804-371-9744	8:15AM – 5PM	dit1.state.va.us/scc/division/clm/index.htm	Corporation Records, Limited Liability Company Records, Fictitious Name, Limited Partnership Records, Assumed Name
Washington	Secretary of State, Corporations Division	PO Box 40234, Olympia, WA 98504-0234	505 E Union, 2nd Floor, Olympia, WA 98504	360-753-7115, 900-463-6000 (Records)	360-664-8781	8AM-4PM	www.wa.gov/sec/corps.htm	Corporation Records, Trademarks/Servicemarks, Limited Partnerships, Limited Liability Company Records

Data provided by BRB Publications. A leader in the research of public record sources.

BRB Publications, 1971 E Fifth St, Tempe AZ 85281, 480–829–7475, 800–929–3811, 800 929–3810 (Fax)

State Name	Provides	Attention	Mailing Address	Courier Address	Telephones	Fax	Hours	URL (St. Main, Sec of State, or Other)
West Virginia	Corporation Records, Limited Liability Company Records, Limited Partnerships, Trademarks/Servicemarks	Secretary of State, Corporation Division	State Capitol Bldg, Room W139, Charleston, WV 25305-0776	304-558-8000	304-558-0900	8:30AM-4:30PM		
Wisconsin	Corporation Records, Limited Partnership Records, Limited Liability Company Records	Department of Financial Institutions, Division of Corporate & Consumer Services	PO Box 7846, Madison, WI 53707-7846	345 W Washington Ave, 3rd Floor, Madison, WI 53703	608-261-9555	608-267-6813	7:45AM-4:30PM	badger.state.wi.us/agencies/dfi
Wyoming	Corporation Records, Limited Liability Company Records, Limited Partnership Records, Fictitious Name, Trademarks/Servicemarks	Corporations Division, Secretary of State	State Capitol, Cheyenne, WY 82002	307-777-7311	307-777-5339	8AM – 5PM	soswy.state.wy.us	

Data provided by BRB Publications. A leader in the research of public record sources.

BRB Publications, 1971 E Fifth St, Tempe AZ 85281, 480-829-7475, 800-929-3811, 800 929-3810 (Fax)

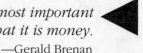

Those who have some means think that the most important thing in the world is love. The poor know that it is money.

—Gerald Brenan

2
Moves You Can Make to Maximize Your Cash Flow

Overview

Every month, most people and businesses prioritize their bills to determine which ones should be paid first. Some bills, such as the rent or mortgage, utilities, and phone, unquestionably come first. The others get placed in a different pile—the pile of bills that get paid if money's available.

In going through this pile, people consciously or unconsciously assign priority to some bills over others depending on what is in their best interest. Your job, therefore, is to remind the customer that paying you on time is most certainly in his best interest. In short, your goal must be to get your invoice to the top of that pile, because that, in a nutshell, is the key to maximizing your cash flow.

This chapter will focus on certain ideas to help you do just this.

Payment in Advance

Certainly the best way to maximize your cash flow is to minimize the possibility of loss. It's pretty hard for a customer to stiff you if he's already paid you in advance. In businesses that offer customized products, such as printed business cards or advertisements, deposits are a *must*. If you are operating a service business such as accounting or engineering, where most of your charges arise out of time spent on a project, strongly consider charging a retainer representing payment for the first phase of the work.

Deposits or retainers accomplish several purposes. First, they enable you to cut your losses if the customer later reneges on the deal. Second, they have the psychological effect of binding the customer to the transaction. He's already invested in it now, so he may as well follow through. The third advantage of deposits is more subtle. In essence, payment of a deposit makes it hard for a customer to protest payment terms such as total fee or hourly rate if he's shown through his payment that he knew what the terms were.

► TRAP FOR THE UNWARY

Note that deposits do carry one trap: If they are not properly documented, acceptance of a deposit could enable an unscrupulous customer to assert that he had understood the deposit to have been the full fee. For this reason it is very important to obtain the customer's acknowledgment of the terms of the transaction. A good practice would be to have the customer write "1/3 deposit" (for example) on the memo line of the check or, at the very least, make sure the word "deposit" appears on a receipt of acknowledgment provided to the customer.

Accept Payment by Credit Card

Although credit-card companies will deduct a percentage of every amount charged as payment for providing this service, having your customers pay this way passes the risk of default (for the most part) on to the credit-card companies. What's more, as we move closer and closer to becoming a "cashless society" where all business is conducted with credit cards, debit cards, and electronic transfers, your customers will appreciate the convenience.

Now, I realize that the acceptance of credit cards may be self-evident for retail outlets. Most service industries are, however, decidedly behind this curve. For that matter, contractors working in the residential market, such as landscapers and plumbers, rarely enable their on-site personnel to accept payment via credit card on the spot. Today, handheld units make this method of payment, complete with verification, accessible to even the smallest of businesses. If you want and expect payment at the time of service when those services are rendered at the customer's home or office, look into this possibility.

Arrange Loans for Your Customers

Recently, I came home to observe that I had a water bed where my lawn had been. It seemed that the pipe bringing water from the pipe under the street to my house had broken and that I was in the course of starting my own underground lake.

After I got over what could only be described as a sort of morbid fascination with my very first grass bubble, I called a plumbing company. They sent out a gentlemen who was no doubt very proficient in his field but who was notably less impressed by my ground balloon than I had been. In fact, other than telling me it would cost more than $2,000 to dig a trench, find the problem, and replace the pipe, he seemed bored by the whole thing. For my part, the $2,000 quote caused something other than boredom, though it most assuredly put an end to my amusement.

Many businesses routinely trade in purchases of $1,000 or more. Some, like my plumbing adventure (and you didn't think I could make that story relevant), are unexpected by the customer. Rather than using your company's resources to extend credit for large purchases, why not explore the possibility of working with a local bank or financing company?

Such a relationship will not only earn goodwill among your customers by providing them with another payment option, but it will also pass the risk of nonpayment to someone else—namely, the bank.

Check Verification Services

Not unlike credit cards, check verification services allow you to transfer the risk of nonpayment to them in exchange for a percentage of each transaction. Although such services may not be worthwhile for businesses that only accept the occasional check, you may want to look into them if payment by check, especially by one-time customers, is a major part of your revenue.

Billing Practices

As far as collection is concerned, your bills are where the rubber meets the road. Good billing policies, consistently applied, are the foundation upon which your company's financial health will rest for years to come. The following sections provide you with rules as well as options you may want to consider in creating or revamping your company's policies.

Send Clear and Understandable Invoices

Never make it difficult for customers to pay you. If your bills aren't clear, they will be paid late . . . if at all. Case in point: Take a look at your next doctor's bill and ask yourself, "Did I understand right away what I owed versus what my health insurance covered?" If not, I'd be willing to bet that you let the bill sit until you had the time to analyze it and/or call someone to answer your question.

Everything you do should be geared toward making it exceedingly easy for your customers to pay you. The flip side of that coin is making it difficult for your customers to find an excuse to delay payment. Understandable invoices are a crucial part of this process.

Make Sure Your Bill Is Never an Unpleasant Surprise

The only time your customers should be surprised is when they open your invoice and the bill is *lower* than they expected (and this is a lawyer talking). The best way to ensure that a customer will pay your bill late (if at all) is to shock him with a higher-than-anticipated total.

You should generally have a pretty good idea of the kind of bill the customer is expecting—at least within a certain range. If at any point you become aware that the bill is likely to exceed that total, contact the customer *immediately*. I recommend that you obtain the customer's approval of the higher cost over the phone and then follow up with a letter or fax confirming the customer's authorization to proceed.

If a confirming letter is not practical, make sure that you document the oral authorization to proceed in the customer's file. Write down the date and time of the conversation, who participated, and what was said. You may find this record to be very useful later if the higher bill is ever questioned.

Getting the Bill to the Customer

Your bills won't get paid if they don't get there. Make sure you are sending them to the correct address. If the customer moves, you want to know. Make sure your files are up to date and that you always have a correct phone number. If your correspondence is returned by the post office with a forwarding address sticker, make sure the new address is posted to your file.

In addition, if your customer is a business, always send the invoices to a specific person with a specific title (e.g., Jane Doe, Accounts Payable) rather than merely addressing them to the company. Your invoices will receive more attention that way, and you will always have a specific person to contact in the event of a problem.

Charge Interest

In chapter 1 we discussed how the establishment of an interest-charging policy stops slow-paying customers from borrowing your money interest-free so that they can pay their other "more important" debts. Including your interest-charging policy on your invoices solidifies the policy. This statement, at the bottom of your invoices, serves as a reminder to the customer that it is in his best interest to place your bill at the top of his "to be paid" pile.

Most companies with this policy print the following statement at the bottom of their bills: "Interest at the rate of ____ percent per annum (__ percent per month) will accrue on all balances not paid within ___ days from the date of this invoice." (Use this language, if you are not already, and fill in your own terms.)

In addition, always make sure that your invoices reflect the actual interest that has accrued since the last invoice was sent. This way, the actual dollars and cents behind your policy will be shown to the customer every month.

Finally, when appropriate, have your office staff remind customers when payments are due at the time they purchase the goods or services for which they will be receiving a bill.

Options

Not all billing policies suit every business. Nevertheless, here are some options to consider for increasing your cash flow and reducing your bad-debt write-offs.

Consider Sending SASEs with Your Bill

You may be surprised how a self-addressed, stamped envelope ("SASE") slipped into a bill speeds up the collection process. There really is a delay when customers have to address their own envelopes and get their own stamps. Even without the prepaid postage, the simple inclusion of a self-addressed envelope can work wonders for your collection rate.

In fact, you may want to try an experiment. Enclose a SASE in the bills you send to half your customers (i.e., *A* through *L*) and determine for yourself if the improvement to your cash flow isn't worth the nominal extra cost of printing self-addressed payment envelopes.

Allow Discounts for Prompt Payment

Many businesses improve their cash flow by offering customers a discount for payment within ten days. You could even have this discount apply to the customer's *next* order, thereby giving them an incentive to use you again (while helping your company build up a base of prompt-paying clients). Even a small discount will be noticed by your customers. Two percent is customary.

Send Bills on the 15th of the Month

Studies have shown that people are used to paying their bills at the end of the month. Consequently, many businesses that send out their bills on the first of each month find themselves waiting thirty days for payment with even their most prompt-paying accounts. On the other hand, businesses that send out their bills on the 15th of the month are often paid within two weeks by customers writing checks on that same end-of-month cycle. Receiving payment a couple of weeks early with no additional effort on your part could do wonders for your financial peace of mind.

Send Bills by Fax or E-mail

While this may not be ideal for every business, more and more companies are using fax machines and even E-mail to save stamps and instantly transmit their bills to the customer. The advantages are obvious: (1) saving on stamps and envelopes; (2) instantaneous delivery; and (3) virtual assurance that the customer receives the bill.

The successful employment of this practice depends on the customer's cooperation. Otherwise, you run the risk of putting off some customers by appearing "too hungry" for your money. What's more, if this billing practice does not fit in with the customer's established procedure for processing invoices, using this method would be counterproductive.

My final caveat is that faxes and E-mail sent to a general mailbox are like postcards—anyone can read them. If your customers would prefer not to have their account information broadcast to anyone who happens to walk by the fax machine, you could wind up losing a client for a perceived lack of discretion.

Bottom line: Don't fax first and ask questions later.

Recognize the PR Value of Your Bills

Most people don't think of it this way, but bills are the strongest and most consistent communication most companies have with their customers. After all, they arrive at your customer's office every month, and you better believe they get read—every line, every month. Your job is to use that kind of attention to your advantage by emphasizing how much your company is actually doing for the money.

▶ "AND I THOUGHT YOU WERE EXPENSIVE"

Not long ago, I found myself in conference with the president of a large company I had represented for the past five years. Although I had worked on several large cases for this client, all with successful outcomes, I knew that he still used another attorney as general counsel to handle his day-in, day-out questions and concerns.

When I asked why, he told me that he felt I was just too expensive. "Too expensive?!" I was shocked. I don't bill my clients for everyday phone calls, I often reduce my hourly rate for long or involved litigation, and I don't charge for office expenses, unlike the other attorney he had been using.

"During the last case I handled for you, we must have talked fifty times," I said. "You never saw charges for those conversations on the bill. When an associate does research and takes longer than I would have, I don't bill for the extra time; and you never get nickel-and-dimed for things like copies, long-distance calls, or faxes. How can you say that I'm too expensive?" I asked.

The fact of the matter was, he never realized how much work the case required compared to the amount he had actually been billed for. From that month on, I began putting all time and expense entries on my bills, often followed by the words "no charge" in bold typeface.

I have never had that complaint since.

Appendix

Model Invoice with Interest and Attorney's Fee Language

Your Company
615 Your Street
Baltimore, MD 21202
356-7297

Joel Client
105 West Street
Towson, MD 21204

Re: Chesapeake Project

Date	Services Rendered	Hours	Charge
10/1	Initial Client Conference	1.5	$ 120.00
10/6	Site Review; Telephone conference with client	3.5	$ 280.00
10/12	Preparation of documents	2.0	$ 160.00
10/16	Revision and finalization of documents; Conference with client	2.5	$ 200.00
Total		**9.5**	**$ 760.00**
Expenses:			
10/12	Enlargement and mounting of documents		$ 75.00
Balance Due Now:			**$ 835.00**

Payment is due upon receipt. Interest at the rate of 18% per annum (1½% per month) will be assessed on all balances due and unpaid after 30 days. In the event this account must be referred for collection, client is responsible for payment of all expenses including reasonable attorney's fees and court costs.

Model Model Invoice with Account Agreement Reference

Your Company
615 Your Street
Baltimore, MD 21202
356-7297

Joel Client
105 West Street
Towson, MD 21204

Re: Chesapeake Project
Account Number: 43213

Date	Services Rendered	Hours	Charge
10/1	Initial Client Conference	1.5	$ 120.00
10/6	Site Review; Telephone conference with client	3.5	$ 280.00
10/12	Preparation of documents	2.0	$ 160.00
10/16	Revision and finalization of documents; Conference with client	2.5	$ 200.00
Total		**9.5**	**$ 760.00**
Expenses:			
10/12	Enlargement and mounting of documents		$ 75.00
Balance Due Now:			**$ 835.00**

The terms and conditions set forth in the account agreement for the account referenced above shall govern the payment policies and obligations of each party to this transaction.

3
Recognizing and Reacting to the Danger Signs

Overview

The sooner you recognize danger, the better your chance of avoiding it. In this chapter we shall discuss how to recognize the most common danger signs soon-to-be slow or nonpaying clients exhibit, as well as some office policies you can put into effect *now* to minimize your risk of loss.

Be Sensitive to the Warning Signs

Just in the normal course of business, your company inevitably amasses an extraordinary amount of useful information on its customers. The ability to act on it frequently separates successful businesses from those holding going-out-of-business sales.

- Are the client's payments slowing up?

- Is the client failing to return your phone calls?

- Has the client bounced one or more checks recently (even if he makes good on them later)?

- Has the client asked you for additional time to pay?

If you notice any of these warning signs, **do not continue to extend additional credit** unless you are still satisfied that there is a good explanation and that the client is still a good risk. While you may want to make your decisions on a case-by-case basis, the fatal sin is to ignore these warning signs or get sucked in by one explanation after another, allowing your business to become overexposed to the risk of default.

► THE ILL-FATED SCHLIMAZEL DEFENSE

About a year after I graduated from law school, I defended a client who was brought up on no fewer than seven different traffic-related charges. Although he had explanations for all of the alleged transgressions, I knew that the judge would listen to only about 3.5 seconds of my defense before making up her mind. I couldn't present seven different explanations in 3.5 seconds. Consequently, I told my client that my only hope would be to come down on him before the judge did.

"Your Honor, my client is what is known in Yiddish as a schlimazel. If you are unfamiliar with the term, allow me to elaborate. A schlemiel is a person who spills soup; a schlimazel is the person he spills it on. My client is such a person.

"You see, Your Honor, only a schlimazel could rack up seven different violations five blocks after leaving his house. And although I am perfectly capable of presenting an exculpatory explanation to the court for each of the violations, I would rather speak to the court about punishment. If the aim of justice is to match the penalty to the crime, then I submit that the most appropriate punishment our legal system can devise is to leave my client to his own devices and grant probation before judgment."

When the judge stopped laughing, she said: "Counsel, it may not be law but it's common sense—wherever you have seven different explanations, you have one very real problem. Nevertheless, for entertainment value alone, I'll grant him probation."

Bottom line: Unless you're willing to laugh off a deadbeat client, remember that too many "good" explanations are still probably hiding a potentially bad problem.

Track Your Accounts Receivable

From the day your bills go out, you should keep track of each account to determine how long it takes each customer to pay. This task may have been daunting thirty years ago, but the advent of inexpensive accounting software has made it relatively simple. Regardless of whether you do this on computer or by hand, examine your accounts monthly to ensure that you are extending credit only to the customers that deserve it.

But remember, tracking your accounts receivable is not an academic exercise. The health of your business depends upon your doing something with the information.

Ask to Get Paid

Sounds too stupid to mention, doesn't it? Ask for your money. Everyone does that, don't they? (I answer with a resounding "NO.") Even in today's business world, many people believe a discussion involving money to be *unseemly.* Sure, they'll send an invoice, but actually mention the topic to the customer over the phone or (gasp!) face-to-face? Never.

I'm sure it would not surprise you to learn that I find this stance not only archaic but counterproductive. Of all the techniques discussed in this book, perhaps the best way to ensure payment is to address the topic directly with the customer. It may be the easiest thing in the world for someone to refrain from writing a check, but it would be immeasurably harder for that same person to do anything other than promise payment when speaking directly with you.

Generally speaking, people keep their promises. Putting fashionable cynicism aside, people who can look you in the eye or speak directly with you on the phone and lie about their intention to pay you are comparatively rare. So if the bill is overdue, don't just keep resending the invoice, ask for your money.

▶ FLIP SIDE OF THE COIN: DON'T BE A PAIN

In order to be an across-the-board resource for our clients, my firm maintained a number of relationships with lawyers in other fields with whom we worked closely when the need arose. These firms would bill us for the work and we, in turn, would forward the invoice to the client for payment. We would pay the consulting firms as soon as the client paid us.

One of these firms has a particularly zealous tracking system for its accounts receivable. If a client had not paid by the 35th day, we would get a call on the 36th . . . and the 38th, and the 41st, and so on until the bill was paid. Now this firm has NEVER been stiffed, but sometimes business clients particularly institutions, take 60 or even 90 days to pay. It's the cost of doing business . . . or our business anyway . . . but the bills are always paid.

Now this consulting firm does exceptional work . . . and we hate working with them just the same. In fact, we've gone to considerable lengths to find a comparable firm just to have somewhere else to go. All of this because the firm employs a "harassment style" collection system which, while not speeding up payment, actually discourages business.

► ADDRESS THE PAYMENT ISSUE WHEN YOUR CLIENT STILL NEEDS YOU

It is astonishing how quickly today's hero can become yesterday's news. If a customer has an urgent project or is desperately in need of your services, make sure he pays you when that need is still uppermost in his mind. Often, once the customer's crisis has passed, so has the urgency with which he will write you a check.

► YEAH, BUT WHAT HAVE YOU DONE FOR ME LATELY?

Very early in his practice, an attorney who shall remain nameless (although he's mentioned on the cover of this book) defended a client in a small contract claim. While the client was supposed to pay the bills monthly, more often than not, he'd skip a month and then make only a partial payment.

It wasn't that the attorney didn't notice, but rather that he had gotten to be friends with the client and really believed in the case. The attorney figured that he and the client were a team and that the client would pay the bill when he could.

As trial loomed closer and closer, the attorney questioned

the client about the bill only to receive rather vague assurances. Although it crossed the attorney's mind to insist upon payment behind the threat of withdrawing from the case prior to the trial, the thought was dismissed out of hand . . . because . . . well . . . he and the client were friends and friends just don't do that.

Flushed with victory and good will following a successful defense at trial, the attorney returned to his office confident that a check would virtually walk in the door behind him. Instead, the client sent a Christmas card thanking the attorney for his help and advising him that he was going out of business and moving to Florida. He would send a check "when he got settled." The attorney still waits unpaid.

Bottom line: Make every effort to get paid when you are still needed.

Keep a Record of Every Client Contact

Every communication with the customer doubles in importance as soon as the bill is even one day overdue. Make sure your office staff keeps a record of *every* customer contact. Your records should be kept in the customer's file and should reflect:

- The date and time of the communication.

- The type of communication (e.g., telephone, letter, E-mail, etc.).

- Who initiated the contact.

- Who participated in the communication—both on behalf of the customer and on behalf of your company. (*And please, use full names, not just initials.*)

- What was said (i.e., did the customer agree that he owed you money and call just to ask for more time to pay? Did he question the bill? Did he threaten to sue your company if you try to collect? Did he promise to pay?).

- When did the customer say you could expect payment?

These records will not only help you review the tenor of the relationship should you have to decide on more decisive action, but they can also serve as valuable evidence. Even though you are the one who wrote the communication log, judges take contemporaneous notes very seriously. The more detailed, the better. As we'll discuss in later chapters, your word, your notes, your records . . . they're all evidence in your case against the customer should push come to shove.

Even if you do obtain payment without having to resort to collection efforts, this kind of log can be helpful if the situation ever arises again. You can compare notes for similarities or serious differences that could make *this* the time that the customer fails to come through.

What If the Customer Is Being Sold?

Recently, I received a call from a client advising that one of her long-standing customers was being sold. She had been dealing with this company for almost ten years and working with it over the past two years to clear up a $30,000 delinquency that had accumulated on the account. Now, with the balance hovering around $10,000, it looked like a new owner was stepping into the picture. My client wanted to know her best move.

There are two cardinal rules in this scenario: (1) obtain a renewed payment commitment and (2) let no one off the hook.

Obtain a Renewed Payment Commitment

Often, the new owners will have an interest in continuing to do business with long-standing vendors. Use this to your advantage by insisting upon the execution of an account agreement that expresses all terms for future business *as well as* repayment of the overdue balance. Remember, just because there are new owners doesn't mean that the company shouldn't be held responsible for past bills. If you never had an account agreement with the former owners, this is a golden opportunity to insist on one. Moreover, you should make your willingness to conduct business in the future contingent upon a commitment to repay the past balance and sign a commercial account agreement along the lines discussed in chapter 1.

Don't Let Anyone off the Hook

When I first began working with my client, we created a commercial account agreement that she felt comfortable presenting to her customers for signature. Having obtained not only the company's commitment but also the principal's personal guarantee, my client was in pretty good shape to insist upon the payment of the past-due balance. Nevertheless, the seller insisted that his sale of the business let him off the hook and that he was no longer responsible for payment of any company debts.

Not true. If you have a personal guarantee, it doesn't go away simply because the company was sold, unless the guarantee specifically says so. Assuming that there is no specific "termination-if-sold" provision in the agreement, the personal guarantor is still on the hook.

One of the primary rules of business is that the more people you can look for to get your money, the better. Take an apartment complex as an example. If Person A rents an apartment and decides, in the middle of the lease term, that she has to leave, the lease will often allow her to find a subtenant to finish out the lease term. But even if Person B moves in as a subtenant, Person A is still on the lease and can be sued if Person B fails to pay rent.

Why give up another potential source of money?

▶ THE "NEVER LOOK BACK" SELLER

There are two ways to sell a company—an asset sale and a stock sale. While the nuances of both are far beyond the scope of this book, suffice it to say that a stock (or membership interest) sale results from a transfer of the whole company, lock, stock, and barrel, while an asset sale only transfers ownership of some or all of what the company owned.

For our purposes, the primary difference is that an asset purchaser usually has no obligation to assume debts accumulated by the company prior to the sale, whereas a stock sale usually transfers company debts along with the assets to the new owner.

This is yet another reason to aim for a personal guarantee. With a personal guaranty, absent some language to the contrary, the sale of the company will do nothing to wipe out the debt owed to your business.

My advice to my client was to work up what we called an "Assumption Agreement" which basically confirmed that the new owner had acknowledged and assumed the company's past balance as a continuing obligation. That agreement, combined with a new Commercial Account Agreement signed by the new owners, allowed my client to continue doing business with the new owners of her long-standing corporate customer on her terms, while maintaining her entitlement to all money owed.

Model Telephone Log

TELEPHONE LOG

Date: _____ Initials: _____ Next Action: _____
Next Action Date: _____
Telephone call with: _____
Left message: ☐
Comments: _____
_____
_____
_____

Date: _____ Initials: _____ Next Action: _____
Next Action Date: _____
Telephone call with: _____
Left message: ☐
Comments: _____
_____
_____
_____

Date: _____ Initials: _____ Next Action: _____
Next Action Date: _____
Telephone call with: _____
Left message: ☐
Comments: _____
_____
_____
_____

A man isn't a man until he has to meet a payroll.
—Ivan Shaffer

4
Dealing with Problem Customers

Overview

After you have identified your problem customers as discussed in chapter 3, the next step is dealing with them. What are you going to do with the knowledge? How are you going to prevent a small problem from becoming a larger one?

In this chapter we shall discuss the most effective ways of handling the problem you have just identified—from what to say to how to say it.

Stop Giving Credit to Overdue Customers

You should be extending credit to prompt-paying customers, not late-paying ones. If someone's account is overdue, CUT HIM OFF. Place the account on a special "watch list." This is a list that is *always* on the desk of the president and the department manager, in addition to wherever else it may be.

If any customer on the watch list is still placing orders, make sure he is doing more than paying COD. Each of these customers should be making payments on top of cash on delivery for new orders so that their balance is actually decreasing.

The customer's payments should also be taken into account in your decision to extend additional credit or fulfill additional orders.

For example, if the customer made a payment of $100, you should only fulfill an order with a $75 maximum value. This way, even on a revolving account, you will be minimizing your exposure.

▶ "HOW CAN I STOP EXTENDING MR. X CREDIT? HE'S ONE OF MY BEST CUSTOMERS"

Nothing irritates me more than this question. (OK, a few things do, but nothing within the scope of this book irritates me more than this question.) Unfortunately, few questions are asked more than this one, so I spend a lot of time annoyed. Here it is, once and for all: **If a customer is not paying you on time, he is not a good customer**.

Too many companies worry about offending customers who habitually stiff them for thousands of dollars. If you have a customer like this, you should ask yourself whether you REALLY care if he is offended by your efforts to collect your money. In other words, if he never uses you again, wouldn't you actually be better off?

If not . . . if this is a customer who eventually does pay and whose business (for referrals or otherwise) is worth keeping, then I still encourage you to tighten the reins a little. Remind the customer that he doesn't have unlimited credit. Chances are, he knows he's taking advantage and is just waiting to find out how far you can be pushed.

Bottom line: If you are not *willing to do the work or deliver the products for free, be firm and consistent in your collection practices—across the board.*

Decide When to Take More Forceful Action

Studies have shown that an invoice that goes unpaid for 60 days has only a 70 percent chance of ever being paid. After 90 days, the chances decrease to 45 percent, and after 120 days, there is only a 20 percent chance that you will see any money.

Your options: (1) legal action, (2) send the account to a collection agency, (3) become your own collection agency, or (4) do nothing.

We can eliminate number four right off the bat. You bought this book, didn't you? So let's move on to consider the other choices.

Collection agencies write stern letters, make phone calls, and take one-third to one-half of all the money they collect as their fee. I would recommend sending an account to a collection agency only if (1) you do not have the time or personnel to track your overdue accounts, or (2) you do not believe the account you are sending is actually collectible. In all other situations, you should become your own collection agency first, and possibly consider legal action later.

▶ DON'T SEND LETTERS FROM A PHONY COLLECTION AGENCY

Some business send out collection letters on official looking stationery with ominous sounding names like "Credit Investigation Bureau, Inc." or "Bonded Debt Collection Services." That's OK, as long as they know what they're doing. There are a good number of laws and regulations that apply to these practices, whether the "agency" is actually set up as a separate business or is merely a fictional name for use on stationery.

I strongly recommend that you consult with an attorney prior to sending out any letters or initiating any communications with non-paying customers using any name other than the actual name of your business. Should you ignore my recommendation and proceed in this manner, you could wind up payment your customer more in damages and penalties than he owed you in the first place.

Set a Schedule of Contact with the Debtor

If a bill is overdue, never let more than thirty days go by without contacting the customer. Sending another bill (even one with an interest charge) is not enough. Consider placing an "overdue" stamp on the next month's invoice. Handwritten notes have also proven to be extremely effective. Of course, the most effective way of getting attention is through personal contact. Phone calls or, when appropriate, visits can be very helpful in obtaining payment from a reluctant customer.

Remember to be polite and to give the client a way to save face. Be firm, but first ask if the services or merchandise you sold was satisfactory. Ask if the customer received the invoice or had a question. Most important, ask when you can expect payment. Get a commitment from the customer. If the customer needs a little bit more time to pay, fine. You may benefit more by giving it to him than by forcing a confrontation. Either way, listen to what your customer is telling you—both verbally and between the lines.

You may find it helpful to create a policy of alternating phone calls with letters for a certain period of time. I often advise that suit should be filed if the debtor does not respond within ninety days— enough time for two phone calls and three letters, with a reasonable response time after each contact. Consider the following schedule:

Day 1: Send invoice (due on Day 30).

Day 35: Call debtor (simply to make sure the invoice reached him) and to inquire as to any payment problems—usually for use with new or problem customers).

Day 45: Send first collection letter.

Day 60: Call debtor second and last time before filing suit and send second collector letter.

Day 85: Send third and final collection letter.

Day 95: File suit.

Contacting the Debtor

No matter how many contacts you decide to have with the debtor during the course of your own collection process, you should ALWAYS observe these rules:

1. Keep it civil and under control.

2. Adopt a sterner tone with each contact.

3. NEVER give the debtor a reason to sue you.

Be Professional

Most people, at some time in their lives, have missed a payment or found themselves short of cash. Remember to treat the debtor as you would like to be treated in that situation. Don't try to humiliate him. Translation: Screaming "DEADBEAT" at the top of your lungs is unlikely to put money in your pocket. Try, instead, to identify the problem and work out a solution. You may find that you will not only get paid but that you will also save a customer well worth having.

A good technique may be to provide the debtor with a ready-made excuse. Acknowledge that he may have been extremely busy and just didn't put your invoice at the top of his pile. As time passes most people's reluctance to call snowballs. What had first been a hesitance to acknowledge slower-than-required payment becomes doubly difficult as the debtor must first apologize for not having contacted you *and then* apologize for the past-due bill.

Even if it strains you to provide the debtor with an excuse or show any understanding after having been strung along, it will be far easier for the debtor to call you (even with his tail between his legs) if he knows he won't be chastised for his lack of response and can simply move on to address the business at hand.

If you cannot be friendly, at least be businesslike. You have a job to do—either induce the debtor to pay or get information from him that is useful in court. If you find the conversation is becoming personal and unproductive, say so, advise the debtor that you are hanging up, and break the connection.

Finally, make sure these instructions are given to anyone on your staff charged with the responsibility of contacting the debtor. Because they work for you, you are responsible for their actions. If a member of your staff harasses the debtor while making a call on your behalf, you could very well be sued or subjected to civil or even criminal penalties.

Be Firmer with Each Contact

Regardless of whether your first "collection" contact with the debtor is by phone or letter, it should always be more inquiring than hostile. If, after that contact, you do not receive payment within a reasonable amount of time, turn up the pressure.

You may want to advise the debtor that his account has been frozen (if he intends to do business with you again—if not, it's an empty threat) and that you will only accept cash up front for goods or services. Furthermore, you may advise him that his account has been "placed in collection."

As you continue through the process, you should advise the debtor that you will be filing suit against him if payment is not received within a certain amount of time. Please feel free to refer to the model collection letters I have placed at the conclusion of this chapter and adapt them for your use.

Never Give the Debtor a Reason to Sue You

Several years ago newspapers all across the country ran an article announcing an $11 million verdict against a collection agency for unfair and harassing collection practices. Granted, this case represented an extreme, but the message from the jury to debt collectors was clear: If you cross the line from legitimate collection efforts to harassment, you will be the one forced to pay.

Avoid Making Threats

Threats of physical harm are illegal. Consequently, advising the debtor that unless he pays up within ten days, he will be receiving a visit from Tony "the Enforcer" Avocado can be harmful to YOUR well-being. The only acceptable threats concern actions you can take, such as filing suit and, if your business is so equipped, having the debtor's failure to pay recorded in his credit history.

Call at an Acceptable Hour

The only thing worse than screaming "deadbeat" at the top of your lungs or threatening a visit from the Enforcer is doing it at 2:00 A.M. It may be tempting, but don't do it. Not only won't this get you your money, but it could place you on the wrong end of a lawsuit for unlawful use of the telephone. (Yes, that is a real charge under many states' penal codes.) An "acceptable hour" is anytime between 8:00 A.M. and 9:00 P.M.—you know, the hours during which you're continuously talking to people trying to sell you long distance.

Call at an Acceptable Location

If the debtor is an individual rather than a business, and you have any reason to believe that the debtor is not allowed to receive personal calls at work, DON'T CALL HIM THERE. This rule may seem like a needless courtesy extended to someone who owes you money, but it's not. If you give the debtor any reason to file a countersuit against you for damages, he will do it. Getting him fired or demoted certainly gives him that reason (in addition to reducing the chances that the debtor will have the money to pay you).

Bottom line: Call the debtor at work. If, however, you are told—even by the debtor himself—that he is not allowed to receive personal calls at work, stop. Ask the debtor when a good time to speak with him is, get a phone number or place to meet, and continue the conversation there. IF the debtor fails to keep the appointment, he is as good as telling you that informal proceedings will not be successful and that your only hope of collecting the money is to file suit.

The Fair Debt Collection Practices Act

Don't Become Your Own Worst Enemy

The Fair Debt Collection Practices Act (FDCPA) is a law enacted to prevent harassment of debtors by creditors or their representatives. Now, you might ask why anyone cares to stop harassment of debtors. The answer is twofold: First, almost everyone is a debtor at some point in his life; and second, left unchecked, overzealous claimants and collection agencies had gotten debtors fired from work, ruined reputations, and threatened families with physical danger, often for debts about which the debtor has a legitimate dispute. Congress stepped in.

All of the rules for communicating with the debtor discussed in this chapter may be found in the FDCPA and its progeny. Review them carefully. Suffice it to say that if you violate its terms in attempting to collect the money owed your company, you may wind up buying yourself a lawsuit, fines, and penalties instead. If you think your practices may violate the FDCPA, check with a qualified attorney before you persist in the questionable behavior.

Instructing Attorneys and Collection Agencies

It may surprise you to learn that many state legislatures are enacting new laws to protect not creditors but debtors. These laws make it easier for debtors to sue the companies that come after them for anything from harassment to intentional infliction of emotional distress. Even more alarming, chances are your general-liability business policy will not protect you from the expense of defending this kind of lawsuit, let alone paying off a judgment should you lose.

While you may be able to control actions taken by your employees, your obligation under these laws may not end there. In the eyes of the law, attorneys and collection agencies you hire are your agents. Their actions may be imputed to you and to your business. In plain language, anything *they* say or do can be used against you.

Your best defense to these claims is to document your requirement that any attorneys and collection agencies you engage abide by the Fair Debt Collection Practices Act. It may sound silly, or like another piece of useless paper, but one letter from you, on your company letterhead, sent at the outset of your relationship with the company or attorney may be your best evidence that you were not aware of and did not condone your "agents'" departure from fair debt collection practices. An example of this letter is included in the appendix at the conclusion of this chapter.

Appendix

Sample Collection Letters

First Collection Letter

[Date]

[Contact's Name, Title]
[Street Address]
[City, State & Zip Code]

Re: [Describe Services or display invoice/account number]

Dear [Contact]:

    In reviewing our records, we noticed that we have not yet received payment from you for the balance due on your account. As you are aware, we agreed that all outstanding balances would be paid within thirty (30) days of billing. The current balance is $_____.

    If you have already sent your payment, thank you, and please disregard this letter. Otherwise, we would appreciate your sending in your payment immediately.

    Finally, if you have any questions or concerns about the bill or [the goods sold or services performed], please call me upon receipt of this letter so that we may discuss these issues.

    Thank you for your prompt attention to this matter. I look forward to hearing from you soon.

                Very truly yours,
                [Your Company]

                [Signatory and Title]

Second Collection Letter

[Date]

[Contact's Name, Title]
[Street Address]
[City, State & Zip Code]

Re: [Describe Services or display invoice/account number]

Dear [Contact]:

As you are aware, your account with us in seriously past due. Your current balance is $_____. Although we would like to work with you to resolve any difficulties in bringing your account forward, we are nearing the point at which we will be forced to take appropriate legal action against you to collect the balance due on your account.

We regret the fact that you have chosen to ignore our telephone calls and previous correspondence. Nevertheless, you should be advised that ignoring this situation will not make the problem disappear. We encourage you to call [contact person] **IMMEDIATELY** if you would like to address this matter without the unpleasantness that more formal collection efforts would bring.

Please do not fail to contact us now. If we do not hear from you within ten (10) days from the date of this letter, we shall assume that you do not want to resolve this matter informally and we shall proceed accordingly.

Very truly yours,
[Your Company]

[Signatory and Title]

Final Collection Letter

[Date]

VIA CERTIFIED MAIL,
RETURN RECEIPT REQUESTED
[Contact's Name, Title]
[Street Address]
[City, State & Zip Code]

Re: [Describe Services or display invoice/account number]

Dear [Contact]:

Please accept this letter as **NOTICE** that we will be pursuing a formal collection action against you for the balance due on your account unless payment is received **IMMEDIATELY**. Such actions may involved filing suit, reporting your failure to remit payment to the appropriate credit agency, or other remedies permitted by law. Your current balance is $_____. Payment must be received at our offices no later than the close of business on [date].

We regret that we have been forced to take this route, but you have left us no choice. If you wish to avoid the prospect of having a judgment entered against you, and possibly having your wages subject to garnishment and/or having your personal property sold at auction to pay the balance of your account, please contact [contact person] now.

Please do not fail to contact us.

> Very truly yours,
> [THE COMPANY]

[Signatory and Title]

Instruction Letter to Attorneys and/or Collection Agencies

[Date]

VIA FACSIMILE AND FIRST CLASS MAIL
[Customer's Name]
[Street Address]
[City, State & Zip Code]

Re: Collection Practices

Dear _____:

As you know, our company is tough on debtors and has engaged your firm as part of our effort to get paid for our efforts. While we would like (and expect) you to act forcefully in pursuing these accounts, it is this company's absolute requirement that all [agencies/attorneys] working with us respect the debtor's individual rights.

State and federal laws, such as the Fair Debt Collection Practices Act, endow each debtor with specific rights and place strict limitations upon actions which any creditor may take in pursuing a debt. We anticipate and, in fact, require that your firm will abide by both the letter and spirit of these limitations. Any actions taken outside the limitations imposed by these laws and regulations are unauthorized and are taken outside the scope of any agency which may be deemed to exist.

If at any time in pursuing accounts on our behalf, you feel that you are unable to abide by local, state, or federal laws and regulations, please return our files to us immediately and refrain from taking any further action.

Thank you for your continued attention to these instructions.

Very truly yours,

[Company]

[Signatory]

Going to Court

The only person who hears both sides of an argument is the fellow in the next apartment.

—Anonymous

5

Alternative Dispute Resolution: Mediation and Arbitration

Overview

Court dockets are crowded. Litigation can be expensive and time-consuming. People who didn't happen to go to law school can sometimes find the rules of evidence confusing. Enter alternative dispute resolution, or "ADR."

The subject of ADR is often embraced by so-called litigation reform experts who see ADR as the answer to crowded dockets and expensive trials. In practice, however, ADR often brings as many disadvantages as it does benefits.

In this chapter we will discuss what is meant by alternative dispute resolution, when and how you can use it to your advantage, and what to beware of when you see an ADR provision in someone else's contract.

What Is Alternative Dispute Resolution?

The "alternative" in "alternative dispute resolution" means anything that is not court. ADR would, therefore, include referring the dispute to a neutral third party or even an informal settlement discussion among the parties themselves—either with or without a facilitator.

When contracts, lawyers, or judges talk about ADR, what they mean is some other process, outside of litigation, that will either push the parties toward reaching a settlement or provide a different forum for arguing the case. The two most frequently discussed types of ADR are mediation and arbitration.

Mediation

Definition

Here's the lawyer's definition straight from *Black's Law Dictionary:*

> **Mediation**. Intervention; interposition; the act of a third person in intermediating between two contending parties with a view toward persuading them to adjust or settle their dispute. Settlement of dispute by action of intermediary (neutral party).

> Translation: settlement conference.

Mediation is what your friends did when you and a playmate had a fight. They listened to the problem and suggested a solution you could then accept (or take your ball and go home). Anytime someone outside the dispute works with the parties to settle the issue, one could say that the issue was being "mediated."

The two most important things to remember about mediation are: (1) It is nonbinding and (2) it is confidential.

Even if, after hearing each side of the dispute, the mediator expresses her opinion that one person owes the other everything claimed, either side is free to ignore the mediator's remarks and walk away. The mediator will not have the power to force a settlement upon either side. She can try to move both sides toward a settlement. She can even provide her opinion as to what a judge would rule. A mediator does not, however, have the power to issue a ruling or bind the parties to her decision.

The confidentiality of the proceedings is equally important to remember. As an example, let's say that your company is claiming $2,000 from a customer as a result of the customer's failure to pay for three separate orders. Now in a court of law, you may fight to the death for that $2,000, refusing to give an inch. However, in your heart of hearts, you acknowledge (quietly to yourself when no one else is looking) that the customer may have a point when he says that he never authorized the third order. In fact, you have a sneaking suspicion that your staff messed up on it in the first place.

If you realize, as most people do, that it would be better to settle a claim than to litigate it, particularly when the other side may have a point or two in its favor, you are a prime candidate for mediation. The problem is figuring out how you can be honest and admit the possibility of an error without risking that admission being thrown up in your face at trial if you are unable to reach a settlement. The answer is confidentiality.

Trained mediators will have all sides sign an acknowledgment that anything said in mediation is absolutely confidential. No statements can be mentioned in court, and the mediator cannot be made to testify about the discussions or her opinions on the case. This way, both sides can honestly work toward settling disputes without worrying that their candor will cost them later on down the road.

Often, both sides cannot be counted on to find a mutually agreeable, neutral third party to hear the competing arguments and facilitate a compromise. Consequently, quite a few private companies and organizations exist, in large part, to provide a structured procedure, a neutral location, and trained mediators. An easy way to find these companies is to consult business-to-business yellow pages or enter "mediation" in any Internet search engine, as many such organizations maintain an Internet presence.

How a Mediation Is Conducted

Mediations can take place almost anywhere. In my experience, they usually take place in a conference room, preferably at a neutral site such as the mediator's office or the office space of a third party. There need not be anything special about the room—mediations have no need for the trappings that characterize courtrooms.

While mediations can be conducted in any number of ways, the basic pattern remains the same. First, the mediator will convene the session with all parties (and their lawyers, if applicable) in one room. She will review the purpose, rules, and procedures involved and ensure that each party signs a confidentiality agreement, as discussed above. If the mediator has not presented a confidentiality agreement, ask for one.

In about half of the mediations I have attended, each party had already been asked to submit a brief description of the claim from their point of view, as well as a summary of negotiations that had already taken place and any settlement demands or requirements. In the other half, the mediator approaches the session cold and must take more time with the parties initially to understand the issues and positions.

Either way, you should be prepared to tell the mediator what you will either accept or offer in settlement. Of course, this figure would not be your bottom-line offer but rather one that sets the tone for the negotiations from your side.

Now remember, if you really want to give the mediation a fair shot at success, your demand must be realistic. Don't make it so high that the person on the other side wouldn't have to pay that much even after his worst possible outcome in court. Such a move would almost certainly cripple a negotiation before it got under way. Instead, your position should be staked out on the high side of reasonable.

▶ THAT DEER-IN-THE-HEADLIGHTS LOOK

I can't tell you how many people I have seen walk into mediations with what must have been days of preparation—papers, notebooks, slipfiles, charts, etc.—only to be completely surprised by the question: "So, what are you looking for?" If you are unable to tell the mediator in one concise sentence what you want to accomplish or what it will take for you to settle, you are not prepared.

Once the mediator has met with everyone at once and gained an understanding of the issues, positions, and personalities, she will ask one side to leave the room so that she may speak privately with the other. There is no magic or advantage to which side goes first. Each will get its turn.

In the private session, the mediator will most likely be more vocal than at the opening of the mediation. She may explore your claims a little more closely, almost the way an attorney might on cross-examination. *Do not get defensive.* What she does to you, she will do to the other side as well. Her job is to make you understand that it is in your best interest to compromise—that your position has some weaknesses.

I always tell my clients that the mediator will likely come in to us and explain how our case is worth $1.98 and urge us to take any settlement and run like a bunny. In half an hour the same mediator will be telling the other side why our case is worth one billion dollars and that it would be in their best interest to offer us anything within their power to pay. Then, with the dollar signs having been suitably removed from both sides' eyes, the mediator can begin working the sides toward the middle.

As the mediation progresses, everyone involved will begin to get a sense as to whether it has a chance to be successful. Sometimes, the two sides are just too far apart to make likely the chances for settlement. In these cases, it is better to cut your losses and end the session. If, however, both sides genuinely want to work toward a settlement and real potential exists, mediations my last for hours, even days. A good mediator will leave no stone unturned in her discussions with each side in order to wring out a compromise all can live with.

▶ THERE IS NO SUBSTITUTE FOR A TRAINED MEDIATOR

There is a world of difference between a neutral party and a trained mediator. Both may fulfill the same role and call themselves the same thing, but a trained mediator understands how to cajole and muscle people toward a compromise. Often, each party understands the need to settle and is simply too stubborn or worried about losing face to act in his or her best interest. A trained mediator can spot openings, will not get discouraged, and will work to move things along.

Many court systems and bar associations have training programs for mediators. Moreover, the organizations of which I spoke earlier often require mediators to complete a course of training before they can be added to the roster. Check out the mediator's credentials if at all possible. With a trained mediator, the chances of reaching a successful conclusion more than double. That's a good thing. After all, it's your time you're spending.

The Mandatory Mediation

Many contracts now require the parties to mediate disputes as a mandatory prerequisite to filing suit. In other words, the contracts provide that suit may not be filed unless the parties have tried and failed to reach a solution through mediation. Don't shy away from this requirement—either by scratching it out of the other guy's contract or by refusing to add it to your own. Too many settlement opportunities are missed because each side is afraid that mentioning the possibility of compromise is a sign of weakness. A mandatory mediation eliminates this fear by placing settlement on a mandatory agenda.

I do not, however, recommend that mediation be made mandatory (say that three times fast) in every situation. Often an early mediation will eliminate litigation in smaller claims, especially where the cost of hiring a lawyer dwarfs the amount at issue.

In claims involving hundreds of thousands of dollars, however, the differences are often great enough to require some fact-finding and discovery (in the legal sense) before meaningful settlement talks can be held. In these types of claims, I prefer a mandatory settlement conference thirty to sixty days prior to trial or arbitration rather than before any papers are filed.

Court-Sponsored Mediation

A number of states offer prospective litigants the option of participating in a court-sponsored mediation. This means that if the parties agree, the court will appoint a mediator, most often an attorney, to meet with the parties and attempt to settle the case before trial. Where small claims are concerned, I have two words of advice: DO IT. You have nothing to lose and you may save yourself (and the court system) a great deal of time and aggravation.

Preparing for the Mediation

Negotiations are won or lost on preparation. Period. End of story. It is one thing to go into a mediation and demand money. It is quite another to go in, demand money, and demonstrate to the other side how effectively you can prove your entitlement to it.

Recently, I attended a pretrial mediation with my client in a construction claim. My client did the work and the owner failed to pay. We had one notebook with all documentation organized and easily accessible. The other side had a pile of unattached papers. Need to locate an invoice? We had each one tabbed. Want to know if we actually worked on such and such a date? All daily reports were organized chronologically. Have to verify an expense? All receipts for supplies were photocopied and arranged in the notebook by date in their own separate section.

You could see the other side wilt. The lawyer not only had to talk to his client about the merits of our position but also had to grapple with the powerful yet unspoken argument: "Do we really want to face that in court?"

Say it nicely if you will, but the fact of the matter is that solid preparation can not only document your claim but break the other guy's spirit—make him lose his willingness to fight. That is your goal.

When you prepare for your mediation (or arbitration or trial for that matter), think about what papers you will need to prove each point of your argument. Then, place them in an order where you can retrieve them instantly. Having done that, you have completed half of your preparation. Now look at it from the other side. What arguments does the other side have?

If you think your customer plans to dispute the amount of work you devoted to the project, organize and bring time sheets, payroll stubs, or anything else that will help you counter that argument. If he plans to state that your work was unauthorized, bring any correspondence, inspection reports, or signed tickets that may speak to the contrary. If applicable, photographs (originals or color copies) really are worth a thousand words.

You cannot be too organized. Try to anticipate the mediator's questions. She will undoubtedly want to see any agreements and/or modifications to the contract upon which your claim is based. Have copies handy. A good way to organize your documentation is in a notebook. I'm a big notebook fan. Files are fine, but you're still flipping papers and giving the appearance of someone who just threw things together. Computer spreadsheets on a laptop are also impressive, as long as you have hard copies for everyone to review.

I would also type (not handwrite, but type) a separate sheet itemizing your claim for the mediator's easy reference. If you can establish your itemization as the reference point for the mediation, such that everyone is working off of your sheet, so much the better.

In essence, your goal, as I shall reiterate in the chapter on trial preparation, is to make it incredibly easy, perhaps even irresistible, for the mediator to follow your exhibits and documentation straight to the conclusion you want her to reach. Even though she is not empowered to render a ruling, the establishment of a viewpoint favorable to your position can be very helpful to you.

Finally, if the mediation ends unsuccessfully, take back your exhibits. The other side may want to keep them because doing so would better help them prepare for trial. In my view, if a settlement cannot be reached, there is no reason why they should leave the mediation with more information than absolutely necessary. Don't be squeamish. Ask for all papers back. It's your right.

How Much Should You Say?

Rarely are there surprises so devastating that their use would guarantee a win at trial. In those circumstances you may want to think twice about tipping your hand in mediation. Other than that, I would not hesitate to explain the strengths of your case in detail. Weaknesses are another story. If you want to acknowledge weaknesses by compromising a little, fine. I would not expound on them or give the other side more information on a damaging subject. Confidentiality agreement or no, you can't unring the bell. Once a statement is made, you can't make the other side forget it was uttered.

Of course, the advice dispensed above presumes that you believe the mediation has a decent shot at succeeding. If there really is no chance of reaching a real settlement and you (and/or the other side) are appearing just because you have to, the less said the better.

Arbitration

Definition

Here's the lawyer's definition straight from *Black's Law Dictionary:*

Arbitration. The reference of a dispute to an impartial (third) person chosen by the parties to the dispute who agree in advance to abide by the arbitrator's award issued after a hearing at which both parties have an opportunity to be heard.

An arrangement for taking and abiding by the judgment of selected persons in some disputed matter, instead of carrying it to established tribunals of justice, and is intended to avoid the formalities, the delay, the expense, and the vexation of ordinary litigation.

Translation: an informal, binding trial.

Arbitration is what your parents did when you and your siblings needed an issue decided.[1] It wasn't mediation—at least not in my house—it was arbitration . . . final. (If you now believe arbitration involves staying in your room, forget that example and keep reading.)

There are three things to remember about arbitration: (1) It's binding; (2) there are even fewer rights of appeal than there are with a court trial; and, (3) there are no rules of evidence—everything comes in.

Unlike mediations, arbitrations are binding. Mediators make recommendations. Arbitrators make rulings. In fact, arbitrators typically have even more power than judges. In every state that has adopted a version of the Uniform Arbitration Act (and that is the vast majority), an arbitrator's ruling can be appealed only for very limited reasons such as evidence of fraud, corruption, or failure to consider significant evidence.

This latter point—the fact that in certain circumstances an arbitration award may be overturned for failure to consider certain evidence—arbitrators routinely let everything into evidence. In fact, it would be accurate to say that there are no rules of evidence.

▶ SAY A LITTLE PRAYER FOR ME . . .

In 1992, I represented a general contractor in an arbitration which arose out of the construction of a convent. The Order

---

[1] I am, however, mindful of Bill Cosby's observation that "parents are not interested in justice; parents are interested in quiet."

sought millions of dollars from my client as a result of some real and some perceived construction defects.

When the lawyers for the Sisters presented their arbitration exhibits, I noticed that buried among the construction daily reports, correspondence, and photographs were hymns, pictures of church outings, and prayers. Every bit of it was accepted into evidence by the arbitration panel.

How an Arbitration Is Conducted

As with mediations, arbitrations are conducted without the trappings of the courtroom. Most often, conference rooms are used. I've had arbitrations in Holiday Inns, library conference rooms, and lawyers' offices across the country. All that is needed is a table upon which one can spread out exhibits and the right number of chairs.

Unlike court, where evidence is received by the judge one item at a time as it is introduced by the testimony, arbitrators usually accept all evidence at once. As I'll discuss in greater detail in the preparation section, I've always found it best to prepare an easy-to-follow notebook for the arbitrator that can be presented right at the outset.

At the appointed time, the arbitrator will begin by explaining the procedures and applicable rules, following which he will allow the claimant to make an opening statement (if desired). An opening statement is a short, concise explanation of what the claimant intends to show. Many arbitrators will dispense with opening statements, preferring to get right to the witnesses, but most will allow them if one side or the other wants to make one.

Once opening statements are finished, the claimant—the person filing the claim—begins to present his case by calling his first witness. The questioning of witnesses is much less formal than it is in court. One of the main characteristics of arbitrations is informality. The arbitrator doesn't want to hear stilted legal-type questions. He wants to hear normally phrased questions that get to the bottom of issues. What's more, you won't hear any objections in an arbitration. The arbitrator will listen to everything (unless or until he gets annoyed).

After one side finishes questioning a witness, the other side will get an opportunity. The two sides can go back and forth with the same witness until they have no more questions to ask or the arbitrator puts a stop to it and tells the witness to go home.

Arbitration follows the same general pattern as trial, and you can read more about the order of things and tips on witness presentation in chapter 15. Each side gets its chance to present all of its witnesses and question all those presented by the opposition. The arbitrator will then ask for closing remarks—a chance for each party to summarize its points and argue its position.

It is rare that an arbitrator will rule immediately after the presentation of evidence. In fact, I've never seen it happen. Usually, the decision will be announced in a terse statement within thirty days of the arbitration's conclusion. Don't expect a detailed report summarizing the arbitrator's opinion as to each issue. Arbitrators can have their rulings overturned if they fail to consider a significant issue. Consequently, they usually don't reveal what they considered at all. Just a two-line who-won, who-lost statement.

Preparing for the Arbitration

Remember my notebooks from the mediation section? I'm even more serious about them here. The easier it is for you and the arbitrator to find a necessary exhibit, the closer you are to winning your case even before you start. When it comes to arbitration (or any proceeding for that matter), preparation is my personal mantra.

When assembling an arbitration notebook, you must first sit back and consider the order in which your case should be presented. Sometimes, you should divide documents by type—agreements, correspondence, estimates, account ledgers, and so on. Other times, particularly when you have multiple claims (e.g., claims arising out of several different orders), you might want to group all documentation supporting each claim together under one tab. Still another option is to group documents and pictures together in the order in which they would be introduced and discussed by witnesses.

To figure out the best organization for your case, I recommend you sit down and write your closing remarks. What do you hope all of your evidence shows? What do you hope to be able to explain to the arbitrator? If you write your closing remarks in a clear, concise, and persuasive way, chances are you will find your exhibit organization in there somewhere.

The Arbitration Clause

There is a huge difference between an option and a command. Nowhere is this more true than in law. In order to have any meaning at all, arbitration clauses written into contracts must be mandatory. If the arbitration paragraph states that "any disputes arising out of this contract *may* be submitted to arbitration," either side may decide against arbitration, thereby negating the provision. On the other hand, if the paragraph reads: "Any disputes arising out of this contract *shall* be submitted to arbitration," the provision is mandatory and the parties are not free to avoid arbitration unless all sides to the dispute agree.

Pros and Cons of ADR

The major advantage to mediation is that it provides a scheduled time to explore settlement. Neither side has to be the first to propose compromise, so neither side risks being perceived as having blinked first. Equally as important is the potential savings of time and money by settling differences rather than airing them in court. As we'll discuss in the chapter on settlement, the vast majority of cases are settled before they ever reach trial. The avoidance of the expense and delays inherent in a fully tried case constitutes the major advantage of mediation.

Many people cite also expense as a major advantage arbitration maintains over trial. And while it's true that arbitration is less formal and often takes less time (certainly than a jury trial), it is not necessarily a cheap option.

Arbitrators are paid by the parties. Fees can run well over $1,000 per day, per arbitrator. In larger cases, where an arbitration panel of three may be needed for weeks at a time, the prospect of a judge paid by the taxpayers begins to look really good. What's more, organizations such as the American Arbitration Association make their money by charging filing fees well over and above those customarily charged by the state and federal court systems.

"Yeah, but . . . ," arbitration proponents would say, "arbitration does away with all of the prelitigation discovery like interrogatories and depositions (see chapter 13) that can run up legal fees, costs, and time spent on a case." This is all true. Nevertheless, one can also run up substantial bills in arbitration just through the production of exhibits, many of which would never be needed or admitted in court. In fact, about ten years ago I served as counsel in an arbitration where our side's photocopying bill . . . *the photocopying bill* . . . exceeded $50,000. So cheap isn't always the watchword.

My bottom line is that I never like to proceed to arbitration in any matter that can be handled by the small-claims court. Arbitration inevitably takes more time and money than court. In larger cases, arbitration is usually less expensive.

There are other differences in addition to cost. First, an arbitrator is usually someone conversant with the subject matter. Let's take a construction dispute as an example. If you proceed to court on a construction matter, which may involve a review and discussion of plans and specifications, you will be talking to a judge who probably presided over two divorce trials last week and will be moving on to hear a petty theft case after he decides your dispute. In other words, he may be no more conversant with construction drawings than the average person on the street (so don't even get me started on trying technical claims before a jury).

Arbitrators, on the other hand, are selected by the parties from résumés provided by the arbitration organization. As a result, arbitrators are usually much more familiar with the nature of the claim. Sometimes this makes no difference. Other times it can mean the difference between an arbitrary result and a well-reasoned ruling.

A further difference concerns the arbitrator's power. An arbitrator has absolute power. She can ignore the state law or enforce it. If an arbitrator decides that the statute of limitations is fifteen years, then in that room the statute of limitations is fifteen years, even if it may be three years everywhere else.

For my purposes, I always prefer arbitration if my client's case is longer on justice than on law. Thus, if my client's position is more appealing from a fairness perspective even though the technical, legal wording of a contract or statute cuts against him, I choose arbitration every time. The reverse is also true. If I am looking for enforcement of the letter of a contract or law, despite what may be seen as a harsh result for the other side, I always look to a judge.

As you can see, there are a number of factors to consider. Nevertheless, where smaller cases are concerned, cash is king. I'd go with the less expensive alternative, which is usually court. Larger cases bring in a number of other factors such as those discussed above. I would encourage you to consider all of these with a qualified attorney or adviser.

How Arbitrators and Mediators Are Selected

The selection method depends upon how the parties arrived at the proceeding. If the parties agreed among themselves to refer the matter to a separate organization for mediation or arbitration, the organization will assemble a list of people in your area qualified to preside. Each side can eliminate those people it determines are unsuitable, whether because the person knows one side, has a real or perceived bias, or lacks the qualifications to understand the subject matter. Each side then ranks in order of preference the remaining choices and forwards its selection sheet to the organization (without copying the other side). The organization will then select that individual who ranked highest on both sheets and advise the parties of the selection.

If, on the other hand, the parties are participating in a court-sponsored mediation or arbitration, the court will select the appropriate individual and notify the parties of its choice.

Logistics

Following the selection of the arbitrator or mediator, the designated person will set up a conference call with all parties to make arrangements for the proceeding. At that time you can ask any questions you may have about how the proceeding will be handled, location, and length of time. These phone calls are always informal and are conducted simply in order to ensure that everything goes smoothly. If, prior to the actual proceeding, you have a question or develop a scheduling conflict, you will be directed to call either a case manager assigned by the organization or the mediator or arbitrator.

This is a court of law, young man, not a court of justice.
—Oliver Wendell Holmes Jr.

6
Do You Have a Case?

Overview

People in our country tend to view the legal system in one of two ways, either with unwarranted optimism ("All I really need to do is show up and the judge will know I'm right") or unrelenting pessimism ("The system is not meant to work for people like me"). The fact of the matter is that the system can work for anyone as long as they follow the rules.

When it comes to the legal system, however, simply being right isn't enough. You must meet all of the requirements for bringing your case to court or you won't even get a chance to tell your story to the judge.

This chapter discusses the major requirements your case must fulfill. Please do not skip this chapter, thinking, "I know I'm right. I'll just skip to the chapter on how to file suit." This mistake could cause you to waste an enormous amount of time and effort.

► **"PROPERLY PRESENTED, YOU SHOULD PREVAIL"**

This was the advice I received from the senior partner when I, as a new lawyer, confessed my doubts about an upcoming trial. "Properly presented, you should prevail."

Sure, this was an innocuous way of saying "If you don't win, it's your fault," but the statement also held a larger truth. Odds are the judge won't know either party or any of the facts before the case is called for trial. For this reason, an awful lot hinges upon presentation. If your case is disorganized or if you fail to understand and clearly state what you want the judge to do, the best facts in the world will not help you win. In litigation, presentation may not be everything, but it's close enough.

As you read through this chapter and the ones to follow, think about the best presentation of your own claims . . . and heed the advice of my old senior partner.

Who Should File Suit?

First things first—you need to know who is suing the debtor. Said another way: "To whom is the money owed?"

If money is owed to *your business* by a nonpaying customer, your business owns the claim against that person. Consequently, the claim should be filed in the name of the business. On the other hand, if the money is owed to you personally, the claim should be filed in your name. This distinction will make a big difference in your case, as we shall see in the sections to follow.

▶ YOU CAN BUY AND SELL YOUR CLAIMS

Even if the amount of money owed to your company is large enough to require the company to hire a lawyer, many states allow a simple way around the rule. Remember that companies may only represent themselves without a lawyer up to a claim amount, depending upon the state (see chart, pages 114–117). Individuals, however, are free to represent themselves without an attorney no matter the claim amount.

Simply put, you, as an individual, can buy the rights to the claim from your company. Let's say the customer owes your company $3,000 and that you must file in Maryland, where the small-claim ceiling is $2,500. You have two choices: (1) Your company can hire a lawyer or (2) your company can "assign" or sell the claim to an individual who, as we know, is not required to hire an attorney.

In order for the sale to be recognized as legitimate, you (or some other individual) should buy the claim for a fair percent-

age of its face value. This price should depend upon how difficult the claim may be to win or collect. For example, you could
buy a $3,000 claim from your company for, say, $1,000. You
must pay your $1,000 to the company. Now all of the rights to
the claim belong to you. You can then follow the instructions in
this guide and proceed to court without an attorney. Note that
there is no precise formula for deciding how much you should
pay for the claim.

I do have three warnings:

First, the sale of the claim must be real. You cannot simply
take over your company's claims without paying for them and
then return any money recovered to the company, the less your
expenses. This is akin to perpetrating a fraud on the court. You
must pay for the claim, and anything you recover belongs to
you personally.

Second, make sure the debtor does not have a claim against
the company. You may be buying his lawsuit against your company right along with your claim against him.

Third, you may actually lose your money. When you buy a
claim, what you are really getting is the right to go to court
against the nonpaying customer. While you make a profit if you
force the customer to pay in full, there is also a chance that you
will lose the suit or be unable to collect on the judgment after
you win in court.

*Bottom line: I do not recommend that an individual buy a com-
pany's claims, but doing so is something to think about. Before
you decide to make a policy of selling your company's claims to
an individual, consult a lawyer. Your lawyer can execute an
assignment agreement and advise you on the legal consequences
of this agreement.*

Do You Have Enough Evidence?

Before an attorney can look at your case and say, "Sure, go ahead
and sue, your case looks good," he has to discuss proof. An attorney has to make sure that you have the necessary evidence to
prove your claim.

To sue a customer for nonpayment, you must prove (1) that the customer accepted your goods or services and (2) that he did not pay for them. In legal terms, when you sue your customer because he did not fulfill his obligation to pay, you are suing him for "breach of contract." Consequently, you must prove not only that your client did not perform his end of the bargain but also that you did—that is, that you provided the goods and services you said you would and that they were of the promised quality and quantity.

► ## MAKE SURE YOUR WITNESSES ARE WILLING TO GO TO COURT

Although it's true that witnesses can be forced to appear in court once they're served with a subpoena, you are always much better off if a witness testifies voluntarily rather than being forced to do so. Consequently, if your case depends on the testimony of one particular person (especially if that person is not one of your employees), make sure he knows ahead of time that he may have to appear if the case goes to trial. Discussing the issue with your witness in advance saves you some unpleasant surprises later. What's more, keep in constant contact with your witnesses throughout the litigation and make sure they know the date and time well in advance.

Once the person agrees to testify, always serve him with a subpoena. Let him know when he will be served and set up a convenient time to have the subpoena delivered. Service of a subpoena is your best protection against witness who suddenly decides he has better things to do than appear in court.

If a material witness is unavailable to testify on the date assigned by the court, request a postponement of the trial, as shown in chapter 12.

What Is a Contract?

A contract is an agreement. It can be oral or it can be set down in writing. A contract can be a fifty-five-page typed, single-spaced document drafted in Latin by a firm of five hundred $300-per-hour lawyers, or it can be a handwritten purchase order.

The next time you start out asking yourself "Did we have a contract?", think instead, "Did we reach an agreement?" The fact of the matter is that most businesses don't do business with fifty-page contracts. One-page estimates, signed purchase orders, two-page account agreements—these are the "contracts" upon which most businesses are built.

When you have your customer sign a purchase order or estimate, you have a contract. When you and your customer exchange correspondence where a proposal is extended by one and accepted by the other, you have a contract. And of course, when your customer signs your commercial account agreement, you have a contract. But it's more than that. As we will discuss, a contract can be any type of agreement.

When the law speaks of a "breach of contract," it asks whether someone failed to live up to an agreement. If the answer is "yes" (most particularly when the customer fails to live up to his end of the bargain by paying you), your next task is to figure out what you have to back up your side of the story.

If You Have a Signed Contract

If you have a signed receipt, purchase order, or contract, great. You have hard, convincing evidence of your claim. But if you don't have that kind of written documentation, don't worry. There are other ways of proving that the client accepted your services.

If you have a signed contract, please skip to the section titled "Have You Incurred Damages?"

If You Don't Have a Signed Contract

As a lawyer, I am frustrated by few things more than hearing my client say, "I can't prove it; it's just my word against his." Nothing could be further from the truth. Judges make decisions every day in which one witness says one thing and another witness says another. Simply put, if the judge believes your testimony more than he believes the testimony given by your nonpaying customer, you'll win.

You can sue your nonpaying customer even if he never signed a contract. In most cases, the simple act of accepting your goods or services made him legally obligated to pay for them. In fact, the vast majority of business today is still conducted on the basis of the so-called oral or "handshake contract." The law calls this something else: an "implied contract."

A restaurant is a good example of a business relying on implied contracts. I'd be willing to bet that the last time you went to a restaurant you simply sat down, ordered your meal, and began eating without ever having signed an agreement stating that you would pay the check when it arrived. The fact that there was no written agreement just doesn't matter. By accepting the service—in this case the preparation of the meal—you agreed to pay for it. The contract was implied. Just let someone catch you walking out of a restaurant without paying, and you will see how binding an implied contract can be!

Similarly, oral contracts are common when ordering goods or services. If you call for a pizza delivery (OK, it's late as I'm writing this and I'm hung up on food), they will tell you the price, and you will decide whether or not to accept it. Later, when the delivery person comes to the door, he will expect to be paid based upon your oral contract.

You Most Prove Both Sides Understood the Terms

Both sides must have understood all of the material terms of the agreement for it to be enforced in court. The legal term for this kind of agreement is "a meeting of the minds." If, for example, you bring your car in for an oil change and that oil change is performed, you are obligated to pay for it. If, however, the garage changes your oil AND decides you need a complete brake job, you are not obligated to pay for the brake job, because that service was not part of the oral agreement you made.

Bottom line: All you need is proof that the customer accepted goods or services from you, that he accepted the payment terms beforehand, and that he did nor pay in full.

So where do you find that kind of proof?

- *Witnesses:* Anyone eighteen years or older and competent to testify can go to court and swear under oath that the nonpaying customer accepted the goods or services. The witness could be yourself or any other person who was in a position to see the customer's acceptance.

- *Partial Payment:* A partial payment from the customer would go a long way toward proving acceptance of the product or services. After all, why would someone pay for something, even in part, if the goods were never delivered or if they were completely unacceptable? Evidence of partial payment would be a receipt, charge slip, canceled check, or even testimony from a bookkeeper.

- *Correspondence:* When compiling your evidence, don't forget letters you may have sent to the nonpaying customer demanding your money, especially if a postal receipt shows that the customer received them. Perhaps even more important are letters the customer sent to you. In evaluating the customer's letters, look for what the customer didn't say. If you feel the customer is only making up an excuse to hide the fact that he can't afford to pay you, earlier correspondence (before the excuse occurred to him) in which nondelivery or the total inadequacy of your services is not mentioned can have a very large impact on a judge's decision.

Limitations on Oral Contracts

Most states set very strict limits on the kinds of oral contracts that can be enforced in court. This is because oral contracts are less reliable than those documented in some way. If there is nothing in writing to document an agreement—not even a letter of confirmation or receipt—most states will enforce only an oral contract for a very low monetary value.

Moreover, if the oral contract is for services, most states place strict limits on the time of performance that can be compelled. For example, in Maryland, an oral contract will not be enforced unless the amount of money involved is less than $500, and, in the case of services, it will not be enforced unless the services can be performed in less than one year.

If, however, the person against whom you are trying to enforce the oral contract admits the existence and terms of the agreement

OR if the agreement is evidenced by his performance, even in part, you can get around this rule and enforce an oral agreement.

Bottom line: If the deal is important to you, make sure something in writing reflects the terms.

Have You Incurred Damages?

It is not enough to show that your customer broke an agreement to pay you. You must also show that you sustained damages as a result of his actions. While this may seem puzzling (along the lines of "why is he bothering to mention such a basic point?"), the fact of the matter is that it is not always the case that a failure to pay results in damages. If you are able to answer "yes" to any of the following questions, you have incurred damages for which you are entitled to file a claim. If, on the other hand, the answer to all of these questions is "no," you have no case.

Did You Perform Work or Deliver Goods?

Your business has clearly incurred damages if you performed work or delivered goods for which you did not get paid. This is the most common type of damages for which claims are made in breach-of-contract cases. (If this is true in your case, skip to the section titled "Will the Court Hold Your Customer Responsible for His Bill?")

Did You Incur Any Expenses Because of the Agreement?

Let's say the customer placed an order for a custom-made part or for some goods you normally don't keep in stock. If your company spent money to stock or manufacture the items and the customer canceled the order, those expenses are legitimate damages that may be claimed against the customer in court.

Note that the absence of a written agreement will cause a judge to scrutinize the reasonableness of your actions. In other words, the judge will want to ensure that the customer knew what you were going to be doing on his behalf and that you gave the customer a reasonable opportunity to cancel the order.

Did You Lose or Turn Away Business Because of the Agreement?

Many businesses, especially those that perform services—medical and professional practices, construction companies, cleaning services, and the like—can only handle so many customers at one time. When these businesses are booked, they either have to postpone work for other customers or turn away the business altogether. If your company turned away business in anticipation that you would be doing work for a customer who later canceled the contract at the last minute, this lost business constitutes a claim for which you can file suit.

Let's take a look at the possibilities:

- If you are unable to get another customer in the wake of the first customer's cancellation, your damages are the amount your first client promised to pay you, less the costs you would have incurred fulfilling his order. In other words, your damages are the anticipated profit.

- If you do get another customer who pays you a smaller amount, your damages are the difference between the profit you would have made from the canceling customer and those you earned from the second job you accepted to fill the gap.

- If you find another customer who pays you an equal or greater amount than the first would have, you DO NOT have any damages. Consequently, regardless of how wrong the first customer may have been in canceling your agreement, you would not have a case.

As an example, imagine you are in the deck-building business, and someone approaches you about building a large deck on the back of his house. You reach an agreement with the customer as to design and price, and you estimate that the job will require the commitment of two workers over a two-week period.

Let's imagine further that you are approached by another prospective customer about doing some work during the same period. Because you're a small company with other jobs already booked, you cannot take on any more business and you turn this customer away.

Later, if the first customer cancels the contract, you will have lost the opportunity to perform work for the second customer. You have, therefore, incurred damages. Your damages are the lost profits from the first customer's job.

Note that even if the profits for the second customer's job would have been greater, your losses are limited to what you lost from the first job. The reason is that your suit arises out of the first customer's wrongful cancellation of the contract. Had he not canceled, you would have performed the work, made the profit, and turned away the second job. Thus, the lost money directly attributable to the customer's wrongful action is the profit from Job #1. And remember, that is what you are asking the judge for—to compensate you for all losses you suffered as a result of the customer's actions.

Now remember, your damages must be capable of calculation with a reasonable degree of certainty. In other words, you can't get too crazy with the numbers and "what-if" scenarios. In our example, it should be fairly easy for you to add up the amount of profit you would have earned on each job. You would simply add up your costs—labor, equipment, and so forth—and subtract them from the price the customer agreed to pay.

What you can't do is speculate wildly about what could have happened. For example, even if the second customer you turned away was a large developer, you would not be able to claim as damages against customer number one all 1,500 decks you would have been hired to build over the next two years had you only been free to take on customer number two, done a good job, and then gone on to be his number one deck builder on the East Coast. This is nothing other than speculation, and no judge would ever allow it as a reasonable measure of damages.

Legal key: "Reasonable damages" are those that are not calculated with the assistance of a crystal ball.

If the first customer in our example cancels the contract in time for you to fill the appointment or sell the merchandise to someone else (assuming you made the same amount of money from both customers), you haven't lost anything. For example, let's assume that the first customer who ordered the deck cancels the order, and you were able to place another customer in that same time slot for a job on which you made an equal or greater profit. You came out even (or better) and, as far as the court is concerned, you have no case.

If, however, you are able to replace the canceling customer's time slot only with something less profitable, the difference between the two jobs constitutes your damages, and it may be worth filing suit after all. Here, let's assume that you would have made a $2,000 profit on the first job. When the first order was canceled, you booked a job for a second customer on which your company made only a $500 profit. You would be entitled to claim $1,500 in damages against the canceling customer.

Note that you have a duty to mitigate damages. This means that you should book the most profitable replacement job you can find. For example, if you have a choice between two jobs with which to replace the first customer's order, one bringing in a profit of $500 and the other $750, assuming there is no reasonable business purpose for selecting the lesser job, you must select the job yielding the most profit. In essence, if you are planning to sue the first customer, you will not be allowed to take the lower-paying job just so you can sue the canceling customer for more money. This is called the *duty to mitigate damages*.

You Cannot Recover for Pain and Suffering

Yes, I know. When you add up all the time it took to get your paperwork together, call the customer numerous times requesting payment, send collection letters, and finally file suit and go sit in a courtroom, we're talking hours that could have been spent much more productively on your business. I also know that all of this time was lost solely because someone wrongfully refused to pay. (Really frosts your shorts, doesn't it?)

In the eyes of the law, it doesn't matter. You will not be able to recover for the time lost by you or your office staff in pursuing collection. Tempting as it may be to slap a $300-per-hour price tag on your time and add it to your claim, resist the urge. Doing so will only take away from the other, more meritorious aspects of your case. I describe this rule as: "Never dilute twelve-year-old Scotch with tap water." Make sure every aspect of your claim is solid and keep the frivolous parts—those on which you have no shot to collect—at home.

Will the Court Hold Your Customer Responsible for the Bill?

Regardless of how good your case is, the court will hold your customer responsible for paying your bill only if he is old enough and mentally competent. At the risk of stating the obvious, the customer with whom you reach an agreement must be legally recognized as capable of entering into a binding contract. For example, a five-year-old child would not be held responsible for any bills that she incurred, even if she were the actual patient or ultimate customer. The reason for this is that the courts will not enforce a contract against anyone who may not have been able to understand the nature of the agreement or the concept of financial responsibility.

Although a five-year-old child is clearly not responsible, teenagers or persons afflicted with mental disabilities such as Alzheimer's disease or Down's syndrome (two classes of people which, according to many parents, share many of the same characteristics)[1] are often more difficult calls.

If a person suffers from a mental illness or condition (for example, senility) that undermines her ability to understand the terms of the agreement, she will not be held responsible. Intoxication at the time the contract is entered into may result in the contract being held unenforceable. Regardless, in all cases a decision rests on the specific facts placed before the court.

Please note that you cannot refuse to do business with someone unless you have a valid reason to suspect impairment. There are variety of laws (a discussion of which is well beyond the scope of this book) that protect the rights of the disabled.

Refusing to conduct business with someone because of disability is not only unjust, it can also be extremely hazardous to your company's financial health. However, if a potential customer is clearly impaired (drunk, for example) or underage, you should use your best judgment when deciding whether he or she is capable of entering into a binding contract.

---

[1] It should be interesting to see the protests arising out of that statement!

Is Your Claim Too Old?

If you have to blow the dust off of the customer file before you file suit, chances are you're out of luck. Often, as part of an effort to take control of their finances, businesses will clean out their filing cabinets and find accounts with outstanding balances on which no action has been taken for years.

While these businesses should be commended for their efforts, these older claims may not be worth the paper they're printed on. The reason lies in what is known as the statute of limitations. A statute of limitations can be thought of as an expiration date. Limitations can run anywhere from one year to twelve, with three years being the average. States vary and limitations periods change depending upon what kind of case and when it's brought, so call your court clerk and ask about the statute of limitations for a collections matter before you file suit.

For the sake of discussion, let's assume that the statute of limitations is three years. The next question, of course, is, "Three years from what?" Well, the time limit certainly does not begin to run until the date on which the customer should have paid the bill. In other words, where the statute of limitations is three years and the customer's payment was due July 1, 2000, you would be able to file suit until June 30, 2003. Often, however, you will have more time than that. The laws of most states provide that you will have three years from the most recent of certain significant events described below.

The Last Payment

Let's assume that your customer owed you a payment of $1,000 on January 1, 2000, and didn't come through. After reading the last section, you know that the statute of limitations on this account started on the date the payment was due—January 1, 2000, and that you would have until December 31, 2002, to file suit.

If, however, on May 1, 2000, your customer makes a payment on account of $250, he has just started the statute of limitations time clock all over again. Assuming no further payments or admissions of the debt (see the next section), you would have until April 30, 2003, to file suit, assuming a three-year statute of limitations.

Admission of the Debt

Let's assume the client ran up a bill of $2,000. Further assume that payment was due on January 1, 1997. Unfortunately, when the due date rolled around, your client was unable to render payment.

No mention is made of this balance and no bills were sent out until December 1, 1999—one month before the statute of limitations expires (or "tolls"). On December 5, 1999, in response to several messages left by your office manager, the customer calls and says something along the lines of the following: *"I'm really sorry I haven't paid. I know I owe you the money. Please don't file suit. I intend to pay you, I just need more time."*

This simple conversation has just restarted the statute of limitations. The only proof of this conversation you need is the word of the person at your office who took the call (and, if you followed my advice from chapter 1, your office manager's telephone log). Your office manager (or the person taking this call) will have to testify at trial.

Note that this kind of admission restarts the statute of limitations anytime it's made—not just if it's made within the original limitations time period. Thus, in the above example, the admission could have been made in February 2000.

Contracts Signed Under Seal

Contracts can provide for a longer limitations period. Moreover, certain laws, such as the Uniform Commercial Code or state laws concerning contracts signed under seal, may provide for a longer-than-standard limitations period. For example, in many states, the words above the signature line on a contract that read "Witness this day my hand and seal . . ." combined with the word "(SEAL)" at the end of each signature line, often in parentheses as shown here, increase a three-year statute of limitations period to twelve years.

(And you thought the appearance of "SEAL" at the end of the signature line merely meant some lawyer got bored.)

Filing Suit on a Partially Paid Bill

If your company did not authorize a customer to pay in installments, your company can file suit against that customer if he made only a partial payment. As an example, the customer owes your firm $1,500 and the terms of the agreement called for full payment within thirty days. If your customer pays only $250 within the month, you are free to file suit for the remaining $1,250.

If you did authorize the customer to make installment payments, and the customer missed a payment, paid late, or did not pay the minimum payment due, you may be entitled to file suit for the remaining account balance or solely for the amount of the missed payment(s), depending upon the agreement reached with the customer. If you and your customer have worked out an installment agreement, the amount you can sue for depends upon what the agreement says. I recommend that any installment agreements and promissory notes contain an "acceleration clause," which simply states that the customer's default will allow you to accelerate the entire debt so that all of it is deemed to be immediately due and owing.

If Your Case Falls Short of These Requirements

If, after reading this chapter, you find that you have one or more problems with your claim but that you are determined to file suit, it would be a good idea to consult with an attorney to consider your next step. If your case fits all of the requirements outlined here, your claim is probably resting on a solid legal foundation and you should proceed to the next chapter.

7

Can You Use This Guide to File Suit?

Overview

All but a handful of states allow businesses to file suit without hiring a lawyer in what are known as "small claims." Individuals can file suit without a lawyer regardless of the amount of the claim. In this chapter we shall discuss when individuals and businesses can use this guide to file suit on their own without hiring a lawyer. We shall also review the important legal terms we will encounter during our all-expenses-paid guided tour of the legal system.

What's more, even if your business must hire a lawyer to file suit, this and subsequent chapters will enable you to understand the process, perform more of the preparatory work yourself, and save hundreds, if not thousands of dollars in the time that your attorney would otherwise spend.

Small-Claim Processes Throughout the United States

In establishing their court systems, each state reached a determination that smaller claims should be streamlined. Simply put, there are more of them and they are less likely to be valuable enough to justify the expense of hiring a lawyer. For these reasons, those claims that each state (for whatever reason) decided should be "small claims" are characterized by form-driven procedures and less formal trials. In other words, small claims are meant to be presented by regular people.

There is no rhyme or reason for one state to have established $2,500 as a small-claim ceiling while another settled on $5,000. The level is controlled by each state's legislature and may change from time to time. The chart on the following pages sets out the small-claim ceilings as they exist at the time of publication for each state. Note that a small claim is the principal, calculated without interest or costs (such as bounced-check fees).

You may want to mark the chart that appears on the following pages with a bookmark or (gasp!) dog-ear the page, as we will be referring to it in a number of later chapters. In this chapter, we will only concern ourselves with the first three columns—the state, the small-claim ceiling, and whether or not a business can file a small claim in court without hiring a lawyer.

Comparative U.S. Chart

STATE	SMALL CLAIMS AMOUNT	Can a company represent itself without an attorney in small claims? (Y / N)	Is there discovery in small claims? What kind? a. Interrogatories b. Request for docs c. Depositions (A B C)	Is there a judgment-by-mail or judgment-by-affidavit procedure whereby the plaintiff does not have to appear if no defense filed? (Y / N)	What kind of post-judgment discovery is allowed? How are debtors assets located?	What kind of execution on judgment is allowed? a. Garnish wages b. Garnish bank accts c. Garnish personal prop d. Lien & foreclosure on RE (A B C D)	Are form and procedures standardized throughout the state? (Y / N)
ALABAMA	$3,000.00	Y	A	Y	Interrogatories	A B	Y
ALASKA	$7,500.00	Y	None	Y	Oral Examination	A B C D	Y
ARIZONA	$2,500.00	Y	None	Y	Oral Examination	A B C D	Y
ARKANSAS	$5,000.00	N	None	N	Depends on County	A B C	N
CALIFORNIA	$5,000.00	Y	None	N	Oral Examination	A B	N
COLORADO	$3,500.00	Y	None	N	Interrogatories	A B C D	Y
CONNECTICUT	$2,500.00	Y	None	Y	Interrogatories & Oral Examination	A B C	Y
DELAWARE	$15,000.00	Y	None	Y	Interrogatories	A B C	Y
D.C.	$5,000.00	N	A B C	Y	Interrogatories	A B	Y
FLORIDA	$5,000.00	Y	B C	Y	Ints. & Oral Exam	A B C	Y
GEORGIA	$5,000.00	Y	A B	N	Interrogatories	A B D	Y
HAWAII	$2,500.00	Y	A B C	N	Interrogatories	A B C	N
IDAHO	$3,000.00	Y	None	Y	Interrogatories — from Sheriff	A B C	Y
ILLINOIS	$2,500.00	N	None	Y	Oral Examination	A B C	N
INDIANA	$6,000.00	Y	A B C	Y	Oral Examination	A B C	N

State	Amount						
IOWA	$4,000.00	Y	None	Depends on County	Y	A B C	N
KANSAS	$1,800.00	Y	None	Interrogatories	N	A B C	Y
KENTUCKY	$1,500.00	Y	A B C	None	N	A B C D	Y
LOUISIANA	$2,000.00	Yes, depending on nature of claim	None	Oral Examination	Y	A B C	N
MAINE	$4,500.00	Y	None	Oral Examination	Y	A B C D	Y
MARYLAND	$2,500.00	Y	None	Interrogatories / Oral Examination	Y	A B C D	Y
MASSACHUSETTS	$2,000.00	Y	None	Oral Examination	N	A B C D	Y
MICHIGAN	$1,750.00	Y	None	Oral Examination	N	A B C	Y
MINNESOTA	$5,000.00	N	None	Order of Disclosure from Court	N	A B C D	N
MISSISSIPPI	$2,500.00	Y	A B	Oral Examination	N	A B C	N
MISSOURI	$3,000.00	Y	None	By Plaintiff — self help	N	A B	Y
MONTANA	$3,000.00	Y	None	By Plaintiff — self help	N	A B C	Y
NEBRASKA	$2,100.00	Y	None	By Plaintiff — self help	N	A B C D	Y
NEVADA	$3,500.00	Y	None	By Plaintiff — self help	N	A B C D	N
NEW HAMPSHIRE	$5,000.00	Y	None	Court hearing	N	A B C	Y
NEW JERSEY	$2,000.00	Y	None	Subpoena	Y	A B C D	N
NEW MEXICO	$5,000.00	Y	None	Court ordered disclosure	Y	A B C	Y
NEW YORK	$3,000.00	Y	None	Oral Examination	N	A B C D	Y
NO. CAROLINA	$3,000.00	Y	None	Subpoena / Sheriff Seizure	N	A B C D	Y

STATE	SMALL CLAIMS AMOUNT	Can a company represent itself without an attorney in small claims? Y/N	Is there discovery in small claims? What kind? a. Interrogatories b. Request for docs c. Depositions A B C	Is there a judgment-by-mail or judgment-by-affidavit procedure whereby the plaintiff does not have to appear if no defense filed? Y/N	What kind of post-judgment discovery is allowed? How are debtors assets located?	What kind of execution on judgment is allowed? a. Garnish wages b. Garnish bank accts c. Garnish personal prop d. Lien & foreclosure on RE A B C D	Are form and procedures standardized throughout the state? Y/N
NO. DAKOTA	$5,000.00	Y	None	Y	By Plaintiff — self help	A B C	Y
OHIO	$3,000.00	Y	None	N	Oral Examination	A B C	Y
OKLAHOMA	$4,500.00	Y	None	N	Interrogatories and Oral Examination	A B C	Y
OREGON	$2,500.00	Y	None	Y	By Plaintiff — self help	A B C	N
PENNSYLVANIA	$8,000.00	Y	None	N	None	B C D	Y
RHODE ISLAND	$1,500.00	Y	None	Y	Oral Examination	B C D	Y
SO. CAROLINA	$5,000.00	Y	None	Y	By Sheriff	A B C D	Y
SO. DAKOTA	$8,000.00	Y	None	Y	Self Help	A B	Y
TENNESSEE	$4,000.00	N	A B C	N	Interrogatories Oral Examination	A B C D	N
TEXAS	$5,000.00	Y	A B C	Y	By Sheriff	B C	N
UTAH	$5,000.00	Y	None	N	Oral Examination	A B C	Y
VERMONT	$3,500.00	Y	None	N	Oral Examination	A B C D	Y
VIRGINIA	$1,000.00	Y	None	Y	Interrogatories	A B C D	Y

State						
WASHINGTON	$2,500.00	Y	None	N	Oral Examination	A B	N
WEST VIRGINIA	$5,000.00	Y	None	Y	By Plaintiff — self help	A B C D	Y
WISCONSIN	$5,000.00	Y	None	Y	Court ordered disclosure	A B C	Y
WYOMING	$3,000.00	Y	None	N	By Sheriff	A B C D	Y

Do You Need a Lawyer?

First and foremost, you must refer to the chart on the preceding pages to determine if your state even allows lawyers to appear in small-claims court. (Many states have concluded that lawyers merely gum up the works in small cases and that things run more smoothly without them.) If your state allows you the option of hiring a lawyer, consider which of the following three statements reflects the facts of your claim:

- The debtor owes the money to your company rather than to you personally, and the amount owed is your state's small-claim ceiling or less. If this is the case, you CAN file suit without a lawyer, and you may use this guide.

- The debtor owes the money to your company and the amount owed is greater than the small-claim ceiling. In this case, you must have a lawyer represent your business. Consequently, this guide can help you to understand the process and to do some of the work yourself, thereby saving you money.

- The debtor owes the money to a person (rather than to a business). In this case, you CAN use file suit without a lawyer, and you may use this guide.

A few states distinguish among the types of companies that can file suit without a lawyer. For example, an attorney may not be required for corporations whereas one may be necessary for a partnership. If your business is run through a partnership, call the clerk before filing suit without an attorney.

Legal Terms You Should Know

Although I try to keep the "legalese" down to a minimum, there are certain terms that, of necessity, I mention frequently throughout this book and that you absolutely must understand. Most are defined as they arise, but three must be defined here.

Plaintiff: The plaintiff is the person or company filing the lawsuit in court.
Defendant: The defendant is the person or company being sued.

(I've been very nice up until this point by describing this person simply as the "customer." Well, you're suing now. Time to throw off the kid gloves. From now on, the person or company that owes you money will be called either the "defendant" or the "debtor.")

Litigation: The process that begins with filing suit and ends with the conclusion of the case (and the defendant's money in your pocket).

I was going to buy a copy of The Power of Positive Thinking
and then I thought: What the hell good would it do?
—Ronnie Shakes

8
Should You File Suit?

Overview

Despite the ease with which television lawyers win their cases, the reality is that litigation often does more harm to the person filing the suit than it does to the person being sued. The good news is that more than 90 percent of all cases filed in small-claims courts never go to trial. Many times, the debtors pay what is owed almost immediately after being served with suit papers. The thought of being dragged into court is enough to get them to open their checkbooks.

In this chapter I will discuss the hidden and not-so-hidden costs of filing suit in order to help you decide when a case is simply not worth pursuing.

Are You Going to Court for the Right Reasons?

When thinking about taking someone to court, you must put emotions aside and make a purely business decision after considering the costs and benefits of litigation. Too many people rush into court because they just want to make life as difficult as possible for the nonpaying customer. In short, they want revenge.

Revenge is the worst possible motive for filing suit. My advice is this: Make your decisions based upon what is best for your business. If that means that revenge will sometimes take a backseat, so be it. But if you do decide to go to court, go knowing that doing so represents a sound business judgment rather than an emotional reaction that will cost you more in the long run than your nonpaying customer ever did.

▶ **MORALITY AND THE LAW**

What is and is not fair has very little bearing on whether you can win in court. Contracts do not have to be fair. Judges do not have to be fair. Very often, agreements or transactions favor one side over the other. If the agreement is valid under the law, it will be enforced, regardless of whether the outcome would truly be fair to the losing side.

I often tell my clients that morality and the law are two different roads that only intersect and random and infrequent times. (Maybe that's the poet in me.) The point is that your evaluation of your court case must depend upon how much, if anything, you can legally recover, regardless of what a "fair" result would be. For example, if a person doing business under ABC, Inc. owes you money, a judge will not make his other company, DEF, Inc. pay you, even if DEF has $4 billion in cash and ABC is flat broke. It may be fair to force DEF to pay since he same person is in charge of both companies, but that is not the law.

What Is Your Maximum Recovery?

If you were invited to play a carnival game costing $7.50 in which the most you could win was $5.00, it wouldn't take you long to figure out that you were not being offered a good deal. So it is with litigation. Sometimes it may cost you more (in time, effort, and money) to go through a trial than you could recover if you win the case.

This chapter will help you answer the following questions so you can decide if it might be worth your while to go to court.

- What are you owed?

- Can you recover interest?

- Are you allowed to claim anything else (penalties, bounced-check fees, court costs, etc.)?

- Are you prepared to invest the time and effort needed to win?

- Do you have a good chance of actually recovering the money?

What Are You Owed?

The answer to this question is, quite simply, the amount of the debt. In the case of a customer's failure to render full payment when due, the amount owed is what the customer should have paid. (Sounds pretty obvious, huh?) In the case of account agreements, however, the answer may not be as obvious.

Let's say a customer owes you $1,200, and he agrees to make twelve equal monthly payments of $100 to your business. If your client misses the second payment, you may be able to sue for the whole remaining balance of $1,100, or you may be able to file a claim only for the missed payment of $100. It all depends on the wording of the account agreement your customer signed. As I discussed in the first chapter, if your customer signed an agreement that contained an acceleration clause, you could sue him for the whole account balance as soon as he missed one payment. If the account agreement does not contain such a clause, you may be limited to a lawsuit for only the missing payment (here, only $100).

▶ TIP: IT MAY PAY TO WAIT A LITTLE WHILE BEFORE FILING

If you are working with an installment agreement that does not have acceleration clause whereby the entire remaining balance becomes due after one missed payment, consider waiting for three or four missed payments before filing. Depending upon the amount of each payment, adding three or four together makes filing suit worthwhile from an economic standpoint. *If you choose to wait some time before filing suit, make sure to keep track of your customer's whereabouts so you can find him once you decide to proceed.*

Can You Recover Interest?

Yes, if you specifically informed the customer in writing (e.g., on your invoices, estimate, or in a signed contract) that interest would be charged on all overdue balances.

On the other hand, if you did not inform the customer that he would be charged interest on overdue bills, chances are you will not be able to recover interest in your lawsuit. Thus, as I've said before, the key to being able to collect interest is to protect yourself in advance.

Are You Allowed to Claim Anything Else?

In addition to recovering unpaid bills and interest, you may be entitled to force your nonpaying client to pay you additional money.

Statutory Penalties

If someone bounces a check on you, you are allowed to claim not only the face value of the check—the amount you should have been paid in the first place—but also a bounced-check fee (typically $25) and additional penalties imposed in many states. After all, your bank charges you for depositing a subsequently dishonored check, so pass the charge along to the person who's really responsible.

Court Costs

Going to court isn't free. Fortunately, however, you can occasionally recover some of the costs involved. Court costs are the relatively minor fees charged by the court for processing your claim. These costs are usually not more than $15 to $20.

If the judge feels that you deserve it, he will order the nonpaying customer to pay your court costs. However, the judge will order the client to pay court costs only if you ask him to. So by all means, ask.

If you must get an attorney, your entitlement to be reimbursed for attorney's fees almost always depends entirely upon your wording of any billing arrangements you made with your customer in advance. To collect attorney's fees, your contracts, purchase orders, or other documentation signed by the customer must clearly state that he is liable for any attorney's fees you incur in trying to collect on an overdue balance.

You Cannot Recover . . .

- The value of your time.

- Your travel expenses going back and forth to court.

- Compensation for your inconvenience and aggravation.

Are You Prepared to Invest the Time and Effort Necessary to Win?

To paraphrase Winston Churchill's famous line about democracy, the American legal system is the worst system in the world . . . except for all the others. As anyone who has ever filed a lawsuit knows, our court system is sometimes inefficient, intimidating, and time-consuming. You must consider these problems before jumping into the system.

In filing a small claim and pursuing it through trial (and beyond), the largest investment you will make is not money, it's time. It takes time to compile the relevant papers. It takes time to draft the filing document (usually called the "complaint"). If you have to appear in court . . . more time. To decide whether a claim is worth pursuing, you must consider the time commitment *before* you get started.

I have listed below the estimated time required for each step of a typical case. Don't worry about analyzing all of these steps now. They are explained later.

1. Compiling and organizing the necessary documents   60 minutes

2. Drafting the complaint and court paperwork   75 minutes

3. Preparing interrogatories (may be unnecessary)   30 minutes

4. Communicating with the court throughout the case   60 minutes

5. Appearing in court   150 minutes

The total? Six hours and thirty minutes of your time! And that's if everything goes smoothly, AND you don't have to spend any time collecting on the judgment (which could stretch out the time you spend on this claim indefinitely). We're assuming only one trip to court, no discovery filed by the debtor, and no lengthy trial. (The lion's share of that 150 minutes in court is waiting your turn!)

However, the estimate of six hours is for a case that goes all the way to trial. If you are lucky, the debtor could decide to pay up at some point *before* trial. You may also be able to win without going to court. Many states have enacted a procedure that allows the court to award a judgment without trial if the other side fails to contest the claim. In essence, if the defendant doesn't want to fight, you will not have to go to court, and you will receive notification in the mail that you have been awarded your judgment.

Unfortunately, some lawsuits become very time-consuming. If a defendant evades service of the suit papers or contests the claim in court, you may wind up devoting up to thirty hours to the case. It is not uncommon to spend hours waiting in court for your case to be called, sometimes only to have the case postponed and you have to go back on another day. The six-hour estimate should be used only as a guideline in considering whether or not to go forward. As they say on TV, "Your actual time may vary."

The one thing to remember is that the better organized you are, the less time you will have to spend assembling the documents and filing the claim.

Do You Have a Good Chance of Actually Recovering the Money?

Flushed with victory after winning my first trial, I was crushed when the judge explained to me that a judgment is nothing but a hunting license. What he meant was that even if you win your case in court, that does not mean your nonpaying client will pay you on the spot. Instead, the judgment you're awarded by the court merely states that you are entitled to the money.

The court will not, however, throw the debtor in jail if he refuses or is unable to pay. There is no such thing as debtor's prison in this country, and I don't foresee it coming back anytime soon. True, the judgment will go on his record and may ruin his credit, but the court will not actually go out and get the money for you. You may have to do a lot of work to actually get your money back. This postjudgment work is another factor to consider before you file suit.

Remember my six-hour time estimate? It did not include the time needed to track down the debtor and force him to pay you after you win your judgment. Although the defendant will sometimes make payment arrangements with you shortly after you win your case, you cannot count on it working out this way.

In some cases no amount of work on your part will get you your money back, such as when you are unable to locate the debtor or he is somehow "judgment proof."

The term "judgment proof" is used to describe people or companies so lacking in money, income, and property that any judgment obtained against them is worthless. Unfortunately, there is no foolproof way to find out beforehand if someone is judgment proof. Certainly, you can pay to conduct an asset search. There are many firms out there that will locate any real estate, personal property (such as cars and boats), and even bank accounts the debtor may have. Nevertheless, these search results, rarely 100 percent accurate, are only a snapshot of assets and accounts that may become obsolete the day after you read the report.

There is some good news, however. A judgment generally lasts for twelve years and is potentially renewable forever. Consequently, if the debtor comes into money, as long as he wasn't discharged from the judgment by bankruptcy, you will be able to get any funds that come into his hands.

Equally as important, judgments often limit the debtor's financial freedom of movement. Many's the time I have received a frantic call from a judgment debtor two or three years after the fact, advising me that the debtor is trying to obtain a mortgage or qualify for some other type of credit and that the existence of the judgment is proving to be a hindrance. You'd be surprised how quickly certified funds can be delivered when the judgment begins to interfere with the debtor's quality of life.

The moral of the story? Before you file suit, you have to evaluate your chances of turning a victory in the courtroom into money. Ask yourself these questions:

- Can you locate the debtor?

- Does the debtor have a job or other source of income?

- Does the debtor have any money or property with which he could pay you?

- Is it likely the debtor could pull up stakes and disappear on a moment's notice?

You don't have to rely on your persuasive abilities to get your money. Once you find where the debtor is keeping or getting his money, the law will help you take it from his pocket and put it into yours. What's more, upon request, the court will order the defendant to provide you with information concerning his assets and accounts. Bottom line: The legal system places a number of weapons at your disposal to use in your fight to get paid. But first you have to find the debtor.

Please note that the appendix at the conclusion of this guide is devoted to a discussion of some inexpensive, easy, and highly successful techniques you can use in trying to locate the hard-to-find debtor.

Can You Locate the Debtor?

There are two times in a case when it is important to be able to locate the debtor—at the beginning and at the end. You need to be able to find the nonpaying customer at the beginning of the case because you must serve the papers on him. "Serving the papers" on the debtor means that he is handed (either through hand delivery or through certified mail for which he signs a receipt) a copy of your suit and a legal notice prepared by the court that informs him of his rights and obligations.

There are some exceptions to this. In unusual circumstances, and when the court is satisfied that all other reasonable measures have failed, the court may allow you to serve the debtor by posting the papers outside his last known address, but you will need special court permission to do this. Getting his permission is not only time-consuming and difficult, but it may be a portent of things to come when it comes time to collect on your judgment. Should you find that you need to have the debtor served this way initially, it would be a good idea to call the clerk's office for information on how to proceed.

By far, the most important time to be able to locate the debtor comes at the end of the case, after you've won your judgment. As we've discussed, a judgment is simply a piece of paper that says that you are entitled to money from the defendant. If you are unable to locate him or any of his assets (such as a house, a car, bank accounts, attachable wages, etc.), your judgment is not worth much more than the paper it's printed on.

Does the Debtor Have a Job or Other Source of Income?

Before you file suit, you should find out if the debtor could pay you if you won. If the debtor is getting money from somewhere, chances are you could redirect some of that money your way.

Of course, the most common source of money is employment. Most states allow you to have the debtor's employer subtract a portion of the debtor's paycheck and put it toward paying you instead. Please refer to the chart on pages 114–117 to find out if the state in which you're filing suit allows what are known as "wage garnishments." In many cases, garnishing the defendant's wages is the best way for you to get paid.

Don't worry if the debtor does not work in your state. If the state in which the debtor is employed allows wage garnishment (refer to the chart on pages 114–117), you can still garnish his wages where he works. I will discuss this process is more detail in chapter 17.

In many cases you may not know whether or where the debtor is employed. If so, there is a way to get the information from the debtor after you win in court. There is a court-ordered postjudgment investigation during which the debtor must tell you under oath where he is employed, how much he makes, when he gets paid, where he banks, and what bank accounts he holds. As long as these items may be used to satisfy your judgment under your state's laws as shown on the chart on pages 114–117, the court will help you get the answers.

The debtor may have other sources of income in addition to wages. While certain types of income (such as child support) cannot be garnished, other types of income (such as that from trust accounts, commissions, rental property, etc.) can be. Chapter 17 will show you how to locate and garnish these income sources.

Does the Debtor Have Any Money or Property with Which He Could Pay You?

Garnishing or "attaching" the debtor's income is not the only way you can get your money. Once you locate his property and/or money, you can have it seized and sold so you can get paid. Don't worry if the debtor's assets are in another state. Most states, as shown on the chart on pages 114–117, allow you to take money from the debtor's bank accounts. In addition, if the debtor has any property such as a house, a car, a motorcycle, a boat, or even a coin collection, the laws of the state in which that property is located may allow you to attach those assets and sell them to pay off his judgment.

Make Sure You Know Who Owns the Property

Appearances can be deceiving. Your customer may look well off, but perhaps he is living off of someone else's income, or maybe the company name appearing on your account agreement is not the one responsible for the fleet of corporate Jaguars you see in front of their building.

Whatever the case, you are not allowed to garnish any asset belonging to someone other than the person or company against whom you have a judgment. For example, if you obtained a judgment against Mr. Jones and his car is actually owned by Mr. and Mrs. Jones, you will not be able to attach and sell it to satisfy your judgment. The reason is that you don't have a judgment against Mrs. Jones, and selling a car that partially belongs to her when she doesn't owe you any money (in the eyes of the law, anyway) would be unfair.

Bottom line: There are many sources of income and assets that could be used to pay you if you win. Just make sure you know who owns them before you go charging ahead full steam.

What Do You Do If the Debtor Is Deceased?

If your debtor is a person, you should know that your claim does not necessarily die when he does. Instead, you simply make your claim against the estate. Follow the same procedures you would use in pursuing the debtor as if he were alive. You will be able to collect your judgment from the estate if it has any assets.

What Do You Do If the Debtor Is Dissolved or out of Business?

A company's income doesn't necessarily stop the day the owners of a business decide to call it quits. It's just like deciding to close your checking account to switch banks. You may decide to make the change on Day 1, but there may still be outstanding checks, direct deposit arrangements, and automatic debits that last for weeks or even months after your decision was made. So it goes with a business.

If a business closes, or even if, as a corporation, the business files papers with the state dissolving the company, customers may still owe it money. In this case, the money that comes in will be held by the officers and directors of the company as trustees. These people are still obligated to pay the company's debts from money the company receives. Consequently, under the right circumstances, it may still be a good idea to pursue your claim even after the doors have closed after the going-out-of-business sale.

Is It Likely the Debtor Could Disappear?

By the time most people in our country have reached the age of thirty, they have heard the Miranda "you have the right to remain silent" warning three thousand times, have witnessed twelve thousand shootings, and have heard the question "Does the defendant have roots in the community?" at least four hundred times at bail hearings. Hopefully all of this experience was gained through television.

Although I made every one of those statistics up, my point is that the same standard used by judges to determine if someone should be released from jail pending trial on minor charges (i.e., "Is the defendant a flight risk?") are useful in your evaluation of whether to file suit.

Does the debtor have family or close business ties in the area? Does the debtor have property in the state? Is the debtor a long-established business with ties to the community? The answer to each of these questions will help you make an educated guess as to whether the debtor is likely or even able to disappear once a judgment is obtained.

Check within your company. Maybe someone knew or still knows the debtor. Perhaps your association with him gave you the impression that he had a good job, had close ties to a trade or business group where he is known and respected, or had good prospects for business growth in the future. On the other hand, perhaps you now know that the debtor lost his job, was in debt up to his eyes, and was likely to become the target of a major criminal investigation.

In other words, if you feel that the debtor is more likely than not to disappear before you will ever get a chance to collect on your judgment, you may want to think twice about devoting the time and effort necessary to file suit and pursue the case through trial. On the other hand, if you believe, knowing how difficult it would be for most of us to pull up stakes and move, that you'll be able to find the debtor once your judgment is awarded, it may well be worth the effort.

Don't Back Off

Yes, my primary rule of thumb is that people, in collecting debts, should base their actions on what's best for them rather than on revenge against the debtor. For this reason, I encourage prospective claimants to look at the cost to them, in both time and money, of pursuing the debt through the court system. Nevertheless, nothing could be worse for a business than to adopt playing the victim as their corporate culture.

This book is written to provide an antidote to the feeling of powerlessness that is often accompanied by the question "What can I do?" The answer is "plenty." When someone refuses to pay you, that person is stealing your money. Your job is to *get it back*. Take my words of caution as factors in making your decisions, but I urge you to err on the side of enforcing your rights.

▶ **PHYSICIAN HEAL THYSELF**

I know a businessman—the head of his own company, no less—who never fails to adopt the same attitude when confronted by a nonpaying customer: "What can I do? If I file suit, I'll either wind up defending some sort of counterclaim, or I'll go through a lot of time and effort with nothing to show for it in the end."

Now, this guy is great at what he does. What's more, he is one of the finest people I've ever known. But this attitude frustrates me no end. He has adopted a corporate-victim mentality. As far as I'm concerned, he deserves what he gets because he refuses (through many justifications and excuses) to stand up for himself.

My advice: If you recognize this attitude developing within yourself, do everything to change it. Fight back against those people who would take advantage of your good nature. Establish a reputation, not only for doing quality work, but for expecting and demanding payment. I guarantee you hat you will not regret your decision.

Oh yeah, the guy I'm talking about? He's a lawyer.

Showing up is eighty percent of life.
—Woody Allen

Showing up in the right place adds another ten percent.
—Eliot M. Wagonheim

9
Where Can You File Suit?

Overview

Just because you live or work in one state doesn't mean that you can walk into any of your home-state courthouses and have a judge resolve your problems with a nonpaying customer. There are a number of rules concerning where you can file your lawsuit. This chapter will let you know whether you can file your claim in your home county and state or if you will have to look elsewhere as a starting point toward retrieving your money.

What Does Your Contract Say?

By far, the most obvious and best place to look to determine where you can file suit is the agreement with your customer. Many agreements, particularly those form agreements originally drafted by lawyers, specifically state where suit can be filed.

Chances are, if the agreement speaks to the issue of where suit can be filed, it will be in a provision titled "jurisdiction and venue." "Jurisdiction" is the power or authority of a court to decide a case. For our purposes, the question of jurisdiction is the question of whether the courts of a particular state have the power to decide a case brought to them. For example, if one Pennsylvania company sues another Pennsylvania company, suit cannot be filed in Florida just because one of the owners happens to spend the winter there. Everything happened in Pennsylvania. Florida courts would not have *jurisdiction* to hear and decide the case.

"Venue" is a term meaning the specific location where the case will be heard. If jurisdiction lies in Pennsylvania, the venue for the suit may be a particular court in York County.

Many times, as in the sample account agreement on page 34, agreements will specifically provide both jurisdiction and venue to save a company from the risk of having to travel in order to obtain a judgment. Take a window manufacturer that I represent as an example. This client manufactures fabulous windows. In fact, the windows are of such high quality that they are in demand throughout the mid-Atlantic region.

If a company from North Carolina takes delivery of a shipment and refuses to pay, my client does not want to have to travel down to Raleigh to file suit. Instead, its commercial account agreements specifically state that "jurisdiction and venue for any disputes arising under the agreement will lie exclusively in a court of competent jurisdiction in Baltimore County, Maryland." This way, in the event of a disagreement, at least my client is playing on its home turf.

If the contract specifies a state other than yours, you will not be able to file suit in your home state unless the debtor voluntarily allows you to do so—highly unlikely.

Bottom line: Check your agreements first. Whatever they say goes. What's more, if you typically use your own agreements in your business (as opposed to being in a business where you customarily have to sign someone else's), you should make sure your agreements are specifically written to allow you to file suit in a location most convenient to you.

And If Your Contract Doesn't Say . . .

If you don't have a contract or if the contract you *do* have is silent about jurisdiction, you'll have to work a little harder to figure it out. For the most part, the answer (at least where jurisdiction is concerned) is obvious—both you and the customer live and/or work in the same state where the business took place, and the transaction had no connection to any other state. No brainer—suit should be filed in that state. Of course, you may still have to choose between different counties to determine venue, so you'll probably still want to review the sections below.

I have placed a worksheet at the end of this chapter, which I encourage you to copy and fill in as you read along. Each of the questions on the worksheet is discussed below. When you finish reading a section, refer to your copy of the worksheet and check the appropriate response. Your completed worksheet will tell you at a glance where you can file suit.

Is Your Claim a Consumer or Commercial Debt?

There are two types of debt (and, for that matter, two types of debt collection cases)—commercial and consumer. The difference between the two depends on the type of debtor. Who owes you the money, a consumer or a business? You need to know which type of debt it is because you can sue a consumer only where she lives or regularly works, but there are a number of places you can sue a business.

This is because the law assumes that businesspeople are aware of their obligations and risks when the enter into a transaction, whereas individual consumers may not be as sophisticated— especially where signing contracts is concerned. Thus, the law offers its greatest protection to the individual.

So how does the law distinguish between consumer and commercial debt? A commercial debt is a debt between businesses. If the defendant originally purchased the goods or services from you for use exclusively in a trade or business, your claim is based upon a *commercial* rather than a consumer debt. Examples would include the sale of merchandise not suitable for home use (such as a forklift), the rendering of corporate accounting services, or the sale of inventory to a store owner for resale.

A consumer debt is between a business and a consumer. If the defendant purchased the goods or services for personal use, your claim is based upon a *consumer* debt. Sometimes it's hard to tell the difference. Please mark your answers on the following worksheet.

Question 1: *Did the debtor purchase the goods or services for resale?*

If the debtor purchased the goods or services for resale, your claim arises out of a commercial debt. Thus, if the debtor bought inventory from you or if your services were used to create a product for sale in the debtor's store, you are dealing with a commercial debt.

If this is a commercial debt, check "yes" and go to Question 3. If the answer is "no," go to Question 2.

Question 2: *Did the debtor purchase the goods or services for use in a business or trade?*

Inventory isn't the only type of goods purchased for use in business. Businesses purchase computers, equipment, office-cleaning services, this guide, and a host of other goods and services for their use in maintaining operations. These purchases constitute commercial transactions as well.

Sometimes the purchase is a judgment call. I have a TV/VCR combination in my office (which supposedly is for viewing videotaped depositions but is really only used for the NCAA basketball tournament). The unit is used in my office, but an argument could be made either way as to whether it was a consumer or a commercial transaction. Bottom line, the presence of this unit in my office or on tax returns as a business deduction (not on mine, but hypothetically . . .) is usually the best way to differentiate the two.

If the debtor bought the goods or services for use in a business or trade, you are dealing with a commercial debt. Check "yes" on your answer sheet and move to Question 3. If the answer is "no," then you are dealing with a consumer debt.

Question 3: *Does your contract say where suit must be filed?*

As we discussed above, the answer to this question will end the speculation. And remember, a contract does not have to be a fifty-page, single-spaced document. It can be the estimate you signed that has terms and conditions on the back (that no one ever reads, except me), or it can even be an exchange of letters confirming an agreement. Review the documents that form the agreement between yourself and your customer first, before you waste a lot of time and effort filing suit in the wrong state.

Question 4: *Where was the transaction conducted?*

Transactions Involving the Sale of Goods

When the transaction involves the sale of a product, the business is deemed by law to have been conducted at the place where the goods were sold. This holds true whether someone walked into your store and made a purchase or if they called, wrote, or visited your Web site and ordered goods for shipment. Regardless of where the order came from, the transaction—the sale—was conducted at your place of business. (Of course, if you're talking about door-to-door sales, the sale is deemed to have taken place at the location the salesperson visited to make the sale.)

Note that in the event that you, as the seller, have multiple offices, you should use the office with which the debtor conducted his business to answer Question 4 on your worksheet.

Transactions Involving the Provision of Services

Services are often another story. While services such as medical examinations and tax preparation necessarily take place at the office of the "seller" (except for medical services from HMOs, which usually involve house calls),[1] other services such as lawn care and house painting are conducted at the customer's premises. Just like the door-to-door salesperson in the discussion above, you must look at the facts of your own transaction to determine where it took place and fill in your answer on your worksheet.

If the business was conducted outside your home state, proceed to Question 5. If the transaction occurred within your home state, you may still have to file suit in the county in which it took place (thereby establishing proper *venue*) and move directly to the next chapter.

---

[1] I crack myself up sometimes.

Question 5: Where does the debtor conduct business?

Even if the transaction did not take place in your home state, there is still a possibility that you can file suit there. A debtor may be sued on a commercial debt in *any* county or state in which he conducts business. Regardless of whether your particular transaction with the debtor took place outside the state, if the debtor conducts business within the state, you may sue him there. Consequently, if the answer to this question is "yes," you may skip the rest of this chapter and move on.

IMPORTANT: MAKE SURE THE COMPANIES ARE THE SAME.

This point has been brought up before, but bears repeating: People can run more than one company. If your debtor is Company A, which never does business in your home state, it does not matter that Company B, run by the same people, is located right in the heart of your state capital. Unless *your* debtor conducts business in your home state, you must answer "no" to this question and proceed to Question 6. Fill in your answer on your worksheet.

Question 6: Does the debtor live in your home state?

If the debtor maintains his primary residence in your home state, you can always sue him in the county in which he lives. Take note: A vacation home does not count. It must be his primary residence. Fill in your answer on your worksheet.

Question 7: Did the debtor sign the contract or reach the agreement in your home state?

You may answer "yes" to this question only if the debtor actually signed the contract in your home state or agreed to the arrangement by phone or correspondence while he was within the state.

Let's take your gasoline credit card as an example. When you obtained your card, you signed a contract with the oil company in which it agreed to allow you to purchase gas, maps, car washes, and snack cakes at any of its stations around the country if you would pay them back with interest.

The credit is actually being extended by their bank, presumably located outside of your home state. The transactions—your gasoline and snack purchases—may have taken place anywhere in the country. Nevertheless, the place where you signed the contract and from which you mailed your payments was your home. That is the only place where you can be sued for your nonpayment. (Otherwise, defaulting credit-card holders would be descending on Houston like a mecca.) Fill in your answer on your worksheet.

Tallying Your Score

Check your worksheet. If you answered "yes" to any one of Questions 4 through 7, you can file suit in your home state. What's more, you may have a choice of counties in your state in which you can file suit. You may file suit in any of the counties you listed in response to Questions 4 through 7.

If You Are Unable to File Suit in Your Home State

Review the worksheet question and, instead of answering "yes" or "no," write down the applicable state where the activity takes place. For example, change Question 6 to read "Where does the debtor live?" and write down the appropriate state. The states you write down in answer to the applicable questions are those states in which you can file suit.

Appendix

Claim Worksheet

1. Did the debtor purchase your goods or services for resale? ( ) Yes ( ) No

2. Did the debtor purchase the goods or services for use in a business or trade? ( ) Yes ( ) No

   If you answered "yes" to either of these questions, your claim arises out of a commercial debt. If you answered "no" to both of these questions, your claim arises out of a consumer debt. You should skip Questions 3, 4, and 5 and proceed directly to Question 6.

3. Does the contract say where suit must be filed? ( ) Yes ( ) No

   If he answer to this question is "yes," you need go no further. Regardless of the answers to the rest of the questions, a valid contract governs where suit must be filed. Thus, if the contract provides where suit must be filed, proceed to the next chapter.

4. Was the transaction conducted in your home state? ( ) Yes ( ) No
   If Yes, specify county: _____

5. Does the debtor regularly conduct business in your home state? ( ) Yes ( ) No
   If Yes, specify county: _____

6. Does the debtor live in your home state? ( ) Yes ( ) No
   If Yes, specify county: _____

7. Did the debtor sign the contract or reach the agreement in your home state? ( ) Yes ( ) No.
   If Yes, specify county: _____

There are two types of people in this world—those who finish what they start . . . and so on.

—Anonymous

10
Preparing and Filing Your Claim

Overview

In this chapter I shall guide you through the preparation and filing of a lawsuit against a nonpaying customer. Whether you have to hire a lawyer or not (consult the state chart on pages 114–117), this chapter will enable you to understand the process, save time and money through superior preparation, and start you on the road toward winning your case.

A Word About Record Keeping

As I discussed in the very first chapter, it is essential that you keep your client files organized and up to date in case you are ever forced to initiate collection procedures for an overdue balance. (Of course, that's not the only reason to keep your files up to date; you may also find the practice helpful in running your business, but I digress.)

Once you file a court case, however, record keeping becomes even more essential. There is an ironclad, never-to-be-broken rule of litigation that can best be expressed in two words: KEEP EVERYTHING.

When I say "keep everything," I mean:

1. Keep a copy of everything you file with or send to the court—letters, complaints with *all* exhibits attached exactly as they were filed, motions, discovery requests—EVERYTHING.

2. Keep everything you receive from the court. Often the court will send you notices telling you anything from your trial date to whether or not the defendant filed a response. Keep them organized in chronological order.

3. Keep everything you receive from the defendant relating to the court case. The defendant should send you copies of everything he files with the court such as a counterclaim, discovery requests, or motions. Keep them organized in chronological order.

I recommend that you create a litigation folder or binder that holds everything sent to or by the court together in chronological order, and tab each document for easy retrieval. For example, a typical litigation binder may have the complaint and summons under tab 1, a notice from the court acknowledging receipt under tab 2, the defendant's answer under tab 3, and so on.

This litigation file should be separate from your original customer file. You should always keep the original customer file intact, copying documents when you need them elsewhere so that you always know where to find a complete set of records on any particular customer.

This way, if you have to go to court, your litigation file will be a complete and organized duplicate of the file the judge will be reviewing. In addition, because it is not uncommon for a paper to be misfiled by the court, your records will enable you to provide the judge with any papers he may be missing at trial.

Getting Started

All small claims start with the filing of a form. Called the complaint in most states (and for convenience referred to the same way here), the form tells the court:

- Who is bringing the suit.

- Who you are filing suit against.

- Why you are filing suit.

- How much money you are seeking.

Every state's complaint form is different. In a few states, forms differ county to county. Nevertheless all complaint forms are created to communicate the answers to the four questions listed above.

To assist you in filling out your state's complaint form, I have reviewed all of the questions and spaces presented on the forms of each state and the District of Columbia. Descriptions of each section are contained within this chapter. Although there may be differences from state to state as to where the information is provided on the form, and even which types of information are called for, you should find everything you need to fill out the complaint form and get started right here in these pages.

Note that not all states require the all of the sections discussed in this chapter.

▶ THE CARE AND FEEDING OF COURT CLERKS

OK. Imagine a job where you have to explain completely foreign procedures to a constant stream of people of every type and description. Most of the people are intimidated, don't understand the terms used, and are ticked off about the circumstances that brought them there in the first place. You have to handle about a thousand forms dealing with every kind of dispute under the sun. And you have to do it efficiently and with a smile.

You've just placed yourself in the shoes of a court clerk.

After having dealt with these people for twelve years in courts all over the country, my admiration for them is limitless. On the whole, I have found clerks to be exceedingly patient and blessedly competent. Treat them that way.

In exchange for a little civility and respect, these people can be your best friends. They can help you navigate the vagaries of the court system, provide you with the appropriate forms (if they exist) and reassure you that there are real human beings in charge of this process.

If you have a question, call them. If you need forms or have a scheduling conflict, call them. While they cannot and will not give you legal advice . . . I'll say that again **clerks cannot and will not give you legal advice** . . . they can be exceedingly helpful. Use them as a resource. That's why they make the big money.

Required Paperwork for Filing Suit

There are two aspects to initiating a small claim: (1) filing the complaint and (2) notifying the defendant that suit has been filed. Not surprisingly, the court has standardized paperwork and procedures for dealing with each.

The Complaint

The complaint form briefly discussed above is the most important document you will file in your case. In simple terms, your case is only as good as your complaint. If you fail to spell out your claim clearly, you run the risk of losing your case or having your case delayed substantially while you try to straighten out your error.

To get the proper complaint form, go the clerk's office located in the courthouse where you plan to file suit and pick one up. Make sure to pick up extras. Not only are they either free or very inexpensive, but it never hurts to be well supplied in case you make a mistake or for the next time you have to file suit.

The Summons

A summons is exactly what it sounds like. It is the document that, when properly provided to or "served on" the defendant, summons him to court to respond to your claim. As we will discuss a bit later in this chapter, you will be required to complete a summons form when you file your complaint. The summons form will tell the court:

- The identity of each defendant.

- Where each defendant can be served with your complaint.

- How you want each defendant served with your complaint (i.e., do you want the court to serve him by sheriff or do you want the summons returned to you so that you can have him served either by certified mail, return receipt requested, or by hand delivery (known as "private process").

The Filing Fee

You must pay a fee to file a case in court. The average small-claim filing fee is $15, but you will have to check with the court clerk to find out your court's fee schedule. Often, the filing fee will depend on the amount of money claimed. If you want the court to have the defendant served by sheriff, there will be an additional fee. Most states also allow people to apply for a waiver of the fee if they are able to demonstrate that they cannot afford it or that payment of the fee represents a substantial financial burden. Check with your clerk for more information.

Completing the Complaint Form

While no one state form has every single section imaginable, I find that the Maryland form has the vast majority of sections used in complaint forms across the country. Now, I won't lie to you; this is incredibly convenient for me as this is the form with which I am most familiar. Nevertheless, it is also very well suited to be used as our model as I proceed through the discussion. Toward that end, I have included it in blank on page 146.

In those instances where the Maryland form does not have a section that appears on other state forms, I shall try to address each of those sections elsewhere in this chapter. If you still have questions about completing one section or another, please call the court clerk.

DISTRICT COURT COMPLAINT FORM

① DISTRICT COURT OF MARYLAND FOR

② LOCATED AT (COURT ADDRESS)

③ CASE NO.
CV

PARTIES

Plaintiff: **④**

VS.

Defendant(s): **⑤**

1.
Serve by:
☐ Registered Mail
☐ Private Process
☐ Constable
☐ Sheriff

2.
Serve by:
☐ Registered Mail
☐ Private Process
☐ Constable
☐ Sheriff

3.
Serve by:
☐ Registered Mail
☐ Private Process
☐ Constable
☐ Sheriff

4.
Serve by:
☐ Registered Mail
☐ Private Process
☐ Constable
☐ Sheriff

ATTORNEYS

For Plaintiff - Name, Address, Telephone No. & Code **⑥**

⑦ DC/CV 1 (Rev. 7/93)

COMPLAINT ☐ $2,500 or under ☐ over $2,500 ☐ over $10,000

Clerk: Please docket this case in an action of ☐ contract ☐ tort ☐ replevin ☐ detinue.

The particulars of this case are:

⑧

FPO

(See Continuation Sheet)

The Plaintiff claims: **⑨**

☐ $ _____ plus interest of $ _____ and attorney's fees of $ _____ plus court costs.

☐ Return of the property and damages of $ _____ for its detention in an action of replevin.

☐ Return of the property, or its value, plus damages of $ _____ for its detention in action of detinue.

☐ Other: _____
and demands judgment for relief.

_____
Signature of Plaintiff/Attorney/Attorney Code **⑩**

Telephone Number: _____

⑪ APPLICATION AND AFFIDAVIT IN SUPPORT OF JUDGMENT

Attached hereto are the indicated documents which contain sufficient detail as to liability and damage to apprise the Defendant clearly of the claim against the Defendant, including the amount of any interest claimed.

☐ Properly authenticated copy of any note, security agreement upon which claim is based ☐ Itemized statement of account ☐ Interest work sheet ☐ Vouchers ☐ Check ☐ Other written document ☐ _____ ☐ Verified itemized repair bill or estimate

I HEREBY CERTIFY: That I am the ☐ Plaintiff ☐ _____ (Owner/Partner/Agent/Officer) of the Plaintiff herein and am competent

to testify to the matters stated herein, which are made on my personal knowledge; that there is justly due and owing by the Defendant to the Plaintiff the sum set forth in the Complaint.

☐ That _____

I solemnly affirm under the penalties of perjury and upon personal knowledge that the contents of the above Complaint are true and I am competent to testify to these matters. The Defendant is not now in the military service, as defined in the Soldier's and Sailor's Civil Relief Act of 1940 with amendments, nor has been in such service within thirty days hereof.

_____
Date

_____
Signature of Affiant

▶ **A WORD OF CAUTION**

While the forms may look easy to fill out, each line must be completed carefully. Please review all sections applicable to your state's form, even if you think you already know how to fill it out. What you learn may not only surprise you, but more important, it may help you strengthen your case.

Section 1: County

Consult the worksheet you developed in chapter 9 and fill in the county in which you decided to file suit. Note that some courts also ask on the form whether the claim is commercial or individual (sometimes called consumer). If this is asked on your state's form, check off the appropriate box from chapter 9.

Section 2: Courthouse Address

Having determined the county in which you will file your claim, you may simply choose the courthouse that is most convenient to you and fill in the address in Section 2.

Note that it is possible that the court system will transfer your case to a different courthouse than the one you designated on your form. Don't be concerned about this. Often, the courts redirect cases depending upon caseload or the location of the parties. You will be notified if your case gets transferred to another courthouse. Simply send all future papers to the new address shown on the notice. This is also the courthouse where the trial will be held, so don't forget to mark it down. There are few things more frustrating that appearing at the wrong place at the right time.

Section 3: Case Number

The case number is the number the court gives your claim after it is filed. Consequently, you should leave this box blank. After processing your complaint, the court will assign a case number, which will then be displayed on all court notices.

Because this number is the court's way of identifying your case, it is extremely important that you place the number on everything you send to the court.

Sections 4 and 5: The Parties

The "parties to the lawsuit" are you (or your company) and the person, people, or company (companies) you are suing.

When filling out these sections, always list the full name of each party followed by the appropriate address. Finding the appropriate address, particularly where a corporation is concerned, is something I shall address in detail later in this chapter.

Note that I have included a sample of a properly completed complaint form at the end of this chapter. Please feel free to refer to it when filling out your complaint.

Section 4: The Plaintiff

The plaintiff is either you or your company. Thus, Section 4 should be filled in with either your full name and address or that of your company, depending upon who is bringing the suit.

The cardinal rule of filling in this section is: USE THE CORRECT NAME. If you win, the person or company identified in this section will receive the judgment. More important, if you use the wrong name (e.g., Don's Clocks rather than the formal corporate name of Don Jackson Enterprises, Inc.), your case may be dismissed. If this happens, you never get a chance to offer any evidence about the debt, and you must start the process all over again by having the correctly named plaintiff file suit. Trust me, I have seen too many lawyers make this mistake for you to overlook the importance of this point.

Remember, the plaintiff is the person or business that rendered a service or provided the goods and did not get paid. Do not make the mistake of using the name of the president of the company, the individual doctor, carpenter, or mechanic who may have done the work, the trading name of the business, or even the name of the person who is doing the paperwork for the claim. Use the actual formal name of that person or company that the customer had agreed, but failed, to pay.

If you are not sure of the exact, formal name of your company, either ask your lawyer or accountant or check the full name shown on your company's tax returns.

Finally, make sure to include the proper address under the plaintiff's name. If you are making the claim on behalf of your business, use your primary business address. Remember, all of the court correspondence will be sent to this address, so make sure it is accurate.

Section 5: The Defendant

The defendant is the person or business that owes you the money. You should fill in this section with the names and addresses of each defendant.

Identifying the Correct Defendant

Naming the right defendant is just as important (and often trickier) than naming the right plaintiff. Ask yourself, "Who is the person or company responsible for paying this bill?" And remember, I'm not talking morally responsible. I'm talking legally responsible. Joe Smith may have looked you in the eye and agreed to the payment terms when he ordered the products, but if the name on the contract is Joseph Smith Industries, Inc., it is the company and not the individual to whom you must look for payment.

The defendant may not be the client himself but rather may sometimes be the client's parent or guardian. Also note that, with companies, the defendant is not the manager or the even the president but the company itself *unless* someone personally guaranteed the debt for the company. For example, Barbara Jones may sign personally to guarantee payment for products bought by Barbara's Cleaning Services, Incorporated. In this case, you would name both Barbara Jones and Barbara's Cleaning Services, Inc., as defendants.

Suing More Than One Defendant

Sometimes, a claim can be made against more than one person or company for payment of your bill. That's fine. *You do not have to worry about choosing the best one.* As long as there are legitimate claims against all of them, name all potential responsible people or companies as defendants. The more legitimate defendants there are, the better chance you have of collecting on your judgment. Moreover, I recommend filing suit against all responsible parties at the same time. Use caution, however; do not name people who cannot be held responsible for your losses.

In a nutshell, I guess what I am saying is:

> Sue them all . . . and let God sort them out.
> (I've always wanted to say that.)

An example of a legitimate claim against more than one defendant would be one arising out of a bounced check drawn on a joint account—name all account holders in the suit. Another common situation involves a contract in which someone personally guaranteed the obligations of another person or company. In this instance, you would name both the original customer and the guarantor as defendants as long as the original client is someone whom the court would hold responsible for the bill (i.e., not a child or adult of diminished capacity).

Naming the Defendant in the Complaint

I can sum up my advice on this subject in three words: "Get it right." Actually, that's my advice on every subject, but it's extremely important here.

If the Defendant Is a Person

If the defendant is a person, use his or her full first and last name, complete with "Jr.," "III," or any other such identifiers. You do not need the defendant's middle name.

If the Defendant Is a Business

Your goal is to put the full, formal business name on the complaint, such as "John Debtor Enterprises, Inc." or "Debtor and Son, Ltd." (Not to second-guess you or anything, but if either of these companies actually became customers and you granted them credit, I frankly think you should have seen trouble coming.)

Finding the correct name may be as easy as looking on a piece of stationery, a check the defendant may have given you, or the sign on the front of the defendant's office. Be warned, however, that any of these places may display the trade name ("Don's Clocks" in our earlier example) as opposed to the full, formal corporate name.

To help you navigate this hurdle, I have printed a chart on pages 37–48 that lists the agency in each state, together with address, phone number, Web site (if any), and hours of operation, with which all corporations must register to conduct business. These agencies will be able to tell you if the company name you have matches or comes close to a company on file. The agencies will also be able to look up registered trade names and tell you the formal, corporate name.

▶ AND YOU THOUGHT ONLY THE COOL KIDS HAD NICKNAMES

As I've alluded to on several occasions, businesses, too, can have nicknames. Generally, these names are selected and used to keep the businesses in the public eye, rather than to keep them from being beaten up on the playground. These are called "trade names."

You may find that you conducted business with "Jon's Pet World" only to discover that their full name is "Jonathan Doe's Pet World and Emporium, Inc." In this case, the best strategy is to include both names on the Complaint as follows: "Jonathan Doe's Pet World and Emporium, Inc. t/a Jon's Pet World." "T/A" means "trading as."

Unlike nicknames, trade names must be registered with the appropriate state agency in order to be valid. And in a perfect world, they would be. Unfortunately, many businesses have been operating under unregistered trade names for years. If you call the state agency and find that it has no listing for the trade name by which you know your customer, use the name you already have from your dealings with the company when drafting your Complaint.

Using the Correct Address

While accuracy is important, *you do not need to serve the defendant at the address listed on the complaint form.* As I shall discuss in the section dealing with service of process, you can have the defendant served by private process in any number of places. If, however, you are asking the court to serve the defendant by sheriff, the court will dispatch the sheriff only to the address identified in the complaint.

Even if you are using private process to serve the defendant, you should make every effort to display the correct address on the complaint so that the court can send the defendant's notices to the proper address. Failure to display the proper address can conceivably delay your case.

If the Defendant Is a Person

Use the defendant's home address, which you should have in your files. If you don't, and you can't find the address in the phone book or some other easily accessible location, try listing the defendant's work address or last known address, if available.

As I said, while it is important, it is not the address on the form that matters so much as having the defendant served with the papers. If you know his habits—where he works, the clubs he belongs to, or even the stores he frequents—you can get him served with enough effort. Please refer to the appendix at the conclusion of this book for more information on tracking down the hard-to-find defendant.

Of course, if the defendant is that hard to locate, you may want to think twice about filing suit in the first place. As discussed previously, filing suit against an absentee defendant may turn out to be more trouble than it's worth.

If the Defendant Is a Business

If the state corporations agency listed in the chart on pages 37–48 does not have a record of the company, use the address of the company's principal office for filling out the complaint. If you're not sure whether the address you have is that of the principal office, you can either call the defendant's business and ask (sounds stupid, but it works) or just use the address you already have.

If the agency does have a listing of the company, it will also have a listing of the person or company authorized to accept service of suit papers. This person is called the "resident agent" (also known in some states as the "registered agent") and is the representative selected by the company to accept service of legal papers. State law requires every company to appoint a resident agent with the state, although some companies either neglect to do this or forget to update the registration when the agent moves or dies. (Gee, that sounds callous.) Note that many states also allow service of suit papers upon a corporate officer.

Most states only require corporations or limited liability companies ("LLCs") to appoint resident agents. If you are dealing with a partnership or sole proprietorship, you simply serve the owner. Should you wish to double-check the policy in your state, simply call the number of the state agency shown on the chart on pages 37–48.

Note that if you are serving the resident agent, it is absolutely crucial that you have the correct one for the company you are suing. If you serve the wrong person, even if the person you served is the president of the company, the judge will dismiss your case. You will be able to refile your claim, but you will not be allowed to proceed to trial until you serve the correct entity or person.

A resident agent does not have to be a person. It can be a company. In fact, there are many companies across the country in the business of being the resident agent for other companies. Consequently, don't worry if the state agency tells you that the resident agent for the company you are suing turns out to be another corporation. And please remember . . . *you do not have to serve the resident agent of the resident agent!*

Please refer to the example complaint form at the end of this chapter to see how you should indicate the resident agent on the form.

If You Can't Find a Listing for the Resident Agent

If the state agency could not find a resident agent, the business you are trying to sue is either a sole proprietorship or partnership, or it is in violation of state law for not having registered a resident agent. Telling the difference between these two situations is usually not too difficult. Check your own company records. See if the customer has one of the following in its name—either printed on its checks (if you ever received one) or on any correspondence:

- Incorporated

- Inc.

- Limited

- Ltd.

- Corporation

- LLC (meaning "limited liability company")

- LLP (meaning "limited liability partnership")

- LLE (meaning "limited liability entity")

- P.A. (meaning "professional association")

- P.C. (meaning "professional corporation")

If so, chances are you are dealing with a company that wrongfully failed to register a resident agent. In this case, the state appoints a resident agent—either the agency shown in the chart or another agency designated by state law. Either way, the agency shown on the chart will direct you as to how to designate the state as resident agent on the complaint.

Note: It doesn't matter if all of this information doesn't fit in the space reserved for the naming of one defendant. As long as the information is there, the court will accept your complaint.

If you do not find any of the above-listed abbreviations or phrases in the company name, you should assume that you are dealing with a sole proprietorship or partnership. Fill in the section with the name and address of the business as you have it in your files. You will serve your papers on the person you were dealing with in your business transaction.

Naming an Out-of-State Company

If you are dealing with an out-of-state company, and you have been unable to find any information for the state agency, *before filing suit* look for information at one of two places:

1. The company itself; and/or

2. Government records from the company's home state.

When calling the company's offices, ask (1) for their full, formal name—tell the person answering the phone that you'd like to send them a letter; and/or (2) for the name and address of their resident agent in your home state. They may not give you any information, but, hey, give it a shot. They might.

A second place to check is the state government for the company's home state. In other words, let's assume you are trying to sue a company that you believe is based in Pennsylvania (or at least has an office there). If you are unable to find any information when calling your state's agency, call the other state's agency shown in the chart before simply assuming that the company you are dealing with is unincorporated. They may simply have neglected to follow proper procedures for doing business in your home state.

Note that in this instance, you would still use your state's agency as the resident agent in your home state because the company did not appoint one of its own. Nevertheless, a call to the company's home state would enable you to find the correct formal name of the corporation.

Section 6: The "Serve by" Option

Section 6 on the Maryland form shows four ways of having the defendant served: (1) registered mail, (2) private process, (3) constable, or (4) sheriff. These options are discussed below.

Option 1: Registered Mail

It is not enough to simply send the defendant the complaint and summons by first-class mail because there is no proof that the defendant actually received them. Without proof (or the defendant's admission through the filing of a response) that the defendant received a copy of the complaint and summons, a court will not enter judgment against him.

Sending a letter by certified mail, return receipt requested (shown on this form as "registered mail") is different. The defendant must sign a postal receipt in order to accept deliver of a letter sent in this fashion. The receipt constitutes your proof that the defendant received the documents. Make sure you save copies of all documents sent by mail, as well as the postal receipts from certified letters and packages.

Depending upon where the defendant is located, it can take anywhere from three to fourteen days before you receive the green return receipt. If you do not receive your receipt within fourteen days, contact the post office from which you mailed your letter.

If this happens, don't delay. Go to the post office and bring copies of all of the documents you sent, including a copy of the receipt you were given when you mailed the complaint. The post office will put a tracer on your letter, and if the receipt was lost, they may be able to provide you with a secondary reply card (yellow) to replace the lost green receipt. This secondary reply card is perfectly valid proof of service needed for court.

Option 2: Private Process Server

A "private process server" is a person who hand-delivers court documents (such as complaints, summonses, and subpoenas) to people. Almost every county in the United States has at least one company in the business of serving defendants in civil claims. You can find such companies by looking in the business yellow pages or even by calling a local law firm and asking for a reference.

As a rule, private process servers are the most expensive and the most reliable way to have the defendant served. Where you may wind up with the wrong signature on a certified mail receipt and the sheriff (as we'll discuss) may give up after three unsuccessful tries, a private process server will keep trying to serve the defendant until you tell him to stop.

I recommend using a private process server if you anticipate that the defendant will be difficult to serve. After all, you get what you pay for. If you want it done quickly and correctly the first time, and you don't mind spending a bit more, service by private process is the way to go.

Private process servers are usually paid a base fee, which can run anywhere from $20 to $75, payable when service is obtained. For an extra fee, many private process servers will also do what is known as a "skip trace" (tracking a runaway defendant). Of course, you should ALWAYS ask about the rates before you hire. In addition, make sure you check in with the process server fairly frequently and place a limit on his activities. You do not want to give the process server free rein only to find that his bill is bigger than the one you are trying to collect from the defendant.

Remember, you can direct the amount of effort the process server puts into serving your defendant. It may be as simple as giving the process server the defendant's home address and having him wait until the defendant gets home in the evening. Of course, more sophisticated or involved forms of tracking cost more money.

Finally, note that the more information you can give the process server about the defendant's habits, the better chance the process server has of serving the defendant on the first or second attempt.

▶ PRIVATE PROCESS SERVICE . . . FOR FREE

Almost anyone can serve a defendant with a Complaint and Summons. The only limitations are that the person serving the defendant must be an adult and cannot be a party to the lawsuit. This means that if your company is the plaintiff, your wife, and even your children (if they are over 18) are allowed to serve the defendant, but your employees are not. If, however, you, personally, are the plaintiff, it may be a good idea to have non-family members serve the Complaint and Summons.

The person who serves the defendant will have to sign a document attesting to that fact, but he will not have to go to trial with you. Ask you small claims court clerk for a copy of the form called an "Affidavit of Service."

Note that this is still considered to be "private process" when you are checking off the "serve by" box on the Complaint.

Options 3 and 4: Sheriff or Constable

Many people don't realize that virtually every county in the United States has a sheriff's office. One of the sheriff's responsibilities is serving defendants in civil cases. Check the fee schedule in your local small-claims court for costs, but the average seems to be about $30 in addition to the filing fee.

You should know that service by sheriff is a bit inconsistent. I have known sheriffs to keep going back to the defendant's home at all hours until they finally succeed in serving him. On the other hand, I have also seen sheriffs make one attempt before returning the papers to the court stating that the defendant could not be served. After that, you would have to request a new summons (if the original had expired) and try to serve it another way.

Despite the expense, however, having the sheriff serve the defendant carries with it the wonderful psychological effect of having an armed officer hand your complaint and summons to the debtor. In many cases, this rather intimidating method has, in and of itself, resulted in the defendant simply paying what he owes in order to end the litigation.

Note that although the complaint form has a separate box for service by constable, the only difference between that and service by sheriff concerns the county in which you are filing suit. If you are interested in having a court officer serve your papers, ask the clerk which box to check on your state's form if you are given a choice. There is no functional difference.

My Recommendations

- If you are suing an individual, have the papers served by private process server or sheriff. People rarely sign for certified letters if they know they're getting sued. Choose between sheriff and private process server depending upon how elusive you believe the defendant will be. If you think he's going to be particularly hard to serve, go with the private process server.

- If you are suing a business that has a resident agent, use certified mail, return receipt requested. Anything else is a waste of money.

► YOU MAY HAVE JUST WON . . .

Would you sign for a letter knowing that you are making it easier for someone to sue you? Neither would most defendants. But I bet you would sign for a letter if you think someone was sending you money. Well . . .

No discussion of service would be complete without mentioning an inexpensive way of getting people to sign for certified letters–fraud. Knowing that people who suspect they're about to be sued generally refuse to sign for a certified letter from the creditor or its lawyer, some people have actually had envelopes printed with return addresses such as "United Beneficiary Locators" or "National Prize Foundation." Debtors sign for the letters and, by the time the debtor realizes he's been sued, he's been served.

I call these creditors "too smart by half." Sting operations may work for the FBI (or maybe not), but obtaining service by fraud renders the service invalid. Thus, marching into court with the debtor's signature on a mail receipt that was obtained by fraudulent means not only risks the dismissal of your case for improper service, but it also jeopardizes your standing in the eyes of the court.

Using Different Methods in the Same Case

As I stated earlier, any of the methods discussed above are valid for obtaining service on a defendant. In the event your claim has several defendants, some of whom may be easy to serve and some of whom may be evasive, you are free to use any combination of these methods.

Section 7: The Attorney

The only reason this information is requested (if indeed it is at all) is so that the clerk will have a contact person. If you are proceeding without an attorney, simply put your own name, business address, and telephone number in the space designated for "plaintiff's attorney."

After your name, you should place the underlined Latin words *pro se*. This tells the court that you are not an attorney. Thus, as an example, this section should be filled in as follows:

John Smith, *pro se*
22 West Pennsylvania Avenue
Baltimore, MD 21204
(410) 555-8500

Section 8: Type of Claim

If you are asked to place your claim in a value range, check the box that corresponds to the principal amount of your claim, exclusive of interest, court costs, and any statutory penalties.

Every case you file against a client for nonpayment is a breach-of-contract case. Consequently, if asked, you should mark the "contract" box because the judge is being asked to make a ruling based upon a contract between the parties.

Section 9: Describing Your Claim

This section is the heart and soul of your case. This is the part where you explain to the judge why you are entitled to the money you are claiming. Now, some courts allow you to attach a separate sheet as a narrative. If your state court allows this, I always recommend it. A separate narrative, which I will show you how to draft a little later in this chapter, will provide the judge with more detail about your claim. It is almost like making an opening statement without the other side saying anything. In other words, it's a free shot. Take it.

Of course, the other reason I recommend this is that many state small-claim complaint forms contain several carbonless copies. If all you write in the narrative section is "please see attached," you can revise your actual explanation to your heart's content. Otherwise, you risk typos, white-out, and a sloppy-looking complaint.

If you are inclined to follow this suggestion, simply place the words "please see attached" in the space allocated on the form for a description of the claim.

▶ A NOTE ABOUT WRITING STYLE

When I prepare a Complaint, I always try to use what has been described to me as the "KISS" method. The KISS method stands for "Keep It Simple, Stupid"—and that is exactly what you should do when drafting your Complaint. The judge is not interested in a lot of needless detail, he said-she said, or questions about the defendant's ancestry. Like Sergeant Joe Friday, the judge wants "just the facts."

After all, the Complaint is only the starting point for your case. You can always elaborate on the details once you testify in court. Consequently, keep your description of events in your Complaint as brief and clear as possible. Aim to fit your entire narrative into one page and at most two pages. Not only do judges appreciate it, but it also makes for a lot less typing.

Using Exhibits

Just as you should think about what you are going to write before you put pen to paper, you should give some thought as to what your evidence is going to be. Very often, certain documents such as a purchase order or contract, bounced check, or invoices tell the story of your claim and should be attached to your complaint. These attachments are called "exhibits."

Put your exhibits in the order in which you want to refer to them in the description of your claim. Chronological order is usually best—meaning, for example, that an estimate or contract would come before a past-due invoice.

Labeling Exhibits

All of your exhibits should be labeled with a number or letter ("Exhibit A" or "Exhibit 1," for example). You can label each exhibit by either typing or writing "Exhibit __" in the upper-right-hand corner of the document.

Please note that each document that you want to refer to separately is a separate exhibit. This means that a three-page letter is one exhibit because it is really one document. Some documents can be grouped. For example, you can put all invoices together collectively as Exhibit 3.

Note: When assembling your complaint for filing, do not send your originals (checks, letters, contracts, etc.) as exhibits. Copies are fine. In addition, make sure to save a full set of all exhibits in a separate litigation file because you will probably want to use those same documents at trial.

Weed Out Unnecessary Exhibits

Try not to be repetitive when deciding which exhibits to include. If the client has not paid you in two years, and you have been sending invoices every month, you do not need to attach all twenty-four invoices as separate exhibits. Instead, I would recommend attaching only the first one, unless you have been showing interest accumulating on the unpaid balance. If this is the case, I would attach both the first one and the most recent one and explain in the complaint that you have been sending invoices every month. One final note: Although I wouldn't attach all of the invoices to the complaint as exhibits, I would bring them to court in case the judge asks to see them.

Filling in the Space Allotted

If you are not allowed to attach an additional sheet, you have a challenge in front of you. You must fit your claim into a one- or two-sentence description. This takes time. Don't try to fill out the form on the fly. Draft your description on a separate piece of paper first and get it how you want it before filling out the actual form.

You may find the following examples helpful:

1. On August 12, 1999, the defendant hired the plaintiff to perform accounting work. The plaintiff fully performed all work requested. Despite demand, the defendant refused to pay the agreed fee.

2. The defendant ordered custom-printed materials from the plaintiff, including business cards and letterhead. The plaintiff provided all material ordered following the defendant's approval of both the quote and the proof. The defendant has failed to pay the agreed amount despite receiving monthly bills from the plaintiff.

3. The plaintiff agreed to provide materials and perform services to complete the defendant's landscaping plan, for which the defendant issued a check in full payment to the plaintiff. The plaintiff completed all agreed work. The defendant's check was dishonored by the bank. To date, the defendant has failed to render payment.

Writing a Separate Description

The Caption

Every paper filed with the court must identify the case to which it pertains. When filing a pleading such as a complaint or a motion, the case identification portion is called the "caption" and appears at the very top of the page. I have printed a sample below:

[Your Company]	*	IN THE COURT
Plaintiff	*	
v.	*	DISTRICT COURT
[John Debtor]	*	
and	*	FOR
[Jim Debtor] individually	*	
and t/a [Jim's Cleaners]	*	_____COUNTY
	*	
Defendants	*	
	*	Case Number: [Number]
	*	

* *

COMPLAINT

Your Company hereby files suit against John Debtor and Debtor's Cleaners, Inc., and for such reason, states as follows:

As I mentioned, the part above the line of asterisks is called the caption, and the plaintiff and the defendant(s) should be identified just as they are on the complaint form. You do not have to print their addresses in the caption on other motions or pleadings once you have filed the complaint. Note that you should leave the space for the case number blank, as this is assigned by the court after you file your claim. Once it is assigned, the case number gets placed in all future captions.

After you display the title of the document below the caption, in this case, a complaint, as well as a simple introductory paragraph that sounds disgustingly formal such as the one shown above, you should write a description of why you are owed money by the defendants.

The Narrative

The description of your claim—the story—is called a "narrative." It should be set in separate, numbered paragraphs that follow in a logical order. Usually chronological order works best, although it is not mandatory. All you have to do is tell the story of your claim. Tell it simply and without embellishment.

Most importantly, you do not have to specify every detail, list every (or even any) conversation, or try to anticipate what defenses your nonpaying customer will raise.

► **ALWAYS ANSWER THE "SO WHAT?" QUESTION**

After writing every sentence in your narrative, imagine the judge hearing the statement you just wrote and asking "so what?" In other words, how does the statement bear on the case? Does it actually influence the outcome?

If you tell the judge that you reached an agreement with the defendant to do something or sell something for money, you held up your end, and the defendant failed to pay you, does telling the judge that the defendant hung up on you when you tried to talk to him about it really get you anywhere? (Wow, that's a long sentence.) It might explain why you're angry at the defendant, but it has no bearing on the case.

If, for every statement you write, you can honestly see why the judge would care in making up his mind, you have successfully answered the "so what?" question and the statement belongs in your description. If not, toss it.

The following is an example of a narrative that should give you some guidance in writing one of your own:

Sample Standard Narrative

1. On [January 1, 1994], [Your Company] agreed to perform services for [John Debtor] for which [Mr. Debtor] agreed to pay [$2,000.00].

2. [Your Company] performed all of the services required by its agreement with [John Debtor].

3. [John Debtor] has breached the agreement by failing to render full payment to [Your Company]. To date, [John Debtor] has paid [$500.00], leaving a total outstanding balance of [$1,500.00 plus interest].

4. [John Debtor] has refused all of the requests made by [Your Company] for payment, as a result of which [Your Company] has incurred damages in the amount of [$1,500.00 plus interest].

WHEREFORE, the plaintiff, [Your Company], seeks compensation from the defendant, [John Debtor], in the amount of [$1,500.00] plus court costs and interest in the amount of [$X.XX] as shown on the attached interest worksheet.

[Signature of Corp. Officer]
_____

[Your Company]
By: [Joe Plaintiff, President]
[Address]
[Telephone Number]
Plaintiff

You may adapt this sample narrative for your case by replacing the items in parentheses with your own information. If you'd like to write your own narrative, make sure to include the following:

• Describe the terms of the agreement. It can be an oral agreement, a written contract, or even an implied agreement.

• Assert the fact that you held up your end of the bargain by completing the work.

• State the fact that the defendant has not paid you.

• State that you have demanded payment. (It doesn't matter whether payment was demanded via telephone conversations, letters, or the sending of invoices, as long as you asked to be paid.)

• Assert the fact that your damages are X dollars.

If you believe your client may come along later and say that you failed to do a complete job or that the price was not what you said it was, let him make that claim and deal with it at that time. You do not need to address those points in your complaint.

Sample Narrative Requesting Interest

1. On [January 1, 1999], [Your Company] agreed to perform services for [John Debtor] for which [Mr. Debtor] agreed to pay [$2,000.00]. The contract between [Your Company] and [John Debtor] is attached to this Complaint as Exhibit [____].

2. [Your Company] performed all of the services required by its agreement with [John Debtor], after which [Your Company] sent bills to [John Debtor] for the amount due. A bill dated [February 1, 1999], is attached to this Complaint as Exhibit [____]. A bill, dated [March 1, 1999], is attached to this Complaint as Exhibit [____].

3. [John Debtor] has breached the agreement by failing to render full payment to [Your Company].

4. [John Debtor] has refused all of the requests made by [Your Company] for payment, as a result of which [Your Company] has incurred damages in the amount of [$2,000.00] plus interest. An interest worksheet showing the calculations for interest due is attached to this Complaint as Exhibit [____].

> [Signature of Corp. Officer]
> _____
>
> [Your Company]
> By: [Joe Plaintiff, President]
> [Address]
> [Telephone Number]
> Plaintiff

Section 10: How Much Is the Claim?

To process your claim properly, the court must be told how much you are owed. Your answer should not include interest or court costs that may be added onto the claim. There is another place on the form where you can indicate the amount of interest you are claiming.

As an example, let's assume that you were claiming the following amounts:

* $1,500 unpaid bill.

- $25 bounced-check charge.

- $1,000 statutory penalty for a bounced check.

- $75 interest.

Your actual claim would amount to $2,525 plus $75 interest, so you would enter $2,525 in the claim box and $75 in the interest blank.

Section 10 also asks whether you are claiming "attorney's fees" as part of your case. Despite that fact that you may be acting as your own attorney, you are not allowed to make a claim for attorney's fees. You should, therefore, either leave this space blank or fill in $0.00.

You will also see a box to check if you want property returned. If you're just suing for money, don't check this box. As an example of when you would check this box, I can recall the case of a woman who was in the business of selling and showing purebred German shepherds. When the defendant's check bounced, the relationship between the parties deteriorated to such an extent (over an issue of how and when to show the dog) that the plaintiff sued to get the puppy back rather than for the money that was owed.

Section 11: Signing the Complaint

Yes, I know this is repetitive with your having signed the narrative, but your complaint will not be accepted by the court without your signature in this area.

If you are filing suit individually, sign your name on the line and cross out everything below the line except the words "Signature of Plaintiff."

If your company is the plaintiff, squeeze the name of your company, followed by the word "by," and have the authorized representative sign. Once again, cross out everything below the line except the words "Signature of Plaintiff."

Section 12: Judgment by Mail or Default

Because of the large increase in the number of collection cases being filed, many states such as Maryland have instituted a procedure that enables a person or company to be awarded a judgment without every having to go through a trial. The reasoning is that if the debt were invalid the defendant would oppose the claim once he was served. Consequently, if the defendant is served with the complaint and does not file anything with the court saying he opposed the claim, then judgment should be awarded without taking the court's time.

If a "Judgment by Mail" exists on the complaint, check it. Otherwise, many states will enter a judgment against the defendant if he fails to answer. This is called a "judgment by default." Either way, it is a mechanism to award judgments without your having to appear in court, as long as there is no dispute raised as to the validity of your claim.

You should always check the Judgment by Mail box, even if you are sure that the defendant will contest the claim. The fact is that it does not take any extra time or money, and it could save you an enormous amount of time and effort.

How Judgment by Mail Works in Theory

Once the defendant is served, he is given a certain amount of time, depending on the state, within which to file a response saying he opposes the claim. If he files the response, a trial date is scheduled. If he does not, the judge will enter the judgment in the amount claimed and the court will notify the plaintiff by mail.

How Judgment by Mail Usually Works in Reality

The court will pencil in a trial date, and the defendant will be advised in the summons that he has a certain number of days to respond or judgment will be awarded against him. Of course it won't, but this is what the defendant will be told.

In reality, even if the defendant does not file a response, he can usually show up in court on the scheduled trial date, tell the judge he has a defense, and the judge will order the trial date to be rescheduled. In such a situation, you would receive a trial/hearing notice within the next couple of weeks.

Bottom Line: If you filed for judgment by mail, do not go to court on the trial date shown on the summons. If you don't receive a response from the defendant by the trial date, you will either be notified by the court that you got your judgment (if the defendant didn't show up) or that your case has been scheduled for a new trial date (if the defendant did show up).

Preparing an Interest Worksheet

If your contract entitles you to collect interest on overdue balances, you should prepare an interest worksheet for attachment to your complaint. This worksheet, which should also be submitted to the judge as an exhibit at trial, shows the calculations you used to reach the amount of interest you are claiming. While you do not have to use one specific format, your worksheet must contain the following information:

- The interest rate.

- The amount of money on which interest is being assessed.

- The length of time over which the interest has been assessed.

Note that you should show the interest accruing from the date on which the debt became due through the date on which you file your complaint. For example, if your billing policy specifies that all bills must be paid within thirty days and the bill went out on January 1, interest should begin to accrue on February 1—the date on which the bill became past due.

Moreover, because it is safe to assume that the judge will not be reviewing the case until well after the complaint is filed, your worksheet should indicate the rate at which interest is accruing. The easiest way to express this is to state at the bottom of the worksheet that interest will continue to accrue at the rate of $X.XX per day. You may find it helpful to use the same format as the sample interest worksheet shown on the following page.

When preparing your interest worksheet, you should add your caption at the top and attach it to your complaint as an exhibit.

Sample *Interest Worksheet*

[Your Company]	*	IN THE COURT
Plaintiff	*	
v.	*	DISTRICT COURT
[John Debtor]	*	
and	*	FOR
[Jim Debtor] individually	*	
and t/a [Jim's Cleaners]	*	_____COUNTY
	*	
Defendants	*	
	*	Case Number: [Number]
	*	

* *

INTEREST WORKSHEET

Principal Amount:		$980.70
Interest:	10% per Agreement of 10/22/98:	

Interest from 5/22/99 through 1/22/00:		
245 days x $.27 per day:		$ 66.15

TOTAL:		$1,046.85
Total Interest:	$ 66.15	
Total Principal:	$980.70	

* Interest continues to accrue at the rate of $.27 per day.

Processing Your Claim with the Court

Once your complaint is all neatly typed, what do you do with it? First, you have to give your paperwork to the court ("file it"); second, you have to serve it on the defendant; and third, you have to advise the court that the defendant has been served.

Filing Your Claim

To file your complaint you need to make several copies of the complaint with exhibits attached—one copy for the court and one set for *each* defendant. Send the original and one copy of the completed form and all attachments for each defendant to the court. Make sure to save a copy for your records. Finally, make sure you bring a check with you to pay the applicable filing fees.

Before filing your claim, it is a good idea to call the clerk in order to make sure that you have filled out all of the necessary forms. Sometimes court procedures change. So even if you become experienced in filing collection cases, you should still call the courthouse in order to make sure that the filing fees and the necessary forms are the same as the last time you filed.

When you call the court, you may be asked what kind of case you are filing so that you can be connected to the person who handles those claims. There are two main types of cases—criminal and civil. Your case, being a collection matter, is a civil case. Accordingly, when calling the court, you will want to speak to the "civil clerk"—the clerk who handles the administration of civil cases.

Filing by Mail

First and foremost, you must check with the small-claim court in your state to see if the court will even accept case filings by mail. Even if they do, I still would recommend filing your claim in person until you become more comfortable with the process and can conduct your business with the court by mail.

While you are certainly free to stuff the papers and check into an envelope and let the clerk sort it out, you will be far better off sending the documents with a cover letter explaining exactly what papers you are filing and what you want the clerk to do once he receives them.

The cover letter that accompanies anything you want filed in the case is called a "letter of transmittal" because it is being used to "transmit" something to the court. A sample of transmittal is shown below.

[Date]
Civil Clerk
District Court of Maryland
for [Baltimore] County
[address]
[city, state, zip code]

RE: [Your Company vs. John Debtor]

Dear Sir/Madam:

Enclosed for filing, please find a complaint with one copy for each defendant with regard to the above-referenced case. I have also enclosed by filing fee in the amount of $_____.

Thank you for your attention to and assistance with this matter. If you have any questions or would like further information, please do not hesitate to let me know.

Very truly yours,
[Your Company]

[Joe Plaintiff]

Processing Time

The court will take anywhere from one to three weeks to prepare the summonses (one for each defendant). If you decided to have the defendant served by sheriff, you will not receive the summonses back from the court. Instead, you will only receive notification that the defendant has been served or that the sheriff has been unable to serve the defendant after several attempts. If this is the case, you can either get the summons back from the court to try to serve it some other way, or, if the summons has expired (see the section below), you can have the summons reissued.

If you have elected to serve the defendant by certified mail or by private process, the court will return the summonses and complaints to you by mailing them to the address you provided on the complaint.

Renewing a Summons

Every state has its own time limit or expiration date before which the summons must be served on the defendant. The number of days during which a summons is valid will be printed right on the form. You must serve the summons and complaint on the defendant within that time period. Otherwise, the summons expires. Since you cannot serve the defendant with an expired summons, you must get the court to issue a new one.

The court will have preprinted request for summons forms that you may get from the clerk's office. Fill in the space provided for "Renewal" and complete the rest of the form with the information requested.

Providing Proof of Service

As stated above, unless you elect to have the defendant served by sheriff, you must not only serve the defendant with the complaint but also advise the court he was served.

When you receive the summons back from the court, you may notice that it comes with several copies. Only one of the forms need be attached to the complaint when you serve it on the defendant. Keep a copy for your file. Finally, a copy should be filled out by the process server and filed with the court. Most private process servers will do this for you. Find out if the one you have chosen is one of these. If not, have them fill out the part of the form where they must describe who they served.

You should advise the court that service has been obtained on the defendant, regardless of whether you had the papers served via registered mail or by a friend. If you had the papers served by registered mail, simply staple the original green receipt to the summons and fill out the portion concerning how and to whom the papers were delivered.

Mail the completed form back to the court along with a cover letter (like the letter of transmittal shown above) confirming that you are enclosing proof of service for filing in this case. If you are serving the defendant by sheriff, the sheriff will automatically file the affidavit of service for you.

Revising Your Complaint After You File It

You can change your complaint after you file it, although this often has the effect of postponing your trial date. Consequently, you should take this option only as a last resort—if you forgot an item of damages or an important fact that you feel could mean the difference between winning and having your case thrown out of court.

Such a revision is called an "Amended Complaint." Some states have actually created a form to enable you to file one. Call the clerk's office to see if such a form is available. If not, or if you do not feel like going to the courthouse to get one, you may prepare one on your own as shown below. The Amended Complaint takes the same format as the narrative that is attached to the original Complaint form.

When you file an Amended Complaint, you do not need to fill out the computerized District Court form that you filled out when first filing suit. You simply need the following printed on regular 8½-by-11 sheets:

- A caption (the section above the line).

- The title "Amended Complaint."

- An introductory paragraph.

- The *complete* narrative describing your case, including your revisions,

- A request for damages.

- Your signature line.

- A certification that you sent a copy of the amended complaint to the defendant.

Everything listed above is shown in the sample Amended Complaint on the following page.

[Your Company]	*	IN THE COURT
Plaintiff	*	
v.	*	DISTRICT COURT
[John Debtor]	*	
and	*	FOR
[Jim Debtor] individually	*	
and t/a [Jim's Cleaners]	*	_____COUNTY
	*	
Defendants	*	
	*	Case Number: [Number]
	*	

* *

AMENDED COMPLAINT

[Your Company] hereby files this Amended Complaint against [John Debtor] and in support of its claim states as follows:

1. On [January 1, 1999], [Your Company] agreed to perform services for [John Debtor] for which [Mr. Debtor] agreed to pay [$2,000]. The contract between [Your Company] and [John Debtor] is attached to this Complaint as Exhibit [____].

2. [Your Company] performed all of the services required by its agreement with [John Debtor]; after which, [Your Company] sent bills to [John Debtor] for the amount due. A bill dated [February 1, 1999], is attached to this Complaint as Exhibit [____]. A bill dated [March 1, 1999], is attached to this Complaint as Exhibit [____].

3. [John Debtor] has breached the agreement by failing to render full payment to [Your Company].

4. On [April 1, 1999], [John Debtor] issued a check for [$500] to [Your Company] to be applied toward his account balance. The check was returned unpaid to [Your Company] by [First National Bank] for insufficient funds.

5. On [May 1, 1999], [John Debtor] issued another check for [$500] to [Your Company] to replace the first check. This check was also returned unpaid to [Your Company] by [First National Bank]. The plaintiff later learned that the check was returned by [First National Bank] because [John Debtor] put a Stop Payment Order on the check.

6. [John Debtor] has refused all of the requests made by [Your Company] for payment, as a result of which [Your Company] has incurred damages in the amount of [$2,000 plus interest]. An interest worksheet showing the calculations for interest due is attached to this Complaint as Exhibit [___].

7. In addition to having failed to render payment for his full account balance, [John Debtor] has also incurred two $25 bounced-check charges which he also failed to pay.

WHEREFORE, the plaintiff, [Your Company], seeks compensation for the defendants, as follows:

a. Compensation in the amount of [$2,000.00] representing the unpaid balance on his account;

b. Returned check charges of $50.00;

c. Court costs.

[Signature of Corp. Officer]
_____
[Your Company]
By: [Joe Plaintiff, President]
[Address]
[Telephone Number]
Plaintiff

CERTIFICATE OF MAILING

I HEREBY CERTIFY that on this _____ day of _____, 19_____, I caused a copy of this Amended Complaint [to be mailed first class, postage prepaid or hand-delivered] to:

[John Debtor] at [Address]

_____
[Your Company]
By: [Joe Plaintiff, President]

Serving the Defendant with the Amended Complaint

As long as the defendant was served with the original complaint, you have to send the amended complaint by first-class mail only. There is no need to obtain a receipt or any proof that the defendant received it, as long as you certify to the court (as shown by the certification of mailing in the sample amended complaint, above) that you sent it to him.

Requesting a Trial Date

When you file your claim, certain states will require you to go through the additional step of sending in a request that the case be set in for trial after the defendant is served. The clerk in each of these states will provide you with this information once you file your case. Read the information carefully and file the request when required. Failure to request a trial date in writing may result in a dismissal of your claim.

COMPLETED DISTRICT COURT COMPLAINT FORM

DISTRICT COURT OF MARYLAND FOR Baltimore County	DC/CV 1 (Rev. 7/93)

COMPLAINT ☒ $2,500 or under ☐ over $2,500 ☐ over $10,000

LOCATED AT (COURT ADDRESS)
120 E. Chesapeake Avenue
Towson, MD 21204

Clerk: Please docket this case in an action of ☐ contract ☐ tort ☐ replevin
☐ detinue.

The particulars of this case are:

CASE NO.

CV

Please see attached

PARTIES

Plaintiff:
    (Your Company)
    (Street)
    (City, State, Zip Code)

VS.

Defendant(s):

1. Jim Debtor
   8511 Ivy Road
   Baltimore, MD 21229
   Serve by: ☐ Registered Mail ☒ Private Process ☐ Constable ☐ Sheriff

2. Jim's Cleaners, Inc.
   7908 Topping Lane
   Baltimore, MD 21293
   Serve by: ☐ Registered Mail ☒ Private Process ☐ Constable ☐ Sheriff

3. Serve On:
   State Department of
   Assessments & Taxation
   301 West Preston Street
   Serve by: ☐ Registered Mail ☐ Private Process ☐ Constable ☐ Sheriff

4. Room 809
   Baltimore, MD 21201
   Serve by: ☐ Registered Mail ☐ Private Process ☐ Constable ☐ Sheriff

(See Continuation Sheet)

The Plaintiff claims:

☐ $ 2,005.70 plus interest of $ 166.64 and
attorney's fees of $ _____ plus court costs.

☐ Return of the property and damages of $ _____
for its detention in an action of replevin.

☐ Return of the property, or its value, plus damages of
$ _____ for its detention in action of detinue.

☐ Other:
and demands judgment for relief.

(Your Company) *Joe Plaintiff*
Signature of Plaintiff/Attorney/Attorney Code

Telephone Number: (410) 555-1212

ATTORNEYS

For Plaintiff - Name, Address, Telephone No. & Code

Joe Plaintiff, President
Your Company
8511 Ivy Road
Baltimore, MD 21229

APPLICATION AND AFFIDAVIT IN SUPPORT OF JUDGMENT

Attached hereto are the indicated documents which contain sufficient detail as to liability and damage to apprise the Defendant clearly of the claim against the Defendant, including the amount of any interest claimed.

☐ Properly authenticated copy of any note, security agreement upon which claim is based ☐ Itemized statement of account ☒ Interest work sheet
☐ Vouchers ☐ Check ☒ Other written document ☒ Invoices, Estimate _____ ☐ Verified itemized repair bill or estimate
I HEREBY CERTIFY: That I am the ☐ Plaintiff ☒ Officer _____ of the Plaintiff herein and am competent
(Owner/Partner/Agent/Officer)

to testify to the matters stated herein, which are made on my personal knowledge; that there is justly due and owing by the Defendant to the Plaintiff the sum set forth in the Complaint.

☐ That

I solemnly affirm under the penalties of perjury and upon personal knowledge that the contents of the above Complaint are true and I am competent to testify to these matters. The Defendant is not now in the military service, as defined in the Soldier's and Sailor's Civil Relief Act of 1940 with amendments, nor has been in such service within thirty days hereof.

9/30/95   *Joe Plaintiff*   For (Your Company)
Date   Signature of Affiant

11
Handling the Defendant's Response

Overview

Now that the defendant has been served with your Complaint and Summons, he will react in one of the following ways:

- He could ignore the Complaint entirely, thus allowing you to win by default.

- He could claim he was not properly notified.

- He could request that the case be decided by a jury (if state law allows jury trials for such claims).

- He could file (or threaten to file) a countersuit against you or your company.

- He could attempt to negotiate a settlement (as I discuss in chapter 14).

Choose the description from the above list that best fits your situation and refer to that section below.

In this chapter I will discuss the various ways to handle the defendant's response to your Complaint. In addition, I will also examine the best ways to deal with the defendant's attorney and when it may be time to consider hiring one of your own.

What If the Defendant Ignores the Complaint and Summons?

If the small-claims procedures in your state provide for judgment by mail as discussed in the preceding chapter and the defendant fails to respond to your Complaint, you will receive your judgment without having to appear for trial. The court will simply send you a notice confirming the date on which the judgment was entered, the amount of the judgment, and any additional amounts found to be due from the defendant such as court costs or interest. Once you obtain your judgment by mail, you will be able to initiate collection efforts as described in chapter 17.

What If the Defendant Claims He Wasn't Notified?

By claiming he was not properly served with your Complaint and Summons, the defendant can force you to have him re-served with a new Summons, thereby postponing the trial. He can make this claim in one of two ways: (1) file a pretrial request that the case be dismissed for improper service or (2) make the argument at trial.

If the Defendant Seeks Dismissal Before Trial

As we discussed, small-claims procedures were created to move smaller cases through the system with a minimum of red tape. For this reason, small-claims courts place a strict limit on the kinds of arguments, called "motions," they will consider prior to trial. That being said, an argument that the case shouldn't even come to trial because plaintiff failed to properly notify the defendant will always be considered.

Since all parties have the right to see what any one of them submits to the court, the defendant should send you a copy of any motion or letter he sends to the court. What's more, even if you do not receive a copy from the defendant, the court will advise you by notice that a motion has been received. The court will also let you know when the issue will be considered (e.g., at trial or at a separate hearing).

If the court sets a separate date to hear the issue or if no date has been indicated, you should file a brief response refuting the defendant's argument point by point. The defendant's arguments will be written in his motion. Simply respond to his argument. You do not have to copy his points or rebut them in the order he arranges his argument. Just tell the court why you feel he's wrong.

As an example, if the defendant states that he did not receive a copy of the Summons and Complaint you sent by certified mail, return receipt requested, you should attach to your response the green mail receipt bearing his signature. If you had the Complaint and Summons hand-delivered, you should attach an Affidavit from that person confirming the delivery. You should also point out any communication you may have had with the defendant in which he discussed the Complaint or otherwise showed that he received the papers.

Your response should be written in the form of the Complaint narrative that I discussed in chapter 10. Start with the caption (which goes on all papers filed with the court), title your response "Response to Motion to Dismiss," write an introductory paragraph, and state your argument in numbered paragraphs.

▶ AS A WHOLE NEW WORLD OPENS UP FOR YOU . . .

Once you get the hang of writing motions, you may find that you simply do not want to return to your previous writing style. Legal style, when correctly applied, can be concise, to-the-point, and fairly impressive.

Consider applying your newly developed skills to school permission slips ("Patrick Smith, student, by and through Charles and Joan Smith, his parents, hereby submits this permission slip for the fifth grade field trip, and for such reason states as follows . . .") or even holiday greetings ("1. That you gave birth to me 34 years ago; 2. That an annual day of recognition has been established to commemorate your efforts as a parent; 3. That this card is submitted in recognition of such event; WHEREFORE, the undersigned wishes you a Happy Mother's Day.")

Sure, you may open yourself up to ridicule and abuse, but take my word for it . . . those people are just jealous.

Mail your response to the court and send a copy to the defendant via first-class mail. It is not necessary to send it certified or otherwise confirm his receipt. Upon receiving your response, the judge will either make a decision based upon the written motions or will schedule a time for a "hearing" when both you and the defendant will have to appear in person to argue about whether the defendant was properly served.

Because pretrial hearings in small-claims court are extremely rare, it is more likely that the court will inform you of its decision by mail or listen to the arguments on the date and time assigned for trial. In the latter case, the court will plow straight through to the trial if the judge decides that the defendant was properly served, or he will dismiss the case for improper service, thereby forcing you to request a new Summons and attempt, once again, to serve the defendant.

If the court indicates that the issue will be decided on the trial date, you do not need to file a separate response. Simply appear as scheduled and wait your turn to discuss the issue with the judge.

► NOBODY'S PERFECT

Whenever you learn about an argument the other side plans to make, whether it concerns improper service or reasons why he doesn't owe you the money, take it seriously. Learning about the other side's argument before the judge does is a huge advantage which too many people let slip by.

Don't just plow ahead without looking at the point from the other sides perspective. Could a judge, who knows nothing about either one of you before calling the case, be persuaded by his argument? If your answer is "not if the judge knew *this* . . ." then figure out how the judge is going to learn *that*. In other words, plan your defense ahead of time. What may seem self-evident to you because you know the case, may not be apparent to a neutral third party.

Equally as important, keep your mind open to the possibility (slim as it may be) that the other side may be right. Maybe he wasn't served. Maybe that's not his signature on the receipt. Sometimes admitting that he may be correct early in the proceeding and working to correct the problem, even if it means delaying the process a bit by having him reserved, can save you a ton of time and aggravation in the long run. The best litigators and business people accept the possibility of error and work to correct it, rather than loudly proclaiming perfection in the face of every objection.

If the Defendant Makes the Argument at Trial

The defendant can also wait until the trial to complain that he was not properly served. Although this may seem a bit absurd considering he had enough notice to show up at trial, a judge will always listen to what someone has to say on the subject. Don't sweat it. After the defendant makes his argument, the judge will ask you for your comments. Simply state the facts.

If you followed the steps discussed in chapter 10, you will have filed an Affidavit of service or be otherwise able to show that the defendant was properly served. Show all relevant documents to the judge and explain why you believe service was proper.

The judge will either overrule the defendant's argument and proceed with the trial or tell you that you have to get a new Summons and have the defendant served properly. The court will then reschedule the case and notify both sides of the new time and date for trial.

What If the Defendant Files a Request for a Jury Trial?

Get a lawyer. If your claim is large enough for state law to allow the defendant to file a request for a jury trial, and the defendant takes advantage of this opportunity, you would be best advised not to go it alone. A jury trial is the most challenging and demanding aspect of the law. (My opinion, certainly, but no one in this book is going to contradict me.) The different rules and strategies used in front of a jury are well beyond the scope of this guide.

What If the Defendant Files a Counterclaim?

Sometimes a defendant will respond to a lawsuit by filing one of his own. If filed in the same action, what would otherwise be called the defendant's Complaint is called a "Counterclaim."

A Counterclaim is basically the defendant's way of saying "I don't owe you money. You owe *me* money." Many times this is merely a tactic the defendant will use to confuse the issue and provide an excuse for his failure to pay you. Even if you're sure this is the case, though, don't fall into the trap of forgetting to consider his arguments. If you fail to go to trial ready not only to present your case but also to refute the defendant's Counterclaim, you will be committing the cardinal sin of walking into court unprepared.

When faced with a Counterclaim, the first thing you should do is call the clerk's office for instructions on filing an answer. Nearly every state and county has ready-to-file forms for contesting a small claim. Some states make these Answers or Notices of Intention to Defend part of the Summons, which can be filled out, detached, and mailed to the court as your denial. Other court systems have forms that require you only to fill in the case name and number, check a box stating that you dispute the claim, and sign on the dotted line. Fill out this paperwork *immediately* when you receive the Counterclaim.

► SERVICE OF A COUNTERCLAIM

A Counterclaim does not have to be served in the same, formal way as a Complaint. Because the plaintiff (you) are already in the case and are aware of the existence of a dispute with the other side, the court only requires Counterclaims to be sent via first class mail. So don't be getting any bright ideas about filing a Motion to Dismiss for Improper Service. Besides, that's my personal philosophy anyway . . . don't expend a lot of effort trying to delay the inevitable. Just outprepare the other side and win at trial.

Do You Need a Lawyer?

In the strict legal sense, you need only refer to the chart on pages 37–48 to see whether the Counterclaim puts you into a class of cases in which a lawyer is required. If the answer is "yes," the inquiry stops there and you should find a lawyer to assist you in the case. If the answer is "no," that doesn't necessarily end the inquiry.

The fact of that matter is that you could walk into any Home Depot or Builders Square and pick up a how-to book that would teach you to build an addition to your house. Even with the book, would you do it by yourself? Most people wouldn't simply because the project is too big and the consequences of failure too great. Most people would call in an expert for a job that big, while attempting smaller projects themselves. So it is with the law.

(You just didn't think I could make that relevant, did you?)

If the defendant files a Counterclaim seeking a few hundred or even a few thousand dollars, you may still be well advised to represent yourself without an attorney, especially if hiring an attorney would cost more than the claim is worth. As the numbers increase, however, so does your risk. If the worst happens, and the judge finds against you on your Complaint and awards the defendant every penny of his claim, could you afford the loss easily? If so, you could chalk it up to a learning experience and move on. If not, and a loss could devastate or even destroy your business, my best advice is to seek the assistance of an attorney.

Please, please, please, when evaluating a Counterclaim, do not rely on your belief, no matter how justified, that "the defendant is a liar and everybody knows that." In point of fact, the judge may NOT know that and, if the defendant manages to remain believable for the twenty minutes of trial, you may find yourself on the wrong end of a judgment.

As a result, you should always consider the Counterclaim from the point of view of someone who has no prior knowledge about the case. If you conclude that his claim has a reasonable chance of success (such as if it is just your word against his), you may want to review the Counterclaim with an attorney for a more objective, expert opinion.

Handling the Defendant's Attorney

Every attorney has his or her own style. Some may try to intimidate you; some may try to bury you in paperwork; some may even try to act like your best friend. Don't fall for any of these tactics. Trust your instincts. More often than not, you will run across attorneys who are just trying to understand the facts of the case and would like to engage in a constructive and fair discussion of each side's point of view. Don't shy away from this conversation just because the person on the other end of the line happens to have Esquire after his or her name.

The bottom line is that you treat an attorney just like you would the defendant. The attorney may be more familiar with the workings of the court than you are, but always remember that you know the facts of the case better than he does. You were there. You know the conversations that were held between your business and the defendant, and you know the services that were provided or the goods that were sold.

Equally as important, treat both the defendant and his lawyer with respect and courtesy. *Everything,* even a lawsuit, proceeds more smoothly if the people involved make an effort to get along. What's more, you may even find the presence of an attorney to be helpful in allowing you to discuss the merits of the case while insulating you from whatever personality conflict you may have with the defendant.

▶ STICKS AND STONES

I can't tell you how many times I would hear, "Well, you know your client is a liar," or some other insult from an unrepresented person on the other side of a dispute. I'd love to know what these people honestly hope to accomplish with statements like that. Do they figure I'd just call my client and tell him I'm through with the case? Or maybe they assume that I'll come over to their way of thinking when I hear the dulcet tones of righteousness coming through the phone line.

Either way, those people should know that personal attacks only make me (or any other listener) think less of the speaker, not of the subject. If you have differences with the other side, fine. That's why they built courthouses. But stick to the merits of the case when talking to or about the defendant . . . and leave the name calling to someone beneath you.

Although I believe that most attorneys approach a case fairly and honestly with an eye toward establishing a constructive dialogue, I am also aware of some less-than-straightforward approaches. Here's how to handle them.

"We're Going to Sue You If You Don't Drop this Claim!"

Definitely the first refuge of the person with nothing to say. If his client had an actual claim to begin with, he would have filed first. This is a fact I never fail to point out. Right away, he's starting from in the hole. I'd also ask the lawyer for information. Have him tell you what claim his client has against you . . . and actually listen to the response.

If the lawyer says that you are liable for the way you handled the original transaction—for example, as an accountant you allegedly gave bad accounting advice—carefully consider this threat and, if you decide that you have nothing to worry about, call his bluff. Nothing subtle about this; it is an attempt to intimidate, pure and simple. The lawyer is just trading on the public's instinctive fear of the court system. Don't let him.

The lawyer may say that your claim is frivolous and that you will be sued for even filing it. Don't be intimidated. If you have followed the rules outlined in this guide, you will have filed a perfectly legitimate claim. After all, the worst thing that can happen is that you won't get your judgment. The best way to handle this tactic is to *calmly* tell the lawyer to do what he wants to do. You can always evaluate the Counterclaim (if he ever files it) when you receive it.

"According to Green v. Brown *You Don't Have a Case"*

Let him tell it to the judge. Lawyers love to intimidate nonlawyers by citing cases. It's like their own little language. Fortunately, the courts handling smaller claims were set up so that you don't have to speak this language. If your state even allows lawyers to participate in a small claim (and several states don't), you shouldn't get overly excited about case law. Judges in these types of cases certainly aren't.

I've said it before and I'll say it again: If you had an agreement with the defendant and you lost money because the defendant failed to keep his end of the bargain, you have a legitimate claim. If a lawyer wants to cite *Diamond v. Hartman, Green v. Brown,* or *United States v. Calimari,* let the judge decide. That's what he's paid for.

"Mr. Plaintiff, as a Lawyer, I Can Tell You You Won't Get Your Money This Way"

What is he, a fortune teller now? Or is he telling you that his client does not plan to obey the judge's ruling? Either way, I view this statement as the most ridiculous yet. What are you supposed to do, agree to see it his way and drop your case?

Always remember, the defendant's lawyer is not your friend. He may be the nicest person in the world, but he has a job to do. He is not working in your best interest. My advice: Listen to whatever the lawyer wants to tell you. You may even find some of it useful. Nevertheless, if you've decided to go as far as filing a claim, there is no reason to dismiss it just because the defendant's lawyer says you won't collect anything. If he's right, so be it, but at least you'll get a judgment.

My last two points on this issue:

1. If the defendant doesn't have any money to pay the debt, how is he paying his lawyer? The response may be the defendant is a relative, but ask; it's fair game.

2. If the defendant truly has no money and is judgment proof, ask the lawyer if he will simply consent to the enrollment of a judgment. After all, if it's uncollectible, where's the harm to the defendant? If he refuses, he's as good as telling you that the defendant does attach some importance to avoiding the imposition of a judgment against him. How much is it worth to the defendant to avoid a judgment? That's your leverage. Use it.

Always remember that some people became clerks because they didn't make the cut to work at the DMV.
—Eliot M. Wagonheim

12
Communicating with the Court

Overview

The court is more than just the building where your trial will be held. It is a living institution that will control and guide every aspect of your dispute. The people who make it run are not judges or lawyers—they are clerks. And despite the quote at the top of the page, they by and large do a fabulous job. Equally as important, clerks are your first, last, and best resource to handle any questions or problems that may arise in your case from filing to judgment and beyond.

In the next few pages I shall provide you with some tips and rules for communicating with the court and protecting yourself in the process.

Get It in Writing

There's a famous journalism adage that, I believe, originated with the renowned Chicago city desk: "If your mother says she loves you, check it out." This statement, and any others that may stand for the proposition that you take nothing for granted, could not be better suited to litigation. Where communicating with the court is concerned, that means get it or at least put it in writing.

Throughout any case you may have any number of telephone

conversations with the clerk. Whether you're asking for a postponement (often called a "continuance") of a trial date or for a renewal
of a summons, you must put it in writing. "Pat from the clerk's
office said the trial was postponed" is no excuse for missing the trial
date if you didn't get something in writing.

Follow up with a letter of confirmation or ask that a new notice
be sent out. Either way, there should be some piece of paper in
your file documenting everything of importance in the case. Telephone calls are fine for a quick answer, but when it counts, get it in
writing.

Copy the Other Side

Everyone involved in a lawsuit has the right to know what any
other party is discussing with the court. For this reason, you should
copy the other side on every letter, pleading, and motion you send
to the court. Send copies via first-class mail. There is no need to
send anything certified, let alone by hand delivery.

Faxes and E-mail

Courts throughout the country are fairly divided on the acceptance
of faxes. Many will accept letters by fax but will insist upon receiving "hard copies" or originals of pleadings and motions. This is uni-
versally true where the pleadings, such as the original complaint
forms, are multipart forms using carbonless copies. Unless you are
specifically told otherwise, if you are going to fax something,
always follow up by dropping it in the mail as well.

E-mail are another story. As of the time of this writing, I know
of no courts that will allow litigants to correspond, let alone file
pleadings, solely by E-mail. Many courts are just coming on-line
now. As a consequence, you may be able to view the court's docket
on-line, but communicating with clerks and filing documents with
the court over the Internet is still a ways off.

Requesting a Postponement

On occasion, the court may schedule your trial for a date on which
you absolutely cannot attend. Perhaps you will be out of town or

have an unbreakable (and important) prior engagement. That's OK. It happens all the time.

As soon as you know about the scheduling conflict, call the clerk and ask if there is a special form that you must file requesting a postponement. Often, courts will have a form for your use but tell you that a request may be filed without using the court's form. As long as the court in your state allows you to file a request for postponement with or without using its own form, it makes no difference which way you choose to make your request.

Either pick up the court's form or create your own request, called a motion for postponement or motion for continuance, as shown on the following page. Include a certificate of mailing at the bottom of it so that the court knows you sent the other side a copy of your request.

Note, if the court allows it, you can also make your request in a letter without going to the trouble of drafting a formal motion.

(YOUR COMPANY)	*	IN THE
(Street Address)		
(City, State, Zip Code),	*	DISTRICT COURT
Plaintiff	*	FOR
v.	*	BALTIMORE COUNTY
(JOHN DEBTOR)	*	
(Street Address)		
(City, State, Zip Code)	*	Case Number: _____
and	*	
DEBTORS CLEANERS, INC.	*	
(Street Address)		
(City, State, Zip Code)	*	
Defendants	*	

*   *   *   *   *   *   *   *   *   *   *

MOTION FOR CONTINUANCE

[Your Company, Inc.], Plaintiff, hereby files this Motion for Continuance, and for such reason states as follows:

1. That the trial of this matter is currently scheduled to begin at 9:00 A.M. on April 15, 1999.

2. That the plaintiff's representative and primary witness is being hospitalized for surgery on April 13, 1999.

3. That the plaintiff would be placed at a severe and unfair disadvantage in its case were the trial to continue without this witness.

4. That the above-captioned case has not been postponed previously.

5. That the defendant's counsel, Cindy R. Diamond, Esquire, has stated that she has no objection to the postponement.

WHEREFORE, Plaintiff, [Your Company, Inc.] requests that the trial of this case be postponed.

_____

[Your Company, Inc.]
Joe Plaintiff, President
1225 Parker Street
Towson, MD 21204
(410) 555-1212
Plaintiff

CERTIFICATE OF MAILING

I HEREBY CERTIFY that on this ___ day of _____, 1999, a copy of this Motion for Postponement was mailed postage prepaid [or hand delivered or faxed] to Cindy R. Diamond, Esquire, 201 Bradley Street, Baltimore, MD 21201, attorney for defendant.

_____

[Your Company, Inc.]
Joe Plaintiff, President

Receiving Notices

From time to time you will receive notices from the court about developments in the case. Whether the notice concerns the scheduling of trial, the receipt of a motion, or the fact that judgment has been entered, keep the notices in your litigation file in the order in which they are received. If the notice concerns the scheduling of trial, make sure you carefully note the location of the courthouse and the time and date of trial.

Don't Get Frustrated

Occasionally, you will run into a clerk who is more eager to get you off the phone than she is to help you with your inquiry. Remember, these people can make life very difficult for you. Don't get frustrated . . . or if you do, don't show it. If worse comes to worse, ask to speak to a supervisor. Then, calmly and professionally explain your original reason for calling and leave personality conflicts out of it.

Trust in God, but count the cards.
—Mikhail Gorbachev

13
Discovery (or Looking at the Other Side's Cards)

Overview

There are three primary rules for litigation known to every trial lawyer:

1. Get your retainer up front.

2. When you're winning, shut up.

3. Never ask a witness a question to which you don't already know the answer.

In this chapter we will discuss the hows and whys of Rule 3.[1]

In essence, adherence to this rule does not require clairvoyance but rather participation in the process known as "discovery." The process of discovery, by which each side has an opportunity to compel answers to relevant questions from the other side prior to trial, is allowed, in one form or another, in every state.

Note, however, that many states do not allow discovery in small-

---

[1]This guide is intended to eliminate Rule 1 by teaching you how to avoid attorney's fees entirely. We discuss Rule 2 in chapter 15 concerning preparation for and appearance at trial.

claims court. If your state does not allow discovery in your specific case, skip this chapter and proceed directly to chapter 15, "Preparation for and Appearance at Trial." To check on whether discovery will be allowed in your claim, please refer to the chart on pages 114–117.

What Is Discovery?

As mentioned above, discovery is the process by which each side gets a chance to look at the other side's case. Discovery is conducted in one of five ways:

1. Interrogatories.

2. Request for Production of Documents.

3. Request for Admission of Facts.

4. Depositions.

5. Informal exchange of information.

Each of these methods, discussed in detail below, enables each side in a dispute to gain a clear picture of the arguments and defenses to be used by the other. Consequently, not only does discovery enable each side to better prepare for trial, but the awareness of the other side's contentions also enhances the possibility of settlement.

Interrogatories

This is the discovery tool that requires the defendant to tell you ahead of time everything he plans to tell the judge. Interrogatories (so-called from the verb "to interrogate") are a series of written questions that the recipient must answer in writing, under oath. States vary on the number of questions that can be asked, but in most small claims, the necessary information can be gleaned without even approaching the limit. Model Interrogatories are included in this chapter and may also be available from the clerk's office.

As you might imagine, the questions are rather straightforward. A defendant may be asked whether she intends to claim that the plaintiff's work or products were defective, and if so, why. Other subjects of inquiry include whether a defendant ever complained about the quality of the work or even contends that the order was canceled. See the model Interrogatories for additional examples of subjects and wording.

Request for Production of Documents

This is the discovery tool that requires the defendant to show you ahead of time each piece of paper or evidence he plans to show the judge. A Request for Production of Documents is . . . well . . . just like it sounds—a request from one side that the other party produce relevant documents prior to trial. These documents could be invoices, items of correspondence, written agreements alleged to exist, workpapers, and so forth.

Often, where discovery is allowed in small claims, state procedures allow you to combine Interrogatories and Requests for Production of Documents in order to avoid the need to file two separate documents. An example of this combination filing is included in this chapter.

Request for Admission of Facts

Usually not available in small-claims actions, a request for admission of facts is a series of statements that the receiving party would be required to either admit or deny in writing. This device is normally employed in more complex cases in order to assist the parties and the judge in winnowing out those issues actually in dispute from those facts on which the parties agree. For example, a given case may focus on the question of whether the plaintiff provided all the goods and services ordered even as the parties agree that the defendant placed an order for materials with the plaintiff at the specified price. A Request for Admission of Facts would establish the areas of agreement—the placement of the order, the prices quoted, and the expected time of delivery—so that the court and the parties can prepare solely to argue the issue of quality of performance.

As with depositions below, this section is included only for the sake of completeness. I do not anticipate that a Request for Admission of Facts would be used in a small claim.

Depositions

Once again, we have ventured into an area you will not need in a small-claims action. In fact, depositions are a good diagnostic tool. If you become involved in a case where depositions are planned, it is a good indication that the time has come to hire a lawyer.

Depositions are the oral counterpart to Interrogatories. While Interrogatories are written questions the recipient is required to answer in writing and under oath, depositions are oral questions, usually asked face-to-face but on occasion over the telephone, to which the other side must respond orally and under oath.

The typical deposition takes place in a conference room. In attendance are the parties, the witness (or "deponent"[1]), and a person known as the "court reporter" whose job is to take down every word stated by any of the participants on the record. No judge is present. The deposition begins with the court reporter swearing in the witness and proceeds for as long as the party who requested the deposition continues to ask relevant questions.

Following the deposition, the court reporter will prepare a transcript of the testimony, which can be used at trial.

Informal Exchange of Information

By far the best way to proceed with discovery, the informal exchange of information presumes that both parties acknowledge the need to understand the other's case. One phone call in which the parties agree to a mutual exchange of information by a specified date eliminates all of the formal discovery filings and time-consuming document drafting in one fell swoop.

If you do succeed in reaching an agreement for the exchange of information, I recommend that you forward a letter to the other side confirming that all relevant documents will be exchanged by the agreed date. Your letter should also specify that additional documents will be sent if either party decides that he or she wants to use something that had not previously been disclosed.

---

[1]The deponent may be a party, but he or she may also be a witness.

When Do You Prepare and File Your Discovery?

As early as possible. Although many states allow you to file your discovery requests long after the debtor files his response contesting your claim, and all states allow you at least a week after the answer is filed, I recommend that you don't wait that long. Instead, prepare them at the same time you prepare your complaint. When you get the summons back from the court, you can then include the requests in the packet with the complaint and summons for service on the defendant.

If you're having the sheriff serve the papers, simply mail the discovery requests to the defendant after you have been notified that the defendant has filed an answer. Either way, make sure you call the clerk's office to find out the deadline for filing your discovery requests. If you miss this deadline, you will not be able to force the debtor to answer your questions.

Preparing Interrogatories

Before setting out to draft your own Interrogatories, you should place a call to the clerk's office. Many states have already prepared model discovery requests for your use, and you may find them in need of only slight revision in order to make them applicable to your case.

As I said, Interrogatories are a series of questions the recipient must answer under oath. While each state has its own limit on how many questions you can ask, you can count on being able to ask between ten and fifteen questions. Of course, the most important question is, "If I go through all the effort of suing you, do you have the money to pay me?" Unfortunately, you can't ask this question now. *You may not ask any questions relating to the defendant's assets or his ability to* pay. First you must get your judgment. Then and only then may you investigate ways to collect on it. I have attached a list of sample Interrogatories in the appendix to this chapter. Feel free to adapt my sample questions to your case or write your own.

When you are finished writing your questions, add a caption. Pay careful attention to the format of the Interrogatories in the appendix. Make sure to include the correct caption (along with your case number if one has been assigned). As with all official documents for your case (except correspondence), make sure it is double-spaced.

Preparing a Request for Production of Documents

A request for production of documents is formatted in much the same way as Interrogatories. If your state procedure does not allow you to combine a request for production of documents and Interrogatories, you should always prepare and send both at the same time. This is because Interrogatories and requests for production of documents are really two sides of the same coin. One asks "tell me everything you know" and the other compels the defendant to "show me everything you have."

As stated previously, the clerk's office may have a model form for your use. If not, feel free to use the sample included at the end of this chapter or to draft your own.

Filing Your Discovery Requests

The actual Interrogatories and document requests are usually *not* sent to the court. Instead, most courts just want to be told that discovery has been filed. The most common way for a court to be told about discovery is by the mailing of a notice of discovery to the court at the same time you send the discovery requests to the defendant. Both the notice of discovery and the Interrogatories may be sent by first-class mail. A sample notice of discovery is given on the following page.

As always, call the clerk's office to check on whether you should file the entire discovery request or if a notice of discovery is preferred.

Sample *Note of Discovery*

[Your Company]	*	IN THE COURT
	*	
Plaintiff	*	DISTRICT COURT
	*	
v	*	FOR
	*	
(John Debtor, et al,)	*	_____COUNTY
	*	
*	*	
Defendants	*	Case Number: [Number]
	*	

* *

NOTICE OF DISCOVERY

I HEREBY CERTIFY that on this_____ day of_____ , 19__,
[Interrogatories or Request for Production of Documents] were
mailed, postage prepaid, to [name] at [address], [defendant's
attorney or defendant].

_____
(Your Company)
(Joe Plaintiff, President)
(Address)
(Telephone Number)
Plaintiff

Responding to the Defendant's Discovery Requests

If the defendant sends you discovery requests, you must respond
fully, promptly, and truthfully. Note that this does not necessarily
mean that you must provide all of the information requested.
Sometimes the truthful answer is "I don't know." For example, if the
defendant asks you to list the dates and describe the substance of
every conversation you ever had with him about the project, you
would have to be a computer to accurately recall this information.
Instead, simply state that you are unable to recall all of the conversations or exact dates (unless you can) and state what you *do*
remember.

Although the formal rules require that your discovery responses be drafted in the prescribed format, small-claims cases proceed much less formally. While I have provided a model of the formal response form, I would recommend doing away with the formalities and responding as follows.

Informal Answers to Interrogatories

Write (or preferably type) out each question asked, followed by your response. Use complete sentences, except when you are asked to respond with a list (i.e., list all people who worked on this project). At the bottom of the last page containing the questions and your responses, place the words: "I HEREBY CERTIFY that the above responses are true and correct to the best of my knowledge, information, and belief" and sign your name (either individually or on behalf of your company, depending upon the identity of the proper party). Always remember to keep a copy of everything you send the defendant for your own litigation file.

Informal Response to Request for Production of Documents

Send the defendant a letter stating that the enclosed documents represent all documents responsive to his requests. In the same letter, list the documents (or categories of documents such as invoices). Keep copies of everything for yourself in the same manner in which the materials were sent to the defendant.

Formatting Your Discovery Responses the Formal Way

Courts have developed a formal style for discovery responses, which usually comes into play in larger, more complex cases. The format is a mirror image of that used for discovery requests. Accordingly, your response (I have used answers to Interrogatories as an example) would resemble the following:

[Your Company]	*	IN THE COURT
	*	
Plaintiff	*	DISTRICT COURT
	*	
v	*	FOR
	*	
(John Debtor, et al,)	*	_____COUNTY
	*	
*	*	
Defendants	*	Case Number: [Number]
	*	

* *

ANSWERS TO INTERROGATORIES

(Your Company), in response to the Interrogatories filed by (John Debtor), hereby files the Answers to Interrogatories set forth below:

INTERROGATORY NO. 1: Please state your name, address, Social Security number, marital status, and occupation.

ANSWER: Joe Plaintiff, (Address), (Social Security number), (Marital Status), Resident of (Your Company).

VERIFICATION

I hereby certify that the facts set forth above are true to the best of my knowledge, information, and belief.

_____

(Your Company)
(Joe Plaintiff, President)
(Address)
(Phone number)
Plaintiff

Your Obligation to Update Your Answers

Answers to Interrogatories must be updated if something happens that changes one of the answers previously given. For example, assume you have asked the defendant to give the name of any expert witness he plans to call at trial, and he responds that he has not yet chosen one. If he later selects an expert witness, he must update his answers to Interrogatories to tell you the expert's name before he will be allowed to call the witness. If you file answers to

Interrogatories and something changes, you will have to supplement your response.

Filing Your Discovery Responses

You file your discovery responses the same way you file your own discovery requests. Either send a notice of discovery (shown previously) to the court at the same time you send your actual responses (plus a copy of the notice of discovery you sent to the court) to the defendant or file the actual response with the court—however you are directed by the clerk.

What to Do If the Defendant Does Not Respond to Your Questions

You may be confronted by someone who simply will not follow the rules. In some cases, the defendant will simply refuse to answer. On the other hand, he may answer only some of the questions or provide only some of the documents. Whatever the case, it is *your* responsibility to speak up and tell the court what the defendant is doing wrong. The judge will *never* look at the file for you and make sure everything is proceeding to your satisfaction. You must report your grievances to the court and ask the court to order the defendant to respond properly.

So here's what you do.

First, Try Calling

Before filing anything with the court, call the defendant or his attorney. Ask when you may expect his discovery responses to be filed. If responses have been filed, and you are dissatisfied with the completeness of a particular response, try to work out your differences with the defendant. Ask him to supplement his response so that it more directly answers your question.

Follow up with a Letter

This is *always* a good idea. If you need to run to the court for help, a written record is always better than your recollection of a conversation. Consequently, if the defendant says he will send you his responses "next week," confirm it in a letter and keep a copy. That way, if he doesn't keep his promise, you have a written record of your telephone call that you can send to the court.

Sample *Letter of COnfirmation*

(Date)

Dear [Mr. Defendant]:

The purpose of this letter is to confirm our telephone conversation on [September 7, 1999]. In our discussion, you stated that you will send me your Answers to Interrogatories by [September 15, 1999]. If my understanding of our conversation is incorrect, please let me know immediately. Otherwise I will look for your Answers to Interrogatories by [September 15, 1999].

Thank you for your attention to this matter

Very truly yours,

(Plaintiff)

Next, Ask the Court for Help

If you want the court to force the defendant to answer your questions, you must ask the clerk about a "Motion to Compel Discovery."

I must warn you not to "cry wolf." Contact the court only if the defendant is being really difficult. You see, the judge is often placed in the position of a harried and harassed parent trying to quiet thousands of screaming children. He will indulge minor infractions of the rules and will not look kindly upon someone complaining about a delinquency of a week or two. And in case I didn't say it before, aggravating the judge is not a good idea.

Your Motion to Compel Discovery might look something like this:

[Your Company]	*	IN THE COURT
	*	
Plaintiff	*	DISTRICT COURT
	*	
v	*	FOR
	*	
(John Debtor, et al,)	*	_____COUNTY
*	*	
Defendants	*	Case Number: [Number]
	*	

* *

MOTION TO COMPEL DISCOVERY

(Your Company), Plaintiff, hereby files this Motion to Compel Discovery, and for such reason, states as follows:

1. That on (May 4, 1996), (Your Company) timely served Interrogatories upon the defendant (John Debtor).

2. The defendant failed to serve Answers to Interrogatories upon the plaintiff as required.

3. Accordingly, the undersigned directed a letter to the defendant dated June 15, 1996, inquiring as to the status of Answers to Interrogatories. This letter is attached hereto and incorporated by reference herein as Exhibit 1.

4. In response to Exhibit 1, the defendant telephoned the undersigned and advised that he was working on the Answers to Interrogatories, and that he hoped to have them completed in the near future.

5. At the current time, the responses are now two months overdue, and the defendant has still not filed Answers to the Interrogatories.

6. The defendant's failure to file Answers to Interrogatories has severely prejudiced the plaintiff in his efforts to prepare for trial.

WHEREFORE, (Your Company) requests that this Court order the defendant to file Answers to Interrogatories within ten (10) days from this date or, in the alternative, bar the defendant from

introducing any evidence, either through oral testimony or documentation, which would have been responsive to the plaintiff's
Interrogatories.

_____

(Your Company)
(Joe Plaintiff, President)
(Address)
(Phone number)
Plaintiff

CERTIFICATION OF SERVICE

I HEREBY CERTIFY that on this_____ day of_____ 19__, a
copy of this Motion to Compel Discovery was (mailed postage
prepaid, hand delivered, or sent via facsimile transmission) to
(Alan I. Smith, Esquire, 201 North Main Street, Baltimore, MD
21201), attorney for defendant.

_____

(Your Company)
(Joe Plaintiff, President)

What Happens Next?

The court will give the defendant about fifteen days to respond to
your Motion to Compel Discovery by explaining to the court why
he has not provided answers to Interrogatories. Whether he actually
files a response or not, the court will send you a notice telling you
how the judge ruled on your Motion to Compel Discovery. For
example, you may receive a notice that the judge has ordered the
defendant to file answers to Interrogatories within ten days.

Sometimes, the notice will tell you that the judge will decide the
issue on the day of trial. While this may seem ridiculous considering
the whole issue concerns your ability to prepare for trial using the
defendant's answers to your questions, this is often the way it is
done.

If this is the case, prepare for trial as best you can. You cannot go into trial just assuming that the judge will see it your way and prevent the defendant from presenting any evidence. As unfair as it may seem, the judge may simply look the other way, decide you had not really been harmed, and direct you to present your case.

Sample Interrogatories with a Request for Documents

[Your Company]	*	IN THE COURT
	*	
Plaintiff	*	DISTRICT COURT
	*	
v	*	FOR
	*	
(John Debtor, et al,)	*	_____COUNTY
	*	
*	*	
Defendants	*	Case Number: [Number]
	*	

* *

INTERROGATORIES

(Your Company), Plaintiff, hereby files these Interrogatories to be answered by (John Debtor), Defendant, with regard to the above-captioned matter and, for such reason, states as follows:

Definitions and Terms

(a) These Interrogatories are continuing in character so as to require you to file Supplementary Answers if you obtain further or different information before trial.

(b) Where the name or identity of a person is requested, please state full name, home address, and also business address, if known.

(c) Unless otherwise indicated, these Interrogatories refer to the time, place, and circumstances of the occurrence mentioned or complained of in the pleadings.

(d) Where knowledge or information in possession of a party is requested, such request includes knowledge of the party's agents, representatives, and, unless privileged, attorneys. When answer is made by a corporation, state the name, address, and title of the person supplying the information and making the affidavit, and the source of his information.

(e) The pronoun "you" refers to the party to whom these Interrogatories are addressed.

Interrogatories

1. Please state your name, address, Social Security number, marital status, and occupation.

2. Please describe each and every conversation you had with a representative of the plaintiff with regard to [describe the transaction] (e.g., the preparation of your tax returns by Joe Plaintiff, CPA). In your answer, please include the date(s) of each conversation, whether such conversation was held in person or over the telephone, the individuals participating in the conversation, and the substance of each conversation.

3. Please describe each and every item of documentation, of which you are aware, concerning the terms of the [transaction]. In your answer, please include a description of the documentation (e.g., purchase contract, correspondence, etc.), the date of such documentation, the parties to such documentation (e.g. the recipient and the signatory), and the substance of the documentation. Please attach copies of such documentation to your Answers to Interrogatories; said attachments may serve as your response.

4. If you claim that you are not obligated to pay the money claimed by the plaintiff, please state all facts upon which you base your contention. Please attach to your Answers to Interrogatories all facts upon which you rely to support this contention.

5. If you claim the plaintiff owes you money or that the plaintiff has caused you to suffer damages in any way, please state all facts upon which you base such contention. Please attach to your Answers to Interrogatories all facts upon which you rely to support this contention.

6. If you claim that the plaintiff did not suffer the damages set forth in the Complaint, please state all facts upon which you base such

contention. Please attach to your Answers to Interrogatories all facts upon which you rely to support this contention.

7. Identify each and every expert upon whose testimony you intend to rely at trial and include in your answer the substance of each such expert's opinion as well as a summary of the grounds therefor. Please also attach copies of every report prepared by each expert, as well as copies of all documents upon which each expert relied in reaching his or her conclusion.

8. If you claim to have a right of setoff against the plaintiff for any reason, please state the exact amount of such setoff, the method upon which said damages were calculated, and all facts upon which your claim is based. Please attach to your Answers to Interrogatories all facts upon which you rely to support this contention.

9. For each claimed setoff listed in answer to the preceding Interrogatory, please itemize each component of damages or reimbursement you are claiming and include an explanation of same. If your damage calculation relies upon a formula, please itemize each figure used in same. Please attach to your Answers to Interrogatories all facts upon which you rely to support this contention.

10. Please identify each and every person whom you believe to have personal knowledge of any facts relevant to the plaintiff's claim. In your answer, please state all facts which you believe to be within the personal knowledge of each individual listed.

(Your Company)
(Joe Plaintiff, president)
(Address)
(Telephone Number)
Plaintiff

Men and nations behave wisely once they have exhausted all the other alternatives.

—Abba Eban

14
Settlement and Negotiation

Overview

Statistics tell us that 95 percent of all cases filed in court settle before they reach trial.[1] Why do so many cases settle? They settle simply because the parties usually come to realize that their differences are not worth the time and expense necessary to go to trial. Equally as important, settlements are usually fueled by each party's unwillingness to risk his or her worst-case scenario.

For the plaintiff, your worst-case scenario is actually one of two possibilities: (1) after devoting all of your time to filing and presenting your claim, you lose, or (2) you win your judgment and are never able to turn it into money. The defendant's worst-case scenario is that he has to pay everything you're asking, including interest and court costs, not to mention the stain a judgment will place on his or her credit.

In this chapter I will discuss the pros and cons of settlement, as well as different options and strategies for maximizing your recovery in a negotiated resolution.

---

[1]OK, I made that statistic up. But whatever the number is (and hey, it could be 95 percent on the button), it's very large and impressive.

▶ THE PRINCIPLE OF THE THING

Always listen when the defendant offers to settle. Even if you decide not to accept his offer, never turn it down before you know what the offer is, just so you can keep suing him on principle. Sometimes I think that more money has been lost in tribute to "the principle of the thing" than in all the world's casinos combined. Even when the actions of a certain defendant just frost your shorts, keep focused on your goal—collecting your money and adding to your bottom line, not aggravating the defendant.

Now, don't get me wrong, as a business lawyer I have certainly had my share of clients tell me that their overriding goal is to sue the defendant into the seventh circle of hell. Nevertheless, after the Prozac kicks in, it is the rarest of clients who doesn't eventually see that accepting *almost* everything and moving on isn't sometimes better than spending the time, money, and aggravation holding out for everything.

As a final word on the subject, I hearken back to that cinematic masterpiece *The People vs. Larry Flynt*. In the movie, Woody Harrelson (Larry Flynt) tells his lawyer, played by Ed Norton, "I'm your best kind of client; I'm rich and I'm always in trouble." Change that line to "I'm rich and I always fight for the principle of the thing" and you'd be a even closer to the mark.

Evaluating the Worth of Your Case for Settlement

Without fail, settlement comes down to a question of whether you are inclined to accept a fast nickel or pursue a slow dime. Now, I can't give you ironclad rules you can use to determine when you should accept a settlement offer and when you should keep pursuing the court case, but I can offer some general guidelines. In evaluating any settlement offer, ask yourself:

Do I really want to spend the time to go through a trial and collection proceedings?

If I win (perhaps after an appeal), will I be able to find the debtor again?

If I find the debtor, can I force him to pay up?

How strong is the defendant's side of the case?

The answer to the first question will undoubtedly change on a case-by-case basis. Because of the circumstances, you may be perfectly willing to spend your life pursuing Customer A for $500 while chalking Customer B's $750 debt up to experience. It's a completely subjective consideration.

Not so with the second question. In the appendix to this book, I summarize certain techniques for finding hard-to-locate debtors. These techniques and more are detailed in any number of fine books on the subject available at your local library. You may want to review the appendix and possibly these other materials as you are trying to weigh the merits of a settlement offer.

Chapter 17 describes methods for extracting money once you find the debtor. You may want to refer to this chapter, as well as to the state-by-state chart of enforcement procedures on pages 114–117, in order to reach your answer to the third question.

Often, it is the fourth question that gets overlooked. People have a tendency to focus so strongly on the presentation of their case that they forget to take a step back and look at things from another angle. In my experience, it is very rare that the defendant doesn't have at least something to tell the judge in answer to the question "Why haven't you paid the plaintiff?" Sometimes the response is a complete fabrication. On other occasions, the defendant's reasoning is misguided but does follow a certain logic. And not surprisingly, there are times when the defendant's explanation is both truthful and persuasive. So persuasive, in fact, that after he's finished, any objective listener would say, "He's right—if that had happened to me, I wouldn't have paid either."

▶ **"I NEVER SAW A PANCAKE MADE SO THIN, IT STILL DIDN'T HAVE TWO SIDES."**

I can't remember where I heard this expression, but it sounds really folksy so I'm going to say that it was something my grandfather always said. (We'll ignore the fact that all of his folksy sayings were in Russian or Yiddish—and focus on the saying itself.)

The fact of the matter is I have not found a more useful expression in law. Whenever a client comes to me and says that he has a slam dunk case, I think of this saying. Regardless of whether you agree with the other side's reasoning, there is always another side. Always. Unless the debt exists simply due to the defendant's inability to pay, you can rest assured that the defendant will be able to offer an explanation to the judge. It is your job to think of that explanation first.

If you were the defendant, what would you say? If you interpreted all facts and documents in the light most favorable to the defendant's point of view, would that give him an argument?

If you can perform this feat of mental gymnastics—forget your arguments and preconceived notions and really examine the facts from the other side—you will be ready to evaluate your case for settlement and, equally as important, ready to counter his arguments at trial, should a settlement not be reached.

Options for Settling Your Case Against the Defendant

Very often, if the defendant had the money to pay you, you wouldn't have had to file suit in the first place. For this reason, it is unrealistic to expect that a defendant with cash flow problems will suddenly be able to resolve them now that you have filed suit. This is just one example of why you may need to be a little more creative in your thinking than "pay me everything you owe me and I'll drop the case." Sure, this may work and, more importantly, may be the only appropriate response in many situations, but if you want to settle your case, you should know that the following options are out there:

- If the defendant pays cash, great; you can drop your case.

- If the defendant can't pay all at once but wants to pay in installments, let him. Just demand that full payment is received before the trial. If you're not paid, go ahead with the trial.

- If the defendant can't pay in full before the trial date but can pay within the next several months, you can request that the court postpone the trial date. Note that you do not have an automatic right to postpone the trial date. Instead, you have to file a request with the court, known as a motion for postponement. (See the form on pages 191–192.) Tell the court in the motion that you and the defendant are attempting to resolve the case and that you would like trial rescheduled to anytime after a certain date. Select a date soon after the defendant is scheduled to make his last payment. If the payments aren't made, your case will still come to trial—only a little later than it otherwise would have.

- If the defendant needs more than four to five months to repay the debt, you have three options, which I have listed below in order of my preference:
  - Enter a Consent Judgment against the defendant.
  - Have the defendant sign a Promissory Note.
  - Place the settlement "on the record."

Entering a Consent Judgment Against the Defendant

A Consent Judgment is just that—a judgment to which the defendant consents. It's a way of getting the judgment you would have received if you won at trial, only without the trial. Obviously, this arrangement is good for you because you don't have to devote all of the time necessary to prepare for trial. It can also be good for the defendant, depending upon the payment terms he is able to work out with you. This is the option I prefer.

To enter a Consent Judgment, both you and the defendant appear in court on the assigned trial date. Instead of trying the case, however, you tell the judge that the case has been settled and that the defendant is consenting to the entry of a judgment against him for a certain amount.

Let's assume, for example, that the defendant owes you $2,000, but he offers, and you agree to accept, $1,700 to settle the matter. Let's also assume that the defendant doesn't have the money right then. When you appear at trial, tell the judge that the defendant has agreed to the entry of a judgment against him for $1,700, which he will pay off in accordance with whatever payment terms you negotiated. Once the defendant confirms that this is, indeed, correct, your "trial" is over.

If the defendant breaks the agreement, you have a valid judgment, and you can begin collection procedures as outlined in chapter 17.

Whenever possible, I recommend that you put a little twist on the example discussed above. As a condition of settlement, I recommend that you push the defendant to agree to the entry of a Consent Judgment against him *for the full amount of the claim* even if you have agreed to accept less in settlement. Thus, in the above example, the defendant would agree to the entry of a $2,000 judgment, which you would then tell the court was "paid in full" upon your receipt of $1,700.

Why do I recommend this arrangement? As an incentive for the defendant to pay. After all, if he pays the $1,700 as he says he will, he has no reason to worry about a $2,000 judgment against him. If, however, he breaks that agreement, you have a judgment for $2,000, and he could have gotten away with paying you only $1,700.

If you do receive full payment of the amount agreed upon in settlement, you *must* tell the court you've been paid in full. Simply call the clerk and ask for the necessary form to file. In most states, it is called an "Order of Satisfaction" and resembles the form shown on the following page. Please feel free to use this form if the court in your state does not have one preprinted for your use.

Note that failure to file this form could result in penalties being levied against you. The reason for this is that the presence of an unsatisfied judgment on the defendant's credit report could hinder his ability to obtain financing or credit. (After all, that's one of the things you count on when filing suit.) If he's made good on the judgment, your failure to report that fact could damage him unnecessarily. And wouldn't he just love a chance to get back at you for harming him?!

[Your Company]	*	IN THE COURT
Plaintiff	*	
v.	*	DISTRICT COURT
[John Debtor]	*	
and	*	FOR
[Jim Debtor] individually	*	
and t/a [Jim's Cleaners]	*	_____COUNTY
	*	
Defendants	*	
	*	Case Number: [Number]
	*	

* *

ORDER OF SATISFACTION

TO THE CLERK:

Please enter the judgment enrolled in the above-captioned matter as "Paid, Settled, and Satisfied."

_____

(Your Company)
(Joe Plaintiff)
(Address)
(Telephone number)
Plaintiff

Have the Defendant Sign a Promissory Note

Often, the defendant is not willing to agree to the entry of a judgment against him, no matter what the settlement terms are. Consequently, a second option is to settle the case by having the defendant sign a Promissory Note.

A Promissory Note is a written agreement between you and the defendant that spells out all of the repayment terms to which the defendant agreed. The Promissory Note can obligate the defendant to pay interest and even your attorney's fees if you have to go to court to enforce the agreement.

I encourage you to use the model Promissory Note attached to this chapter in the appendix and adapt it to fit your particular situation.

Placing the Settlement "on the Record"

Placing a settlement "on the record" means having all parties state and agree to the terms of the settlement in court before the judge. To do this, both sides should appear for trial and wait for the judge to call the case. Instead of presenting evidence, however, you would just tell the judge the terms of the settlement you reached.

This is not the same thing as a Consent Judgment unless the defendant says he is agreeing to the entry of a judgment against him. If he is not, the judge will simply mark the case as settled.

Make sure you agree on the amount and timing of all payments, the applicable interest rate, if any, the total amount to be paid, and even whether the defendant will be responsible for paying your attorney's fees if you have to sue him to enforce the agreement.

Once these terms are explained to the judge (and automatically recorded like any other court proceeding), the judge will ask the defendant to state his agreement to these terms. If the defendant does agree and then breaks his agreement later, you can file suit to enforce the settlement agreement.

You can think of an agreement placed on the record as an oral contract recorded by the judge. If the defendant breaks the contract, you can file suit to have the settlement enforced. You would simply call the clerk and order a copy of the transcript from the court proceeding in which the defendant promised to pay. Your evidence would consist of the transcript and your testimony that the defendant did not pay in accordance with the settlement terms.

By now, you may have realized why this is the method of settlement I least prefer (although hundreds of cases are settled like this every day). After all, it's a pain to order a transcript and file suit again. With a Consent Judgment you wouldn't have to file suit at all—you would already have your judgment. Similarly, a Promissory Note, if done correctly, would at least give you attorney's fees so you can hire someone to go through this for you with the defendant paying the tab. Thus, while placing a settlement on the record is certainly a valid way to resolve a case, you should try using one of the other two methods first.

How to Negotiate a Settlement

Once you decide how much your case is worth, stick to your guns. If you are willing to settle your case, your job then becomes convincing the defendant through negotiation that your case is worth what you say it is.

▶ EVERYTHING IS A NEGOTIATION

Many people are intimidated by the thought of sitting down to negotiate a legal settlement. I don't see why, considering that anyone who has reached adulthood has spend the better part of their lives negotiating. (OK, maybe not the better part, but more than half.) By way of example, I'm going to tell you the wedding ring story. Immediately after the story, I'm going to surprise anyone who actually made it through the whole thing by making every facet of it relevant to the topic of negotiating a settlement. So without further ado . . .

When my wife, Nikki, and I had decided to end our rather lengthy engagement with an elopement to Hawaii, we began discussing wedding bands. It was at about this time that Nikki's father presented her with her stepmother's wedding band. Now Nikki's stepmother, Barbara, was a wonderful, caring lady of great class who had passed away the year before.

When Nikki received this gift, she knew immediately that she wanted it as her own band. The trouble was that the ring, made of rosegold, was rather . . . thick. It looked wonderful on Barbara's long, slender fingers but when Nikki put it on, it looked more like a brass knuckle. I made note of this about a millisecond after Nikki slipped it on her finger for the first time and asked me what I thought. I made an immediate and risky decision. . . I told her. (Relationships are not for cowards.)

As Nikki's face clouded over with the effect of my comparison, I suggested that we melt the ring down and use the gold to make both of our bands. (Yes, it was that big.) Knowing that the she would in every sense be wearing Barbara's ring as her own, Nikki readily agreed.

Upon recommendation, we went to see a local jeweler who was reputedly one of the finest new designers in Baltimore. He agreed to make the rings to our specifications.

After several missed deadlines, Nikki was finally able to pick up the rings on the Thursday before our Saturday morning flight to Hawaii. Hers looked beautiful. Mine looked like a child's first grade pottery project.

The next day, I went to see the jeweler. (Wow, this story has gotten long, but trust me, there is a point to it.) I told the jeweler how much we loved Nikki's ring. It showed his obvious talent in both design and manufacture. I told he we were less pleased with mine. When we examined it together, I pointed out the flaws—the uneven lines, the visible solder, etc. I explained that this was not the ring I could wear for the rest of my life. Even while acknowledging the flaws, he told me that he just didn't see what the big deal was.

It was this. Imagine, I told him, that a magazine was doing a feature story on him. Imagine further that this magazine was going to be read by his every potential customer. In order to do the story, the magazine would choose one piece to extol as representative of his skill. I told him that I bet that if the magazine chose Nikki's ring, he would be very proud, and rightfully so. I wondered what he would think if the magazine chose my ring. Would that be the piece upon which he wanted to be judged?

Without a word, he walked back to his office behind a partition and ordered one of his assistants to refund the charges to my credit card. He never came out. Never apologized. Never said "good-bye."

I shall now go on to describe why and how this story is relevant.

Ground Rules

Keep the Conversation Going

If you are interested in exploring the possibility of settlement, remember to obey the first rule of negotiation: KEEP THE CONVERSATION GOING. After all, you cannot negotiate with a dial tone or an empty chair. Try to be polite (but firm) and businesslike in your manner. Firing off a few nasty comments maybe satisfying, but it may cost you money—the defendant could decide not to work things out, and you may never see your money.

In my heart-warming wedding band story, I knew that if I simply told Nikki my opinion about the ring without offering an alternative, we would have become entrenched in our respective yes/no positions. That wouldn't have served anybody well.

In your case, if the defendant hasn't called you, try calling him—not immediately after he's been served, but certainly at some point before the trial. You lose nothing by testing the settlement waters. If you're concerned that making that first call entails a loss of face, mention to the defendant that the odds are that the judge will ask whether you've discussed settlement before proceeding with the trial. As I tell defendants all the time, "I figure that as long as we know the judge is going to ask, we might as well have an answer. So, have you given any thought to settling this case?" No loss of face, and the conversation begins.

Make an Effort to Understand the Other Side's Needs

Sometimes a customer doesn't pay because of cash flow problems. That customer needs time. Sometimes the customer doesn't pay because of abrupt treatment by one of your employees. What that customer needs is an apology. On still other occasions, cash flow problems prevented the customer from paying in the first place, and now threatening letters and a lawsuit have cultivated a "don't tell me what to do" attitude. That customer needs a one-on-one conversation in which he is treated with respect while working toward a solution. Sometimes, customers have complaints, admittedly minor, and refuse to pay because no one would listen. Your job now is to listen.

Going back to my wedding-ring story, Nikki did not need to wear Barbara's exact ring. What she needed was to keep Barbara's ring (and hence, Barbara) with her symbolically. Identifying *that* need made reaching a solution simple.

Be Civil: Hostility Breeds Hostility

If your goal is to start a conversation and keep it going, stay professional. You don't have to take an interest in the customer's kids, just try to refrain from calling him a deadbeat to his face. (Am I asking too much here?) Treat both him and his views with respect. Even if you disagree with him—which you undoubtedly will—simply point out the areas of disagreement. If neither of you sees a reason to change your point of view, find out if there can be a monetary settlement even if you "agree to disagree" on the issues.

Listen carefully: You may be surprised to find out that the defendant actually has some legitimate disputes with your products or services. Hear him out. Granted, he should have said something earlier (although maybe he did, and you weren't listening), but hear him out anyway. This kind of conversation may save you a great deal of time and money in the long run.

Remember that civility at the end of the discussion is just as important as it is at the beginning. Your reputation may depend not on whether you win or lose but on how you conduct yourself. If the defendant winds up paying you money and you found a way to treat the person with respect, you have much less to worry about when it comes to people discussing your behavior behind your back. And is there anyone running a business today who doubts the importance of reputation?

In point of fact, had the jeweler in my story looked at the ring and said, "You know, I'll tell you that the ring was not my best work. I messed up. I got busy and I'm sorry," I probably would have given him more business later down the road. As it was, his great work on Nikki's ring was completely undermined by his poor work on mine and, *more important,* by his rudeness. Yes, he addressed the situation by refunding the money, but I would have been happier with a result where I received a little less than everything I paid in recognition of the subjective nature of my complaint combined with a bit more grace.

Beginning the Negotiation

Regardless of who initiated the conversation, when you get down to numbers, your priority as the plaintiff is to force the debtor to make the first offer. After all, you have already put your first number on the table by filing suit. Do not fall into the trap of bidding against yourself by discounting your claim before the defendant has put any money on the table. After hearing the defendant's first offer, you can then decide what you want to do.

Using Your Leverage

When negotiating a settlement, feel free to remind the debtor of the inconveniences he may suffer because of the lawsuit:

- There is the embarrassment of being sued and having to appear before a judge to explain his less-than-honorable actions.

- If you win, a judgment will appear on his credit history and, even if paid off, will remain there for seven years. If he does not pay it off, the judgment could stay on his credit record for a lot longer than that and prevent him from buying anything on credit.

- If you win, you may be able to seize and sell the debtor's car, garnish the money in his bank accounts, and/or force his employer to subtract a portion of his wages to pay you directly.

The threat of these actions constitutes a great deal of leverage over the average person. Use it!

▶ THE OPPOSITE OF TALKING

For too many people, the opposite of talking is not listening, it's waiting. If you are one of those people, you have no business conducting a settlement negotiation. Every time the defendant speaks, he increases his chances of providing you with just the information you need to prevail. A never-to-be-broken rule of negotiation is LISTEN.

Not long ago, I represented a client in a lawsuit where both the client's company and the client personally, had been sued. Two months into the litigation, we were on the verge of a spectacular result and discussing the tactics of the case. All the client kept repeating was "I can't have a judgment against me personally. Against the corporation, OK, but not against me personally."

Soon after reaching a very favorable settlement with the other side, the client's check for my fee bounced and all of a sudden we found ourselves (possibly) on the other side of the table. He promised to make the check good for months without result. I remembered his statement when (on one of the rare occasions) I filed suit. Because I represented him, personally, as well as his company, I filed suit against him on an individual basis. Knowing his weak spot gave me leverage. He paid in full within one week of being served.

Negotiating with the Defendant's Lawyer

First and foremost, remember that the lawyer is not the one writing the check. It is the defendant who must agree to any financial arrangements.

As a consequence, a lawyer must have authority from his client to make a firm settlement offer. Ask the lawyer if he has authority to negotiate and make an offer. He may not. Either way, you can negotiate with him; just know going in that you will not be able to settle the case in that one conversation. If the lawyer knows his client, he will have a feel for what his client will and will not accept. Consequently, you can work with him to come up with a figure that he will "recommend" the client pay.

Another thing you should keep in mind when dealing with the other side's lawyer—you know the facts much better than he ever will. The facts of the case are your turf. You were there. You had the conversations or took the order or did the work. And that turf is where the majority of the discussion will be held. Generally speaking, a case in small-claims court is not about new and exciting legal precedents; it's about who's right on the facts. Recognize your knowledge of the facts as a strength.

For other thoughts on handling the defendant's lawyer, review the tips given in chapter 11.

Dismissing Your Case After Settlement

If you entered into a Promissory Note, or if you have been paid in full, you must dismiss your case. Check with your local court clerk for a preprinted form. If none is available, feel free to use those on the following pages.

If, after you filed your complaint, the defendant had not yet filed a notice of intention to defend, all that is required is a notice of dismissal signed by the plaintiff such as the following:

[Your Company]	*	IN THE COURT
	*	
Plaintiff	*	DISTRICT COURT
	*	
v	*	FOR
	*	
(John Debtor, et al,)	*	_____COUNTY
*	*	
Defendants	*	Case Number: [Number]
	*	

* *

NOTICE OF DISMISSAL

Mr. Clerk:
Please note that the parties have reached a settlement in this matter. Accordingly, please dismiss the above-captioned case with prejudice.

_____
(Your Company)
(Joe Plaintiff)
(Address)
(Telephone Number)
Plaintiff

If the defendant has already responded to your complaint by filing a notice of intention to defend, the form you have to file in court to drop your case differs slightly from that shown above. In this case, the form should resemble the following:

[Your Company]	*	IN THE COURT
	*	
Plaintiff	*	DISTRICT COURT
	*	
v	*	FOR
	*	
(John Debtor, et al,)	*	_____COUNTY
*	*	
Defendants	*	Case Number: [Number]
	*	

* *

STIPULATION OF DISMISSAL

Mr. Clerk:
Please note that the parties have reached a settlement in this
matter. Accordingly, please dismiss the above-captioned case with
prejudice.

_____   _____

By: (Joe Plaintiff   (John Debtor)
(Your Company)   (Company)
(Address)   (Address)
(Telephone Number)   (Telephone Number)
Plaintiff   Defendant

Appendix

Sample Promissory Note (with Instructions)

[The following Note is only applicable to commercial debts and not to consumer debts. (See the discussion in chapter 9 if you are unsure which category applies to your debt.) If the debt arises out of a consumer transaction, you may use the note printed below only if you delete paragraphs 6 and 12. As you read this Note, you may come across many unfamiliar terms. That's OK. Use the note as it's written by just filling in the blanks. If the debtor fails to pay, take it to a lawyer. This note is all you need for a lawyer to collect all of your money plus attorney's fees from the debtor.]

_____[1]_____ $_____[3]_____

_____[2]_____ , 19___

PROMISSORY NOTE

FOR VALUE RECEIVED, the undersigned, _____[4]_____ , INC., a Maryland corporation (the "Borrower"), promises to pay to the order of _____[5]_____ (referred to as the "Lender"), at _____[6]_____, or at such other place as the holder of this Promissory Note may from time to time designate, the principal sum of _____[7]_____ Dollars and _____Cents($___[7a]__), together with interest thereon at the rate here after specified which maybe owing to the holder of this Promissory Note by the Borrower, on _____[8]_____ which is the final and absolute due date of this Promissory Note. The following terms shall apply to this Promissory Note.

1. Interest Rate. Interest shall accrue on the disbursed, unpaid principal balance until paid in full at a rate equal to ___[9]____ percent (_[9a]_%) per annum.

227

2. Repayment: The unpaid principal balance under this Note shall be paid___[10]___ (__[10a]___) consecutive monthly installments of principal and interest. The installments shall be in the amount of _____[11]_____ Dollars and _____ Cents ($___[11a]____), each, beginning on _____[12]_____ and continuing on the first day of each of the next succeeding _____[13]____ (__[13a]__) calendar months. The balance of any remaining unpaid principal, together with accrued interest and any and all other penalties, charges, costs, or fees to the extent such sums are still due and owing, shall be due on _____[14]_____.

3. Calculation of Interest: Interest shall be calculated on the basis of a three hundred sixty (360) days per year factor applied to the actual days on which then exists an unpaid disbursed principal balance. Interest shall not accrue until the fifth day of the month.

4. Prepayment: The Borrower may prepay this Promissory Note in part at any time or from time to time without penalty or additional interest. Any such prepayment must be accompanied by interest accrued and unpaid on the amount so prepaid to the date of such prepayment.

5. Late Payment Penalty: Should any payment due hereunder be received by the holder of this Promissory Note more than fifteen (15) calendar days after its due date, the Borrower shall pay a late payment penalty equal to five percent (5%) of the amount then due.

6. Confession of Judgment. Upon any default hereunder, the Borrower authorizes any attorney admitted to practice before any court of record in the United States to appear on behalf of the Borrower in any state court in Maryland in one or more proceedings, or before any clerk thereof, and to confess judgment against the Borrower, without prior notice or opportunity for prior hearing, in favor of the holder of this Promissory Note in the full amount due on this Promissory Note (including principal, accrued interest, and any and all penalties, fees, and costs) plus an attorney's fee equal to fifteen percent (15%) of the amount due under this Promissory Note. The Borrower consents to the jurisdiction of and agrees that venue shall be proper in the Circuit Court of any County of the State of _____. The Borrower waives the benefit of any and every statute, ordinance, or rule of court which may be lawfully waived, conferring upon the Borrower any right or privi-

lege of exemption, stay of execution, or supplementary proceedings, or other relief from the enforcement or immediate enforcement of a judgment or related proceedings on a judgment. The authority and power to appear for and enter judgment against the Borrower shall not be exhausted by one or more exercises thereof or by any imperfect exercise thereof, and shall not be extinguished by any judgment entered pursuant thereto; such authority and power may be exercised on one or more occasions from time to time, in the same or different jurisdictions, as often as the holder shall deem necessary or advisable until all sums due under this Promissory Note have been paid in full.

7. Interest Rate After Judgment. If judgment is entered against the Borrower on this Promissory Note, the amount of the judgment entered (which may include principal, interest, default interest, late charges, fees, and costs) shall bear interest at the highest rate authorized under this Promissory Note as of the date of entry of the judgment.

8. Expenses of Collection. Upon a default under this Promissory Note or any other Loan Document between the Borrower and the Lender, this Promissory Note may be referred to an attorney for collection. If this Promissory Note is referred to an attorney for collection, the Borrower shall pay all of the holder's costs, fees, and expenses resulting from such referral, including attorney's fees of fifteen percent (15%) of the amount outstanding, even though judgment has not been confessed or suit has not been filed.

9. Waiver of Defenses. In the event the holder of this Promissory Note transfers this Promissory Note for value, the Borrower agrees that all subsequent holders of this Promissory Note shall not be subject to any claims or defenses which the Borrower may have against a prior holder, all of which are waived as to the subsequent holder, and that all subsequent holders shall have all of the rights of a holder in due course with respect to the Borrower even though the subsequent holder may not qualify, under applicable law, absent this paragraph, as a holder m due course

10. Waiver of Protest. The Borrower, and all parties to this Promissory Note, whether maker, endorser, or guarantor, waive presentment, notice of dishonor, notice of intention to accelerate the maturity hereof, notice of acceleration of the maturity hereof, and protest.

11. Extensions of Maturity. All parties to this Promissory Note, whether maker, endorser, or guarantor, agree that the maturity of this Promissory Note, or any payment due hereunder, may be extended at any time or from time to time by the holder without releasing, discharging, or affecting the liability of such party

12. Commercial Loan. The Borrower warrants that this Promissory Note is the result of a commercial loan transaction as defined by applicable state law.

13. Choice of Law. This Promissory Note shall be governed, construed, interpreted, enforced, and its validity and enforceability determined in accordance with the laws of the State of _____. The Borrower consents to the jurisdiction of the courts of the State of _____ and, if diversity of citizenship exists between the Borrower and the holder, and a sufficient amount is in controversy, or if some other basis exists for the jurisdiction of the federal courts, to the jurisdiction of the United States District Court for the District of _____, except as to confession of judgment.

14. Notices. Any notice or demand required or permitted by or in connection with this Promissory Note (but without implying any obligation to give any notice or demand) shall be in writing and made by hand delivery, by wire, or by certified mail, return receipt requested, postage prepaid, addressed to the Lender or the Borrower at the appropriate address set forth below or to such other address as may be hereafter specified by written notice by the Lender or the Borrower, and shall be considered given as of the date of hand delivery or wire or as dated on the return receipt if sent by certified mail, or, if delivery is not made by hand delivery, wire, or certified mail after an attempt to do so, then as of two (2) days after the date of mailing by first-class mail, postage prepaid, independent of the date of mail delivery, as the case may be:

If to the Lender: _____[15]_____
If to the Borrower: _____[16]_____

15. Invalidity of any Part. If any provision or part of any provision of this Promissory Note shall for any reason be held invalid, illegal, or unenforceable in any respect, such invalidity or unenforceable shall not affect any other provision of this Promissory Note, and this Promissory Note shall be construed as such invalid, illegal, or unenforceable provision or put thereof had never been contained herein, but only to the extent of its invalidity, illegality, or unenforceability.

16. Tense and Gender. As used herein, the term "Borrower" includes the singular and the plural and refers to all genders.

17. Assignability. This Promissory Note may be assigned by the Lender or any subsequent holder at any time and from time to time.

18. Binding Nature. This Promissory Note shall inure to the benefit of and be enforceable by the Lender and the Lender's successors and assigns and any other person to whom the Lender may grant an interest in the Borrower's obligations to the Lender, and shall be binding and enforceable against the Borrower and the Borrower's successors and assigns.

IN WITNESS WHEREOF, this Promissory Note has been executed by the Borrower under seal as of the (_____[17]_____ day of _____, 19____).

ATTEST: THE BORROWER:
                                 _____[19]_____
_____[18]_____ By: _____[19a]_____ (Seal)
                                 _____[19b]_____ (Title)

Promissory Note Form, Box 1: The Place. Fill in the place at which the defendant is executing the note. There's no need to put in a fall address; the city or town and the state will do.

Promissory Note Form, Box 2: The Date. Fill in the date on which the debtor signs the note.

Promissory Note Form, Box 3: The Amount. Fill in the full amount of the settlement. For example, if the defendant has agreed to make four monthly payments of $300, you would fill in $1,200. Moreover, even if you agree that the defendant will be charged interest running from the date of the agreement to the date of the last payment, the amount filled in should still be $1,200.

Promissory Note Form, Box 4: The Debtor. The debtor is the only person who actually signs the note (because the note only concerns the debtor's obligation to pay). Consequently, put the debtor's full name in box 4. If the debtor is a business, put the full company name as it appears on the complaint.

Promissory Note Form, Box 5: Your Name. Fill in this box with the name of the plaintiff—either you or your company.

Promissory Note Form, Box 6: Where Payments Should Be Sent. In this box fill in the address to which all payments should be sent or delivered.

Promissory Note Form, Box 7 and 7A: The Amount. This is the same amount as shown in box 3. There are two boxes so you can write out the amount in box 7, followed by the numbers in box 7A. For example, if the Promissory Note was for $2,000.50, you would fill in boxes 7 and 7A as follows: "Two Thousand Dollars and Fifty Cents ($2,000.50)"

Promissory Note Form, Box 8: The Final Payment. Fill in the date on which the last payment is due. If payments under your note were to start on January 1, 2001, and continue for six months, you would fill in June 1, 2001, as the date of the final payment.

Promissory Note Form, Boxes 9 and 9A: Interest. Fill in the interest rate, if any, in the same way you filled in boxes 7 and 7A. For example, if you are charging 10 percent interest, you would fill in the boxes as follows: "ten percent (10%) per annum. ("Per annum" simply means "per year.") If you are not charging interest, you can leave these boxes blank or write "zero" in the blanks.

Promissory Note Form, Boxes 10 and 10A: Number of Payments. How many payments will there be? If there are to be five, you would write "Five (5)" in boxes 10 and 10A.

Promissory Note Form, Boxes 11 and 11A: Amount of Payments. Fill in boxes 11 and 11A with the amount of each payment. For example, if each monthly payment is to be $200, you would fill in the boxes as follows: "Two Hundred Dollars and No Cents ($200.00)."

Promissory Note Form, Box 12: When Is the First Payment Due? Fill in the date on which the debtor is to make his first payment.

Promissory Note Form, Boxes 13 and 13A: How Long Are Payments to Continue? Fill in the number of payments the debtor is to make. For example, if the agreement calls for six payments of $200 each, you would fill in boxes 13 and 13A as follows: "Six (6)"

Note that my examples have always concerned monthly payments. There is no requirement that this be the case. If your arrangement calls for weekly payments or quarterly payments, or payments in any other time period, simply replace the word "month" or "monthly" where it appears in the sample note and use the word that best applies to your situation.

Promissory Note Form, Box 14: The Final Payment. Fill in the same date you used in box 8.

Promissory Note Form, Boxes 15 and 16: Addresses. During the course of the payment term, you and the debtor may have to get in touch with one another. One of you may have moved, the debtor may need an extension, or you may have to call the debtor about a past-due payment. This is the purpose served by boxes 15 and 16.

Promissory Note Form, Box 17 and 17A: The Date of the Note. This should be the same date shown in box 2—it is the date on which the debtor signs the note, and it is written as "the 1st day of January, 2001."

Promissory Note Form, Box 18: The Witness. Always have someone sign the note as witnessing the debtor's signature. Although you can be the witness, you should have a third person do it. That way, in case a question ever comes up in court as to whether the debtor actually signed the note, it won't just be your word against the debtor's.

Promissory Note Form, Boxes 19, 19A, and 19B: The Debtor's Signature. I have set this signature box up for a company. If the debtor is a company, fill in the company name (as it appears on the complaint) in box 19. The person who is signing on behalf of the company should place his signature on line 19A and print his name and title on line 19B. If the debtor is not a company, ignore lines 19 and 19B (or delete them entirely), and just have the debtor sign on line 19A.

Write the word "Seal" in parentheses after the debtor's signature as it appears on the form. Under the laws of many states, the use of this format will extend the statute of limitations.

Optional Paragraphs. I have included certain optional paragraphs you ran include or delete depending upon the specific terms of your agreement. Those paragraphs are numbered 1, 3, 6, and 12 on the form on the preceding pages.

Paragraph Numbers 1 and 3: Interest. While I encourage you to charge the debtor interest if you are allowing him to make payments over time, it is by no means mandatory. If you are not charging him interest, delete these paragraphs.

Paragraph Number 6: Confession of Judgment. You MAY NOT use this provision in a consumer transaction. Go back to chapter 9, where I discuss whether your claim is a commercial or consumer transaction.

Paragraph Number 12: Commercial Loan. Delete this paragraph when dealing with a consumer transaction.

Copies. You should keep a copy of the signed note in your files. It doesn't matter whether or not you have the original, although I'd prefer it if you did.

Completing the Note. Often it is not possible to meet face-to-face to negotiate a settlement. If this is the case, discuss all of the terms of the settlement with the defendant and advise him that you will be sending out a Promissory Note for him to sign. If he will not be signing the note in the presence of a witness whom you know, have him get his signature notarized. Many businesses have notary publics who will notarize documents for a small fee. He can then send the signed and notarized note back to you.

Effect of Bankruptcy. Debtors are usually able to escape the enforcement of a Promissory Note (or other obligations) through the filing of bankruptcy. There are several ways to eliminate this risk. First, a provision may be included in the note (depending upon your state law and the facts of your case) that waives the debtor's right to escape this debt through bankruptcy. Note that this is available only in a commercial transaction. Second, it is possible to force the debtor to secure the payment obligation with some sort of collateral.

The exercise of either of these options requires the input of a qualified attorney practicing in your state dispensed after he or she obtains a full understanding of the facts of your claim and settlement.

Professional Advice. As with any legal document, you are well advised to seek the advice of a competent professional concerning the applicability of this form to your specific case.

The opposite of talking isn't listening. The opposite of talking is waiting.

—Fran Lebowitz

15
Preparation for and Appearance at Trial

Overview

Now that you have a trial date, you may think it's time to relax and wait for your opportunity to tell the judge the story of your claim. You could do that, just as you could take an exam without studying, but you probably would be disappointed with the result.

Trials are won or lost on preparation. I'll say it again: Trials are won or lost on preparation.

To prepare for your trial, you must organize your papers and other evidence (trial exhibits) as well as prepare your testimony and your questioning of witnesses—both yours and those the defendant chooses to call. In this chapter I will walk you through every aspect of trial, from preparation to the judge's ruling.

Preparing for Trial

Who Is Allowed to Appear Before the Court?

Each state has its own views as to whether lawyers are allowed to appear in small-claims courts. Quite simply, some states feel that lawyers streamline the process through an efficient presentation of evidence without the personal attacks and irrelevant evidence that can sometimes characterize a nonlawyer's case. Other states feel that lawyers do nothing more than gum up the works. If you haven't already, please refer to the state chart on pages 114–117 to check if you have the option of being represented by a lawyer.

Remember, even if you *can* have a lawyer represent you, hiring one wouldn't necessarily be in your best interest. After all, I wrote this book (in a state where lawyers are allowed in small claims) knowing that clients often wind up paying their lawyer more than a claim is worth. In small claims, absent any complicating factors such as the filing of a counterclaim against you seeking one billion dollars and your firstborn child, I recommend self-help.

Assuming you will not be hiring a lawyer, note that if you filed a lawsuit in your name, you must be the one to go to trial to present your case. The same idea applies to companies; not just anybody from the company can take the case to trial. The company must specifically designate an officer, director, member, or other principal to go to trial on its behalf.

Always check with the clerk's office to make sure that your company's designated representative will be allowed to present your case at trial. Some states require company officers. Others have no such restrictions. Better to find out beforehand than appear with someone who will be barred from speaking on behalf of the company.

Organizing Your Case

Have I mentioned that collection cases are won or lost on organization? Your materials—notes, exhibits, ledgers, and so forth—should be arranged in a folder or notebook and should follow the order of the trial.

When preparing, understand that your notes are your business. You do not have to show them to the judge or to the other side unless you are reading from them while testifying, so don't worry about how your materials look. In a little while I will show you the best way to organize your documents, notes, and witness examinations. First, I would like to acquaint you with the various parts of a trial so that you understand what you will be preparing for.

Elements of a Trial

A trial is evidence sandwiched between speeches. The evidence takes the form of documents or other objects (the business cards you printed for the defendant, for example) and testimony. The speeches are actually brief statements, completely optional, in which you first tell the judge what the case is about (i.e., what she's going to hear) and then, after the evidence, tell the judge what it all meant (i.e., what she heard). These so-called speeches are the Opening Statement and the Closing Argument.

By the time you walk into the courtroom you should have prepared your Opening Statement, the exhibits you plan to use, questions for your witnesses (direct examination), questions for the defendant's witnesses (cross-examination), and your Closing Argument.

Your Opening Statement

Sgt. Joe Friday (yeah, I'm back on *Dragnet* again and I never even watched the show) might have described the Opening Statement as "just the facts." In the Opening Statement each side briefly explains his case to the judge. Don't be surprised if the judge doesn't ask for it; many judges prefer to dispense with the Opening Statements and move directly to the presentation of evidence—especially in smaller collection cases. If you do give an Opening Statement, it should not take any longer than five minutes. Remember, you are there to try your case . . . not the judge's patience.

As with any type of speech, different people have different ways of preparing for Opening Statements. You may require nothing more than a few words written down in front of you as a reminder of your key points, or you may feel more comfortable with every word written out ahead of time. I encourage you to *over*prepare the first few times you go to trial until you are familiar with court proceedings and feel at ease.

Remember to keep it brief; the judge has heard literally thousands of cases just like yours. While the parties may be different people, the situation will probably be all too familiar to him. If the judge has a question, rest assured he'll ask.

To write an Opening Statement, I suggest you summarize your

Complaint in a few paragraphs. When you have finished writing out your Opening Statement, review it carefully. Make sure that you can back up everything you say, either through the testimony of a witness or through an exhibit of some kind.

Bottom line: If you can't prove something you have written into your Opening Statement, cross it out. Just as important: Everything in your Opening Statement must have a direct impact on your case. If you look at any one sentence and cannot provide a concise answer to the "so what?" question, cross it out.

Remember to start with the obvious. Chances are the judge doesn't know you, your business, or the defendant. Tell the judge why you're there. Don't try to be flashy. You are not Tom Cruise in *A Few Good Men.* (If you are and if Jack Nicholson's on the stand, you may want to rethink your decision not to hire a lawyer.)

A model Opening Statement in a standard collection case would be:

"Good morning, Your Honor. My name is Paula Smith and I am the president of Smith Printing Company. On October 16, 2000, we received an order from the defendant to design and print 1,000 business cards and 5,000 sheets of letterhead with matching envelopes. The defendant approved our quote for the work and paid us a 25 percent deposit. We designed the material to his specifications and showed him a blue line. The defendant approved the blue line and we printed his order.

"The defendant has refused to pay us the balance due on the order. We're suing him for the balance of $1,250 plus interest of $116.25."

It is concise. It wastes no time on extraneous facts, and it tells the judge everything you want her to know. In other words, it quickly gets her oriented to what you are asking and what she should be listening and looking for.

Preparing Your Exhibits

As I explained earlier, exhibits are documents or other tangible items relevant to your case. Invoices, estimates, contracts, correspondence, telephone logs, photographs, and interest worksheets are all exhibits that may be useful in you case.

Selecting Your Exhibits

A good starting point (and perhaps ending point) in selecting your trial exhibits is your Complaint. Which exhibits did you think were appropriate when you drafted it? Ideally, your exhibits would tell the story of your claim all by themselves. By this I mean that you would have a document reflecting each stage in your case—what you were hired to do, how much the defendant agreed to pay, how much (if anything) the defendant did pay, how much he still owes you plus interest, and your efforts to collect the balance before filing suit.

Even if you don't have exhibits to reflect *all* parts of your claim, chances are you at least have some bills you sent to the defendant, an interest worksheet showing the judge how much interest the defendant owes you an top of his principal balance, or some type of document reflecting what you were hired to do in the first place.

When I put together exhibits for my own cases, whether the case involves a simple collection issue or a complicated corporate fraud claim, I imagine the judge leaving the courtroom with nothing but my exhibits in his hand. The question I ask myself is: "If the judge happened to sleep through the trial, could he look at my exhibits and tell what my client and I want and why?" If the answer is "yes," then I know I have all the exhibits I need.

As an example, refer to the sample Opening Statement on page 238. The exhibits to be presented at trial would be:

- The defendant's order.

- The plaintiff's quote (perhaps signed by the defendant as approved).

- A copy of the defendant's deposit check (if available).

- The blue line (signed by the defendant as approved).

- A sample of the business cards, stationery, and envelopes printed by the plaintiff to the defendant's specifications.

- The plaintiff's invoice for the balance.

- An interest worksheet showing finance charges.

These exhibits tell the story of an order placed by the defendant for an agreed price, a design approved by the defendant, and work performed by the plaintiff. Everything you need to substantiate your claim is right there.

If you anticipate that the defendant plans to argue that you messed up the job, correspondence from the defendant praising your work (even midway through the project) makes a wonderful exhibit. Almost as effective is correspondence from the defendant that does not mention the defect he is now using as his excuse for nonpayment.

Organizing Your Exhibits

There is no single correct way to organize your exhibits as long as you can find them when you need them. I have always found it easiest to place them in the order in which they will be used in the case. Thus, if Witness A will be discussing the estimate, you may want to keep copies of the estimate clipped to the outline of your questions for Witness A.

Keep in mind that the other side is entitled to a copy of any exhibit you are presenting at trial *at the time you are presenting it.* It doesn't matter if he already has a copy; you must hand him one at the same time you begin using it in court. Consequently, you should always make three copies of each exhibit—one for the judge, one for you to keep with the file, and one for the defendant.

Preparing Questions for Your Witnesses: Sample Trial Worksheet

In legal terms, questioning your own witness is called "direct examination." (Questioning the other side's witnesses is called "cross-examination.") In this section, I shall discuss preparing your direct examinations.

As you have probably seen on TV, witnesses testify using a question-and-answer format. Thus, to use a witness effectively, you must figure out ahead of time what you want the witness to tell the judge. Once you know the key points you want to bring out through each witness's testimony, you will be able to figure out the appropriate questions. It's even better if you have a piece of physi-

cal evidence—an exhibit—to supplement the witness's testimony.
I suggest using the chart below:

Witness:	Point:	Exhibit:
1._____	1._____	1._____
	2._____	2._____
	3._____	3._____
2._____	1._____	1._____
	2._____	2._____
	3._____	3._____

As an example, let's take a case of nonpayment for accounting services. Let's assume that Witness A of Acme Accounting Services met with the defendant, wrote up an estimate that the defendant then signed, and performed the work. Witness B (perhaps Acme's office manager) kept Acme's account ledger, billed the defendant, and spoke to him over the telephone about his overdue account.

In preparing to present the case described above, your notes for your direct exam would look something like this:

Witness:	Point:	Exhibit:
1. A(Salesman)	1. In [October 1995, the defendant asked A to do some accounting work.	1. Phone log
	2. During the conversation defendant agreed to pay [$500] for the work.	2. Contract or the Purchase Order
	3. Acme did the work as requested.	
2. B (Office Mgr)	1. After the work as completed Acme billed [John Debtor] [$500].	3. Ist Invoice

Witness:	Point:	Exhibit:
	2. When no payment was received, Acme continued to send monthly invoices.	4. Invoice #'s 2–8
	3. To date, Acme still has has not been paid.	5. Account ledger
	4. Acme is owed [$500] plus interest through the date of the trial.	6. Interest Worksheet

As you can see, the plaintiff wants to elicit three major points from Witness A and four major point from Witness B, while presenting six exhibits.

Note that this is a rather lengthy presentation for a small claim. Often small claims involve two witnesses—the plaintiff and the defendant. If this is the case, prepare just as you would for a more complicated case—listing each point you want to make and each exhibit you will use. (Just try to avoid the question-and-answer format if you'll be playing both parts. Schizophrenic plaintiffs can put the judge off.)

Sample Questions for Your Witnesses

I encourage you to cover all the key points discussed below in order to solidly establish the facts of your case. Use as many witnesses as you need. I have listed a number of sample questions below. Feel free to use my sample questions or make up your own.

Establish the Relevance of Each Witness to Your Claim

The first part of each witness's testimony should tell the judge why this person is on the stand (e.g., he or she works for your company or has expertise in a particular field). Keep this part of the testimony brief—one or two questions at most—and make sure the questions are relevant. The judge may not care how long a particular person has been in his field unless the defendant plans to question his competence.

Bottom line: Keep this part short, but DO IT FOR EACH WITNESS.

- What do you do for a living?

- Where do you work?

- How long have you worked for (X Company)?

- How long have you been an (occupation)?

Describe the Witness's Familiarity with the Claim

- Do you know the defendant? How?

- Did you ever meet with the defendant? When? Where? What were the circumstances?

- What was discussed at your meeting with the defendant?

Focus the Witness's Testimony on the Claim

- Were you ever asked to do work for the defendant?

- What were the circumstances?

- Did you agree to do the work?

- Describe the work.

- Did you quote a price for the work?

- What payment arrangements did you make with the defendant?

- Did you write up an [estimate, agreement, etc.]?

If so, show the document to the witness and ask the questions set forth in the following section.

- Did the defendant agree to the price?

- Did you do the work agreed to do in the [agreement]?

- Mr. Witness, I am showing you a document [which you will ask the judge to mark as Exhibit 1 or whatever the next exhibit number is]. Do you recognize it?

- Please tell the judge what it is.

- Is that the defendant's signature? How do you know?

You should now ask the judge to accept the document into evidence as Exhibit X. You would ask as follows: "Your Honor, I would ask that this document be accepted into evidence as plaintiff's Exhibit X."

Question the Witness About the Defendant's Failure to Pay

- When was payment due?

- Did you bill the defendant for the balance?

- Did the defendant pay you any money?

- How much?

- Did you call the defendant about the money he owed?

- What did the defendant say?

- Did the defendant respond with any payment?

- How much money is currently owed?

- Have you added interest to the balance owed?

- Did you reach an agreement with the defendant that permits you to charge interest? Where was that term written?

- Did you advise the defendant that interest would be charged on overdue balances?

- What rate of interest did you apply to the overdue balances?

- Did you prepare an interest worksheet?

Now ask the judge to accept the document into evidence as Exhibit X. You would ask as follows: "Your Honor, I would ask that this document be accepted into evidence as plaintiff's Exhibit X."

- How much interest are you claiming?

- Has the defendant incurred any other fees?

- Are you claiming anything else from the defendant in addition to his balance and interest?

Practice, Practice, Practice

ALWAYS rehearse your questions your witnesses. This kind of practice ensures that you and your witness are on the same wavelength. What's more, practice in advance virtually guarantees a smoother presentation at trial.

Preparing Your Own Testimony

In many small-claims cases, the plaintiff doesn't bring any witnesses; he just tells his story himself. If you feel you don't need to bring any witnesses, you would be sworn in just like any other witness. The judge would ask you to tell him what it is you came to say. You would tell your story to the judge in the same way you would explain it to a friend who is pressed for time. Skip insignificant details, keep your story simple and concise, and stick to your key points and exhibits. The judge will ask questions if he wants to, just like he'll generally let you know when he's heard enough.

Preparing Your Closing Argument

A Closing Argument, or summation, is your last word to the judge. Your Closing Argument will bear a pretty close resemblance to your Opening Statement. In your Closing Argument, you will want to briefly and succinctly summarize the evidence you presented. You can use the same outline you prepared for your Opening Statement—just make sure that your Closing Argument recounts what actually happened at trial, not what *should* have happened. Thus, for our purposes here, the only real difference between the Opening Statement and the summation is that the Opening Statement addresses *what the evidence will show* and the summation concerns *what the evidence showed.*

Appearing at Trial

Go to the Right Courthouse at the Right Time

The most important part of the trial is showing up at the right place at the right time. As I said previously, sometimes the court system will transfer your case to another courthouse in the same county where you filed suit. They will always send you a trial notice. Check the address, trial date, and the time on the notice and enter them on your calendar. Few things irritate a judge more than calling a case only to be told by the clerk that one of the parties (or the attorneys) called from the wrong courthouse and will be delayed.

Confirm the Trial Date

Before heading off to court with your witnesses in tow, be sure to call the clerk two or three days ahead of time to confirm that your case is on the schedule. All too frequently a case is postponed for one reason or another and someone doesn't receive a new trial notice. Don't waste a trip . . . call ahead.

What If You're Late?

If you are late, and you either missed roll call or arrived in the middle and did not hear your case called, you will have to get a message to the clerk that you are, in fact, present and ready to appear. This can be tricky because court is already in session. You can do this in one of two ways:

1. Try to catch the eye of the bailiff or the clerk and motion to either of them that you would like to speak with them in the hall.

2. Go outside of the courtroom and tell someone in the clerk's office what happened. They will find someone to slip a note to the judge while he's on the bench.

What If You Miss the Court Date Entirely?

If you fail to appear on the trial date, your case will be dismissed. Nevertheless, unless the judge decides to dismiss the case "with prejudice," you can refile your Complaint and begin the procedure all over again. To find out whether the case was dismissed "with prejudice," call the clerk and ask.

Dismissing a case with prejudice means that you can't refile the claim. If the dismissal doesn't say one way or another, the case has been dismissed "without prejudice," meaning that you *can* refile your Complaint.

Finally, if you decide to refile, reread the section on the statute of limitations in chapter 6 to make sure that you still have a valid case.

So, You're in the Right Courthouse on the Right Date and at the Right Time . . .

When you arrive at the courthouse, the first thing you should do is check the docket sheets. A docket sheet is simply a list of the cases to be called on that particular date and time. Docket sheets are usually posted on a bulletin board or inside a mounted glass-front display case.

Except in small, less-traveled courthouses, there is always at least one sheet for each courtroom. Although most courthouses post them where you can see them upon entering, ask someone where you can find the docket sheets if you do not see them right away. The docket sheet tells you the actual courtroom in which your trial will be held. It also confirms once and for all that your case is on the schedule for that day.

What If Your Case Is Not on the Docket?

If, after reviewing all of the docket sheets, you do not see your case, go directly to the clerk's office and ask why your case does not appear. Have your case number handy so the clerk can look up your case on the system. While it is rare, it is possible that the case was rescheduled within the last couple of days. This is just one of the inevitable costs of doing business with the court system.

The Judge's Role During Trial

The judge can ask questions at any time during the trial, and he can direct his questions to anyone—you, the defendant, or the witness.

The judge's questions always have priority. Answer them immediately and respectfully. Sometimes a judge will ask a question that seems entirely irrelevant to the case. Answer it anyway as if you felt it were completely on point.

The watchword for dealing with the judge is RESPECT. Always treat the judge with the utmost respect, addressing him as "Judge" or "Your Honor." When you are in the courtroom you are like a guest in the judge's house. He makes the rules.

Your Day in Court

Your day in court will usually proceed in the following order:

- Roll call.

- Waiting.

- Opening statement from all parties (optional).

- Presentation of the plaintiff's evidence.

- Presentation of the defendant's evidence.

- Closing argument (optional).

As we discussed, the judge may dispense with Opening Statements and/or Closing Arguments, but you should be prepared to present something anyway.

Roll Call

After finding the correct courtroom, have a seat. It does not matter whether you arrived half an hour before the appointed time or two minutes early. You will invariably encounter my Second Rule of Litigation: The judge will get started late. If your trial notice schedules your case to begin at 9:00, consider yourself lucky if the judge enters the courtroom by 9:30.

DO NOT USE THIS AS AN EXCUSE TO BE LATE YOURSELF. SOMETIMES JUDGES LIKE TO SURPRISE THE LITIGANTS AND GET STARTED ON TIME. (This, of course, brings us to my First Rule of Litigation—prepare to proceed on time, regardless of what you think the judge will do.)

Once the judge enters the courtroom, he will begin taking the roll of all cases listed on the docket sheet for his courtroom. When he calls your case, he will want to know two things:

1. Whether all parties to the case (you and the defendant[s]) are present, and

2. How long the trial is expected to take.

Do not try to explain your case to him at this time, as you will be cut off before your second sentence. He only wants these questions answered so he can start taking cases in the most efficient way possible—from the shortest to the longest proceeding.

When your case is called, stand up, identify yourself as the plaintiff, and tell the judge how long it will take you to present your case. It should not take you more than fifteen to twenty minutes. (You'll get better at estimating once you've been through the process a few times.) The judge will also ask the defendant for a time estimate.

While I encourage you to talk to the defendant before the judge enters the courtroom in order to come up with an estimated time for both sides to present their case, it is not mandatory. Simply tell the judge how long you believe your case will take. Unless your case is unusually complicated, figure each witness will take between five and ten minutes.

Waiting

After roll call, you will probably have to wait your turn. Don't go out in the hall; use this time. Watch the cases before yours. Even if you have been through this process hundreds of times, you can always learn by watching the judge. Try to determine what kind of mood he's in and how he handles cases. Each judge is different. You'll be able to see what points interest the judge, how he runs the trial, and what mistakes he finds in other presentations. No matter how well you prepare, there is no substitute for scouting out the judge.

Opening Statement

When it is your turn, the judge will call out the name of your case and the case number. Take your materials and walk up to the trial table. The other table is for the defendant. (Note that some judges reverse the seating arrangements. If so, they will tell you where to sit when your case is called.)

After you get settled at your table, the judge may ask if you want to make an Opening Statement. (Depending upon how many cases he's heard that day, the judge may ask this question with all of the enthusiasm of someone making a dental appointment.) It's your call. Make one if you want, but remember that an Opening Statement is not necessary in this type of case, and I often don't make one.

Unless them is something unusually complicated about your case or the other side tells the judge he wants to make one, there is no real reason you should insist an making an Opening Statement. Moreover, if the judge seems impatient to get started, forget about the Opening Statement and begin your case.

If you decide to make an Opening Statement, you, as the plaintiff, will go first, followed by the defendant. When it is the defendant's turn to speak, BE QUIET. Although you will undoubtedly disagree with the defendant's statement, you are not allowed to interrupt him. It is not a debate. Instead, you have the chance to present your evidence right after the defendant stops speaking.

Presentation of the Plaintiff's Evidence

Your case begins with your first witness. When the judge asks you to call your first witness, state the witness's name and have the witness approach the witness stand where he will be sworn in.

After the witness swears to tell the truth, you will begin your direct examination. Break out your trial worksheet from above and ask your questions. Equally as important, LISTEN TO THE ANSWERS. Just because you asked the right question doesn't mean the witness will give the right answer. If the witness did not make the point that you wanted made, just ask the same question another way.

For example, if you wanted to establish that the defendant signed the estimate, you might ask: "Did the defendant sign a contract?" If the witness is on a different wavelength and answers "no," stay with it. You might present the witness with the signed estimate and ask him to identify it, along with the defendant's signature. You could also ask if the defendant signed "an estimate" rather than "a contract" as was originally asked.

As each witness testifies, remember to refer to the key points you had outlined for each witness and check them off on your worksheet as the witness testifies to them. Once all of the key points for the witness have been checked off, conclude your examination by advising the judge that you have no further questions for that witness.

After you conclude your questioning of a witness, the defendant will have an opportunity to question him. In cases such as these, cross-examination is often either waived or, if attempted, proves to be a waste of time.

Note that you have the right to question your witness again after the defendant has finished his cross-examination. If the judge doesn't ask you whether you want to do this, you can speak up and tell the judge that you have a few more questions.

The purpose of this "redirect examination" is not for you to repeat what you asked the witness the first tune. Instead, the purpose is to allow you to clear up anything the defendant may have brought out on cross-examination. Redirect examination should only be used in very unusual circumstances. Once you're finished questioning your first witness (and the defendant is finished with his cross-examination), tell the judge that you would like to call your next witness.

After your final witness has testified, you should tell the judge that you have concluded your case.

Presentation of the Defendant's Evidence

Once you tell the judge that you have finished presenting your case, he will give the defendant a chance to present his. If there is more than one defendant, the judge will take them in rum (no special order is required). The defendant's case will follow the same pattern that yours did. The defendant will call his witnesses, question them, and then the judge will give you an opportunity to ask them questions—to cross-examine them.

Cross-Examination

Cross-examination is an art, and very few people, including attorneys, do it well. There are entire books written on the subject, and some people make their living teaching this one subject to aspiring trial lawyers. It is not my purpose here to make you a master of the art of cross-examination. I simply want to provide you with a couple of rules. What follows is what I refer to as . . .

The Ten Commandments of Cross-Examination

1. Ask leading questions (questions that suggest their own answers). Examples include "You did this, didn't you" and "Isn't it true that you said this?"

2. Never ask "why" on cross-examination. It is an open-ended question that gives the witness a chance to go an forever. Remember, you are cross-examining the witness because he testified *against* you. Don't give him an opportunity to say things you don't want him to say during your questioning.

3. KISS . . . Keep It Short and Simple. If you decide to cross-examine, only ask a few questions and then stop. A talented lecturer and trial lawyer, the late Irving Younger, once stated that if a trial was a war, then cross-examination was a "commando raid . . . get in, get out. It is not," he told his students, "the invasion of Europe."

4. If you don't know the answer, don't ask the question. The answer may be more damaging to your case than anything the other side actually brought out in their questioning of the witness. At trial, what you don't know can hurt you.

5. Don't just contradict the witness's testimony in the hope that he will admit he was lying. Only on television do witnesses actually break down and confess. In the real world, unless you have something more than just "your word against his," a witness WILL stick with his testimony regardless of what you say.

6. If you aren't getting anywhere or do not think there is anything to gained by asking any questions, keep quiet. Remember, it is better to say nothing and be thought a fool than to open your mouth and remove all doubt (with compliments to Mark Twain).

7. Ask commonsense questions. If someone says that he refused to pay you because you sold him a defective product, ask him if he ever sent you a letter complaining or filed a formal Complaint against the warranty. Find out if he bought a replacement. People will say anything to disguise the fact that they just didn't feel like paying. Most often, they will try to point a finger at your goods or services. Bottom line: If they made use of your goods or services and did nothing to back up their claim of dissatisfaction, bring that out.

8. As Napoleon once said, "Never interrupt an enemy when he's making a mistake." If you notice that the defendant forgot to ask a question, thereby forgetting to present part of his defense to the judge, don't do the defendant's job for him by asking the witness a question on the subject.

9. Be courteous to the witness even if the witness is lying through his teeth. It will get you nowhere (except perhaps on the judge's bad side) to be abusive or disrespectful. You can and should disagree without being disagreeable.

10. Finally, observe the cardinal rule of trial law—if you're winning, shut up.

Model Cross-Examination

Limit your cross-examination to a few succinct questions. Here are some sample questions for cross-examining the defendant's witnesses. Notice that they all require simple yes-or-no answers:

- You signed the estimate, correct?

- You agreed that if we did the work, you would pay [$500], didn't you?

- You didn't complain about the work after it was completed, did you?

- You only started to complain when we began collection proceedings, right?

- You haven't paid for any of the work, have you?

- You never wrote to us complaining about our work, did you?

Closing Argument

When the defendant has finished presenting his case, the judge will ask each side to make a Closing Argument. A Closing Argument is your final chance to convince the judge that you should win the case.

Although there is no substitute for preparation, part of your Closing Argument will always have to be composed on the spot. Trials rarely work out exactly as planned. You may notice that the judge has a particular question or concern, the defendant may have a different argument than you anticipated, or a witness may have said something unexpected or forgotten to say something you thought he would. Be flexible and summarize your perspective on what actually happened rather than what you thought would happen.

The Judge's Decision

After the Closing Arguments, the judge will probably advise you of his decision. DO NOT ARGUE WITH THE JUDGE WHEN HE IS RENDERING HIS DECISION. By this point, the judge has already heard everything you have to say, and it is his turn to speak. Do not interrupt.

If the judge does not immediately announce his decision, don't worry. He will review the evidence later, and you will be notified of his decision by mail . . . when he gets around to it. Most judges will render decisions within thirty days of the trial.

You will receive a confirmatory Notice of Judgment in the mail a few days after the judge announces his decision—whether at trial or afterward.

"After Reviewing the Evidence, I Find in Favor of . . ."

If you won, CONGRATULATIONS! Enjoy a brief victory celebration (although I recommend that you wait until you're outside of the courtroom) and move on to the chapter that tells you HOW TO GET YOUR MONEY . . . now that the judge has said you deserve it.

Judge: A law student who marks his own examination papers.
—H. L. Mencken

16
A View from the Bench

Overview

With all due respect to Mr. Mencken, it is not his own examination papers the judge is marking, but yours. If you take this to heart, your sole focus leading up to trial should be providing the judge with the answers he is looking for. After all, it does not matter if you're right. It only matters if the judge thinks you're right.

Equally as important as the necessity of being legally entitled to win your claim is making the judge want to find in your favor. In this chapter I turn the floor over to the judges. Over a two-year period, I surveyed more than one hundred judges who routinely preside over the trials of small claims in order to find out how best to win and the easiest ways to guarantee a loss in their courtrooms.

The results of that survey, summarized in narrative form in this chapter, are arguably the most important pages in this book. In all of the other chapters, I have been teaching you how best to take the test. Here, I give you the answers—straight from the horse's mouth.

Courtroom Etiquette

Whenever they see the word "etiquette" used in a sentence, most readers would barely stifle a yawn and flip the page to see where the section ends. *Don't do that.* The observance of courtroom etiquette wins cases. Ignore it, and you could be on the receiving end of a judicial lecture followed by an early departure from the courtroom, regardless of the merits of your case.

Addressing the Judge

The watchword is "respect." Not only does the judge deserve respect by virtue of his status and authority over this small portion of your life, but in a very real sense, by being in the courtroom, you are standing in the judge's house. Nothing will put a judge off faster than giving the impression that you are treating him with less respect than his due.

Stand before speaking to the judge and while the judge is speaking to you, unless the judge instructs you otherwise. When speaking to the judge, refer to him as "Your Honor." In certain circles, referring to the judge as "Judge" is considered rude or a short form of address, but it is usually acceptable. (In other words, I recommend phrases such as "Yes, Your Honor . . ." as opposed to "Yes, Judge.")

Be deferential. You don't always have to agree with everything the judge says, just make sure you disagree in a respectful way. Believe me, in my years as a trial lawyer I have experienced every possible emotion when talking to a judge, from complete agreement to limitless exasperation. Knowing that I wouldn't get anywhere yelling, "You're just not gettin' it are ya, Sparky?" I had to find another, more respectful way of bringing the judge around to my way of thinking.

Part of showing respect means that when the judge starts speaking, you stop. Time and time again I have seen litigants, even lawyers, try to drown out the judge by continuing with their arguments. This may work at the dinner table, but it is much less likely to work in the courtroom. Although I admit that a weak judge may allow someone to get away with it, this is not a good tactic to try.

Addressing the Opposition

In a nutshell, you should act toward your opposition as you would instruct your children to act when meeting an adult for the first time.

They don't have to act like best friends, just polite and respectful.

At the outset, I should note that you should only rarely speak to the other side while in trial, if at all. Instead, your comments should be directed to the judge. If, however, you either have to speak about the other side or you have to address him directly, such as when you're being asked questions on the stand, be polite and respectful.

Many judges cited "being overly aggressive" and "being abusive to the defendant" as two of the best ways to lose in their courtrooms. One of the most important rules to remember in trying a case is that you must park your personal feelings at the door. I've seen litigants who would make guests on the Jerry Springer show look like Miss Manners graduates. Few things alienate a judge faster. Worse, these tactics may make the judge, however subconsciously, begin to sympathize with the other side.

If you must speak directly to the other side, use Mr., Ms., or Dr., as appropriate. Confine the name-calling to the parking lot. Concentrate on presenting your case rather then on showing the judge how much you hate your opponent. As Sergeant Friday used to say on *Dragnet,* "Just the facts." If you're presenting documents to the court, have a copy for the defendant to review—even if he's already seen it—and hand it to him rather than throw it. (Yes, I've seen that done, too.)

Your Nonspeaking Role

When the defendant or the judge is speaking, you will be relegated to a nonspeaking role. Here's how you act: Don't speak. I don't know exactly why some people seem to believe that if they yell "she's lying" at just the right place in the defendant's presentation, the judge will be persuaded to find in their favor. Personally, I've never seen it work, although the resulting tirade from the judge does entertain the audience.

Dress for Success

Judges do not take to Metallica T-shirts . . . at least not when they're on the job. (What they do in their off hours is up to them.) Come to court looking like you respect the process and want to be taken seriously. Dress as you would going to a job interview for a position you really want. This is not to say that you shouldn't walk into a courtroom in anything less than an Armani suit. The watchword is not "elegance" but rather "businesslike."

▶ "AND OUR SECOND RUNNER-UP IS . . ."

Many years ago, a judge told me that he used to advise his clients to dress formally for court. He stopped giving that advise after his third year of practice. At that time, he was representing a lady in a personal injury suit in which she was seeking damages for injuries sustained in a car accident. About a half hour before the jury trial was supposed to start, he was having coffee with a friend in the courthouse cafeteria when out of the corner of his eye he noticed a woman walking to the main entrance of the courthouse. "I didn't know they still performed weddings at this courthouse" he recalled telling his friend.

As it turns out, the person he had seen was not a bride-to-be, but rather his client who turned up in a flowing white dress and a tiara. From that point on, he stopped telling clients to dress formally.

There's no word on how well the jury took to the notion of awarding damages to a tiara-laden plaintiff.

And If You're Not Perry Mason . . .

Be yourself. Don't try to act the way you believe a lawyer would handle the case. Whenever I judge students in mock trials, I find that they get tongue tied trying to think of fancy ways to ask plain questions . . . because that's what they think lawyers do.

The question "What time is it?" becomes "Mr. Witness, could you tell me what, if any, indication is showing on your chronometer?" The overwhelming advice from judges: Forget about trying to be the second coming of Perry Mason. Just make yourself understood, act natural, and make your case.

Trying the Perfect Case: Advice from the Judges

Keep It Simple

An overwhelming number of judges who responded to the survey placed this piece of advice on their list of top five ways to win in their courtrooms. When asked to elaborate, several responding judges explained that too many litigants start in the middle of the story without letting the judge get his or her bearings. "I shouldn't have to listen to twenty minutes of testimony just to figure out that maybe the parties had a written agreement," one judge stated.

The solution: State your case simply and in a logical order. Start with the agreement—who asked whom to do what. Explain the terms. If the agreement is reflected in writing, show it to the judge at the outset of your case. In this same vein, many judges emphasized the need to make sure that the documents upon which you are relying are easily understandable. If your case hangs on a sentence or two, you may want to highlight it so that the judge can go right to it.

Remember, most small-claims courts have very full dockets. In order to move things along, a judge must often listen to witnesses, rule on objections, answer questions, and review documents *at the same time*. It would behoove you to do anything and everything you can think of to make his job easier.

Figuring out what to leave out of your case is as important as figuring out what to keep in. In the words of one judge: "Omit all evidence of why the debt is unpaid unless it has some relevance." Said another way, calling the defendant a deadbeat or explaining to the judge that this guy always passes bad checks or is a known liar won't do anything other than cause you to lose ground with the judge.

On the other hand, many people forget to discuss the reasonableness of the bill they are trying to collect. If you've been in the printing industry for ten years and you are trying to collect a bill for letterhead and business cards, tell the judge that the prices charged are reasonable in the industry. That small statement will go a long way toward proving your entitlement to the money. After all, chances are the judge doesn't know prices in your industry. He may never have ordered the materials or services that are the subject of your case, or, worse, his knowledge of prices may be a decade old. Educate the judge.

Keep It Organized

Not surprisingly, many surveys discussed the impression made by organized files or notebooks over dog-eared and scattered piles of paper. You should never have to shuffle through papers to find what you need. Bring copies of contracts, correspondence, invoices, and receipts for the court, the other side, and witnesses to examine.

"When I see someone sitting there with an organized file, the ability to substantiate all damages sought and with all of the relevant documents at his fingertips, I automatically begin to assume that they know what they're talking about. I begin to view them as the authority on this case simply because they're so organized—especially when the other side is shuffling through papers or forgot to bring the documents he needs." These are the words of one judge who was recounting a recent case in her courtroom.

Another cited what she called the "halo effect" whereby a party who presents an organized claim or defense automatically gains credibility even on those issues where it is just one person's word against the other's.

Bring the Right People to Court

In response to the survey, many judges cited their frustration with people who leave important witnesses back at the office. If the owner of the company shows up, but the person who negotiated the deal, had all conversations with the defendant, and signed the contract is back at the store, chances are that company will lose in court. Now, you don't have to bring everyone who ever had a conversation with the defendant, but if there was one point person who could listen to the defendant's testimony about what happened and say from personal knowledge, "No, that's wrong," bring her.

Anticipate Defenses and Be Ready with Evidence

This goes back to what I've stated previously . . . only now it comes from the judges. Do your best to anticipate what the other side is going to say and come ready to refute it. If there is written evidence against him—such as partial payment on account to show that he had agreed to the charges—bring a copy of his check or the receipt you issued. You must be prepared to hit the ball back over the net.

How to Ensure a Loss: Warnings from the Judges

The Claim Itself

"When a plaintiff gives me a 'deer-in-the-headlights' look when I ask him what he's claiming or how he came up with his figures, it's basically all over but the shouting." So says one fifteen-year judicial veteran of small-claims court. Another asked, "How can someone walk into court not knowing what they want me to do?" It may sound unbelievable, but I was told time and time again that it happens all the time.

Know to the penny how much money you're claiming and how you got there. If you are seeking interest, have your calculations ready. Equally as important, bring your accounting records to show the judge all the charges and payments relating to the account. There are few things worse than making the judge feel that he's being asked to enter a judgment with little or no credible information as to the right amount. A judge is not going to do your work for you. You must spoon-feed him information and lead him to the conclusion you want to reach.

The Witnesses

Too many people forget to prepare their witnesses. If the person asking the questions and the person answering them are not on the same page, nothing will be accomplished. "If only these people would take a few minutes to talk to their own witnesses, a lot of confusion could be avoided." This same judge told me that he could not count the number of times a witness failed to get out a crucial piece of testimony just because he didn't understand the question he was being asked.

"Look," said one judge, "everyone gets nervous. People, even experienced lawyers, sometimes stumble over their questions. But if you have a witness who knows what you want to get out of him, he'll provide the information even if you didn't ask the right question in the right way. The opposite is also true. If the witness doesn't know what you're talking about or tells you he doesn't know when asked a crucial question (such as the amount of the claim or whether the defendant agreed to the terms), it can be fatal to your case."

Bottom line: Prepare your questions ahead of time, outline the points you want to elicit from each witness, and review the questions and information ahead of time.

Note: This is not to say that the testimony should be scripted. It does mean, however, that you should verify the accuracy of all of the information you are seeking from the witness. Better to find out in the hall that the witness can't testify to something—either because she can't remember or because the point you are hoping to make is inaccurate—than to find out for the first time while she's on the stand.

Attitude

Not only is your attitude important, but also that of your witnesses. The same advice concerning respect for the judge, attire, and courtesy to the other side applies to your witnesses as well.

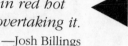

*The happiest time in any man's life is when he is in red hot
pursuit of a dollar with a reasonable prospect of overtaking it.*

—Josh Billings

17
Turning Your Judgment
into Money

Overview

Now that you've concluded your victory celebration, it's finally time
to get down to the business of ACTUALLY GETTING PAID.

As I said, the judge won't take the money out of the defendant's
pocket on the spot. In fact, neither the judge nor the court system
will lift a finger to help you get your money back. The judgment
you won merely gives you the *right* to get your money from the
defendant. Similarly, the legal system provides tools to help you,
but you must do the actual work yourself.

There are three elements in turning your judgment into money.
First, record your judgment so you can sell the defendant's property
if necessary. Second, find out what the defendant's assets and
income are. Third, use the court system to get paid.

States differ on the tools provided successful plaintiffs in order
to collect their money. In this chapter I describe each method of
collection that may be available to you in your pursuit of the defendant's assets. Consequently, as a starting point, refer to the chart on
pages 114–117 determine which avenues of collection are open to
you.

One final word before we get started—up to now the debtor

has been referred to as the "defendant" in court. After the defendant has lost in court, he is called the "judgment debtor." Remember this term, as it may appear on the legal forms you will fill out to collect your money. By the same token, you are now a "judgment creditor."

Getting Started

There are many incentives for a person to pay or "satisfy" a judgment against him—protection of his credit, elimination of further court proceedings, the fact that interest accrues on unpaid judgments, and even the acknowledgment that he fought, lost, and *should* pay, among them. Often, these incentives are enough. Just as often, not.

For those times when the judgment debtor must be compelled to pay, it is up to you to force the issue. As I said previously, a judgment is nothing but a hunting license. Your job, when faced with a recalcitrant debtor, is to use the weapons provided by the courts of your state to flush the debtor's assets out of the woods and into your net.

As a starting point, you must determine three things:

1. Where are you going to hunt for assets and income sources?

2. What assets and income sources are you licensed to hunt to satisfy your judgment?

3. What information do you already possess or know you need?

Do You Have to Search?

Certain states, as identified on the state comparative chart, place the burden of finding assets on the sheriff. These states require the judgment creditor to file a request that the sheriff seize recoverable assets, including bank accounts and a portion of the defendant's wages, to satisfy the judgment. Once you file this form, the sheriff will be dispatched to deal with the defendant in order to secure these assets.

Sure, it sounds easy, but in many cases overworked sheriff's departments result in long delays and incomplete searches. The

solution? Providing the information to the sheriff to reduce or eliminate his investigation time. Read the sections below for more information on doing just that.

Where Are You Going to Start Your Search?

Where does the judgment debtor live? Where is the judgment
debtor's principal place of business—either for the whole company
or for the portion that operates in your area? The Answers to these
questions tell you where to start your search.

Typically, the debtor is based in the state in which you
received your judgment. Sometimes, however, a judgment debtor's
assets—both in terms of cash and real estate—are located out of
state. On those occasions, your first step should be to record (otherwise known as "enroll") your judgment in the state or county
where the assets are most likely to be found. To record a judgment
obtained in one jurisdiction in another state or county, you must
obtain forms from both jurisdictions. In other words, your goal is
to get the original court—the source of the judgment—to talk to
the new court for the jurisdiction that has become the target of
your search.

For example, let's say you received your judgment in a Texas
small-claims court (the "source court") and want to use it to reach
the debtor's assets in Oklahoma (the "target"). You must place two
calls. First, call the clerk for the Texas court where you obtained
your judgment to get copies of the right forms to transmit that judgment elsewhere. Then, call the clerk for the court located in the target jurisdiction to get the form necessary for it to accept the Texas
judgment.

When the forms are filled out properly, the source court will
transmit all of the information necessary to record your judgment in
the target jurisdiction, just as if you had brought the case there in the
first place. Once your judgment is enrolled in the target jurisdiction,
you should proceed with collection as outlined below.

What Can You Use to Get Paid?

Any given state chooses from among the following vehicles for
judgment collection:

1. Interrogatories.

2. Oral examination under oath.

3. Wage garnishments.

4. Bank account and personal property garnishments.

5. Levies on real estate.

Some states allow a judgment creditor to choose from among all four options. Other states limit the available options. To determine the options allowed by your state, please refer to the chart on pages 114–117.

Locating the Debtor's Assets and Income Sources

Most states recognize that just because you won a judgment against someone, he won't automatically pay up. Judgment creditors in these types of cases fall into two categories: those who know the location of the defendant's assets or income sources and those who don't.

If you know the location of assets or income sources your state allows you to pursue to satisfy your judgment, skip to the section that discusses that particular device. For example, if your state allows wage garnishments and you know where the debtor works, you should skip to the section on the attachment of wages. If you do not know where to find the debtor's assets, bank accounts, or income sources, keep reading.

The tools provided by each state for your use in figuring out what assets and income sources the defendant has are one or more of the following:

- Interrogatories in Aid of Execution.

- Oral examination under oath.

- Court-ordered disclosure.

You can choose any option, depending upon your state's laws as shown in the chart. A survey would show a fairly even split of opinion among attorneys as to which method of investigation they prefer. Some like the oral examination because, if you're face-to-face with the debtor, you can ask follow-up questions. Others, like me, prefer the convenience of written questions. After all, once I have the questions on computer, it is easy enough to make the slight changes necessary to adapt them to the current case. What's more, sometimes the defendant doesn't show up for an oral exam. With written questions, there is no chance of wasting a trip down to the courthouse on the oral exam date.

Don't Overlook the Obvious

In your search for the defendant's bank accounts, the information you need may be as close as your file. In many cases, the defendant made at least one payment before he either bounced the check or refused to pay the balance of his account. If you have a copy of the check or if the defendant provided you with information when filling out an account agreement, you know where he banks, and you have his account number. This may not be his only account, but it's a good place to start.

Interrogatories in Aid of Execution: Asking the Defendant About His Finances in Writing

The written questions the debtor is required to answer are called Interrogatories or Interrogatories in Aid of Execution.[1] Like all other aspects of small-claims court procedure, you are required to prepare and file the questions in the specific format discussed and shown in chapter 13. Most states have preprinted forms and model questions for your use. Simply call the clerk and inquire as to availability.

For your convenience, I have listed model questions below in case your state does not make them available or the forms are inapplicable to your situation.

Preparing Written Financial Questions for the Defendant

To prepare questions most likely to be helpful to you in your search for assets, use both your knowledge and your common sense.

---

[1] The process of pursuing collection of a judgment is known as "execution" or "executing on the judgment."

Although the questions below are general, don't forget to use your association with the debtor for specific information about the debtor's assets. Check your files.

Try to remember conversations with him. If he had a piece of vacation property or liked going out on his boat, compose an interrogatory requesting applicable information. For example, if the debtor bought durable goods from you, you know he has at least some personal property. Find out where it is. If the debtor used your accounting services, use your information about his finances for your own benefit and compose specific questions about the location of assets you know he has.

I have listed below a sampling of questions you may choose to use in your own forms—either as they appear here or modified to fit the facts of your case. These are by no means the *only* questions you can ask. They are, however, general questions that, without anything else, will get you the information you need to turn your judgment into money.

Model Questions for a Company or an Individual

1. Identify all of your sources of present and anticipated income and, with regard to each source of income, provide the amount of income and the name and address of the person (natural, corporate, or other entity) from whom the income is to be received. Finally, please attach documentation of said income (e.g., pay stubs) to your Answers to Interrogatories in Aid of Execution.

2. Please state the name, address, and telephone number of any accounting firm that performed work for you from [the date three years prior to judgment] to the present. In your answer, please describe the nature and extent of the work performed, identify the name of the individual accountant performing such work, and identify the inclusive dates during which such work was performed.

3. Identify each and every parcel of real property, fee simple, or leasehold in which you, individually, as a member of a partner-

ship, or as co-owner with any other person or entity, had any interest whatsoever from and after [the date three years prior to judgment], and with regard to each, state the type of interest held, state the names and addresses of all co-owners, identify and describe the deed or other instrument under which you acquired title to the interest held, and state which properties produce any income and the amount of income produced.

4. Give a complete list of all persons who owe you, or any one or more of the partnerships of which you are a partner or member, any money or accounts receivable and/or who are holding any money or credits to which you, or any one or more of the partnerships of which you are a partner or member, is or will in the future become entitled, giving names and addresses, amounts owed or held, date payable, and state whether you consider the same to be collectible or uncollectible. Attach all documents referring or relating to same.

5. List each and every motor vehicle, boat, outboard motor, marine motor, or marine property, business and/or recreational machine, and/or equipment of any kind in which you individually, or as co-owner with any other person, have any interest whatsoever, stating the exact interest which you have therein and the location of the same, and giving, when applicable, the make, model, serial number, title or registration and license number, and with respect to each motor vehicle, boat, machine, or piece of equipment listed above, which is neither your sole property free from liens nor other encumbrances, state the name, address, occupation, and relationship to you, if any, and the precise interest, lien, or encumbrance of each person, company, or corporation claiming any interest, lien, or encumbrance in each item of property.

6. State whether you own or have any interest in any goods, wares, merchandise, money, furniture, fixtures, chattels, old coins or stamps, jewelry or diamonds, stocks, patents, or copyrights and if so, state the value and location of each, the nature of your interest therein, and identify all persons possessing any lien or encumbrance upon all or any part of the personal property, stating fully the type of lien or encumbrance, date incurred

or acquired, face amount thereof, and balance due thereon as of the date answer is given, date balance due, and whether or not payments are in arrears.

7. List all sources and amounts of gross income you have had in each of the last three years, state the total allowable tax deductions for each year, and show the adjusted gross income you reported to the income tax authorities in each of the last three years.

8. State whether you are the legatee, devisee, or beneficiary of any will, estate, or trust fund; and if so, give the nature of the interest, the amount payable, and when it is or will be received and references to any court proceedings. Attach all documents referring or relating to same.

9. State whether, in the last three years, any court or tribunal has entered any judgment(s) in your favor against any person or entity in any cause of action or claim; if so, give the title of said cause of action or claim and the name of the court or tribunal in which same is filed.

10. State whether there is any pending litigation (including workers' compensation claim) to which you are a party, in any court, or administrative agency; or whether there is any action in which you claim or anticipate any settlement or monetary recovery; and if yes, identify the pending litigation or action. Attach all documents referring or relating to same.

11. State whether you paid any debts or allowed any judgments or liens to be entered against you or your property within the last twelve months; giving the nature of the debt, lien, or judgment; the amount thereof; by whom obtained or to whom paid, and the date or dates thereof.

12. Identify all bank accounts, checking accounts, certificates of deposit, or other documents evidencing accounts between [defendant's name] and any financial institution. Attach all documents referring or relating to same.

13. Identify and attach hereto all Federal and State income tax returns, including all amended returns and all schedules and

attachments thereto, from [the date two to five years prior to judgment] to the present.

Model Questions for a Company ONLY

1. Identify and describe any disposition, transfer, or sale of your assets not in the ordinary course of business, including, but not limited to, the winding down of your affairs from [the date three years prior to judgment] through the date on which you respond to these Interrogatories.

2. State whether you are an ongoing business concern; and if not, state why you are no longer an ongoing business concern and the date on which you stopped functioning as an ongoing business concern.

3. Identify and describe the disposition, transfer, or sale of your assets to any person or entity from [the date three years prior to judgment] through the date on which you respond to these Interrogatories.

4. Identify all of your current accounts receivable and attach all documents referring or relating to same.

5. Identify all shareholders, officers, and directors of [name of defendant] from [the date three years prior to judgment]. Attach all documents referring or relating to same.

6. [For use with preceding interrogatory] For each individual identified in your answer to interrogatory No. 5, identify the amount and date of all dividends, salary, bonuses, or other payment to that individual from [the date three years prior to judgment] to the present. Attach all documents referring or relating to same.

7. Identify all interim and/or annual financial statements, income and expense statements, and asset and liability statements of [name of defendant], audited if available, for each year from [the date three years prior to judgment] to present.

8. Identify any of your assets not heretofore mentioned in your Answers to the Interrogatories in Aid of Execution. Attach all documents referring or relating to same.

Creating Your Own Questions

If you decide to prepare your own questions, keep the following rules in mind:

1. *You can ask only about the defendant(s).* If you do not have a judgment against someone, you have no right to their financial information. In other words, a judgment against one individual does not entitle you to information about the financial affairs of that individual's spouse. However, you do have a right to find out if the debtor transferred any of his assets to his wife in an attempt to keep them from you.

    You can also ask any and all questions about the judgment debtor's interests in various assets. Thus, if the debtor is involved in a partnership, you have the right to find out how much the partnership (and hence how much the debtor's share) is worth.

2. *Stay focused.* Although you can cause the debtor a lot of inconvenience by making him produce tons of documents, harassing him is not your goal—getting your money is. Only request information that is likely to be helpful to you in locating assets. In other words, don't ask for bank statements going back five years just because you can. Only ask for the things likely to be relevant and useful.

3. *Keep the questions general.* The more specific a question is, the greater the opportunity for the debtor to avoid giving you information. For example, if you ask the debtor to produce information on all bank accounts held at NationsBank, N.A., he can answer "none" if he moved the account to another institution the day before you filed your Interrogatories. Instead, ask the debtor to produce all information concerning all current bank accounts.

4. *Always request documents.* Documentation is the key to getting your money. You should always require the debtor to produce documents to back up his answer. For example, if you requested information on the debtor's bank accounts, your interrogatory should also instruct the debtor to attach copies of the bank statements to his Answers to Interrogatories.

Oral Examination: Asking the Defendant About His Finances in Person

The other way to discover the defendant's assets is through oral examination—forcing the defendant to come to court and answer your questions under oath. Basically, these are the same questions you would ask in written Interrogatories as shown above. In addition to compelling the defendant to appear in court, you can and should require that he bring his financial records so you can write down relevant facts such as employment information and bank account numbers. (You won't have access to a photocopier while at the courthouse, so take along a pad and pencil.)

To compel the defendant to testify in court about his assets and property, you must file what is normally known as a Request for Order directing defendant to appear for oral examination in aid of enforcement of judgment. This form is available from the clerk's office. Note that each form applies only to one defendant. If you obtained a judgment against more than one defendant, you must fill out a separate form for each defendant you would like to have appear for an oral examination.

A judge will consider the request and sign the Order compelling the defendant to comply. (I've never seen a judge refuse to sign the Order as long as the form is completed correctly.) The completed form, now constituting a court Order, must be served on the defendant. (See chapter 10 for serving instructions.) The Order will specify the time, date, and place for the defendant to appear for the oral examination.

Court-Sponsored Investigations

Certain states (identified on the state law chart) take matters into their own hands if the defendant refuses to pay a judgment. These states issue court Orders that the defendant either come to court to disclose assets to the court or require the defendant to issue a written disclosure directly to the plaintiff/judgment creditor.

The net result is that if the defendant refuses to comply with the court-Ordered disclosure, a bench warrant can be issued for his or her arrest. Pretty powerful stuff! Refer to the state law chart to check out the procedures in your area.

Collecting Your Money!!!

Interest on Your Judgment

Don't forget that interest accrues at "the legal rate" on unpaid judgments. The "legal rate" changes from state to state, but normally is between 6 percent and 10 percent. Unless the judge or notice of judgment from the court says otherwise, this is the rate at which interest will continue to accrue on the outstanding balance of the judgment. Thus, if you received a judgment for $1,000 on January 1, assuming no payments were made, at a 10 percent rate the debtor would owe $1,100 by the next January 1. (Note that this is simple, not compound, interest.)

Planning Your Attack

Now that you know the whereabouts of the defendant's financial resources, it is time to go get them. The state chart on pages 114–117 will tell you what your options include.

If all options are available, when it comes to collecting a judgment, I view bank accounts as the best targets, followed by the debtor's employment, personal property, and, finally, real estate.

Your goal is to collect as much money as you can with as little wasted effort as possible. With that in mind, don't pursue all of the options at the same time. Garnish the debtor's bank account and see how much money you collect before moving on to the next step. Same goes with garnishing the debtor's wages. Wait and see what you get before going through the hassle of locating and selling his car, boat, or van. You may find that only one (or even the threat of one) of the above steps is all you need to collect every penny you're owed.

I often give this a try even if I don't know where the debtor banks. I'll serve garnishments on five or ten banks in and around where the judgment debtor works or lives. About half the time, this "fishing expedition" comes up with an account. If you come up empty or secure only enough money to satisfy part of your judgment, keep going by trying either other banks or other methods of collection.

My second favorite point of attack is wages. Wage garnishments rely upon the employer to deduct a portion of the debtor's wages and send the check for that amount directly to you until the debtor either stops working for that employer or the judgment is satisfied. Chances are you will have to wait a while to collect your judgment in full, but regular payments can do a lot to help your frame of mind.

You should also keep in mind that wage garnishments may still be used even if the debtor is self-employed or is the sole employee of his own corporation. If the debtor gets wages from anywhere, they are subject to attachment as directed by state law. Thus, if you would like to explore this method and you know where and for whom the debtor works, proceed to page 00 and follow the procedure to have a portion of the debtor's paycheck forwarded directly to you. If you don't get enough money from this step to pay off your judgment, keep going.

If the bank account attachment and wage garnishment are either not allowed or don't pan out for you, my third point of attack is directed at the debtor's personal possessions. If you know the make, model, and tag number of the debtor's car, proceed to page 280 and follow the procedure to have the car sold so that the net proceeds can be sent to you to satisfy your judgment. If you don't get enough money from this step to pay off your judgment, keep going.

Finally, my least favorite method of executing on a small judgment—real estate levies. If the debtor owns any real estate (including the house he lives in), you can theoretically sell the property so that the net proceeds can be sent to you to satisfy your judgment.

Making a Withdrawal from the Defendant's Bank Accounts

In legal terms, taking the defendant's money out of his bank account is called attaching or garnishing his account. Garnishments are Orders from the court that the defendant's money be seized by the bank and sent to someone other than the defendant.

The mechanics are simple. First, you must request that the court issue this Order. Request for garnishment forms are available from the clerk free or for a nominal charge. Fill out the form, indicating the name and case designation of your claim, the names of each party, the amount and date of the judgment, and whether any payments had been made to reduce the balance owed.

The Request for Garnishment must then be filed with the court.

Often courts require the payment of a small processing or filing fee—in the neighborhood of five or ten dollars. Copies of the request do not have to be sent to the defendant upon filing, as that would give him a chance to move his bank accounts before the garnishment is processed.

It may take a week or two, but a judge will evaluate the request and, if the form is filled out correctly, issue the Order. All that remains is to serve the Order upon the receiving bank. To ensure proper service, simply call the bank while filling out the form and ask for the name and address of the person to whom the garnishment should be directed. Every bank has a designated person or department to handle these matters, as they are far from unique.

Serve the Order for garnishment received from the court on the bank via certified mail, return receipt requested. There is no need to go the expense of hiring a private process server because no bank will be hard to track down or try to evade service.

Upon receiving the Order, the bank will prepare a response advising as to whether it is holding any assets of the defendant that could be used to satisfy your judgment. If the debtor does not maintain an account at the bank or if there isn't any money in the account, the bank will respond that it is holding no assets. On the other hand, if the bank was able to seize assets, you will be advised of the exact amount.

At this juncture, you will be required to obtain a second Order from the court directing the bank to turn the assets over to you. You see, the first Order directed the bank to locate and seize the money. The second tells the bank what to do with it. Once again, the necessary form is available from the clerk.

Which Bank Accounts Can You Attach?

In states allowing this procedure, you can attach any of the defendant's bank accounts with certain limited exceptions:

- You cannot attach an account the defendant holds jointly (unless you also have a judgment against the other holders, too).

- You cannot attach IRAs or retirement accounts.

- You cannot attach escrow accounts.

Timing Tip

How much you get from your garnishment of the debtor's bank account depends to a large extent on luck. You only get what's available in the account at the time the bank first attaches the money. Furthermore, if there isn't enough money available, the bank will not wait until the defendant's balance is high enough to pay you in full.

As a result, if you happen to serve your garnishment right after the debtor makes a deposit but before any checks are drawn on the account, you win! If, however, you serve your garnishment before he makes a deposit or after clearance of all checks written on the account, you will probably not have much to show for your efforts.

Consequently, I recommend that you always have the garnishment form returned to you for service upon the target bank so you can control when the bank attempts to withdraw your money from his account. Since most people get paid on Friday, I recommend that you serve the bank on a Monday. For the same reason, I also recommend that you not have the garnishment served on a Thursday—when most account balances are at their lowest.

Garnishing the Defendant's Wages

If the defendant is working in a state in which wage garnishments are allowed, and you know his employer's name and address, you can have the employer withhold a portion of the defendant's paycheck and send it directly to you. As long as the defendant is employed in a wage garnishment state, his wages can be garnished whether or not he is a resident there. You will not, however, be allowed to garnish the wages of active military duty personnel.

"Wages" include all compensation paid to an employee including:

- Hourly pay or a weekly or monthly salary.

- Commissions.

- Other regularly paid compensation.

Notes About Garnishing Wages

If There Is Another Garnishment on the Defendant's Salary

If the defendant stiffed you, he may very well have done the same thing to other people. Consequently, you may find that someone else is already garnishing the defendant's wages. This means that the employer is already withholding the legal limit from the defendant's paycheck in Order to satisfy someone else's judgment.

Should this happen, you can pursue one of the other methods of securing payment, or you can just stay put. The employer is obligated to begin withholding money to satisfy your judgment as soon as the first judgment is satisfied. You do not have to refile the garnishment—it continues until either the judgment is paid or the defendant leaves his job.

How Much Can You Take?

You will not be allowed to take the defendant's entire paycheck. The law provides that you are allowed to take only a portion of the disposable wages each pay period. In a nutshell, disposable wages equals net pay. The portion of the defendant's pay that will be sent to you each pay period varies from state to state according to a pre-set formula the employer is obligated to apply to the debtor's wages upon receipt of a garnishment.

How to Garnish the Defendant's Wages

The procedure for garnishing wages is almost exactly like that of attaching bank accounts. Fill out your state's request for wage garnishment form and file it along with payment of the nominal filing fee. Once the judge has signed off on your request, turning it into an Order of garnishment, you should serve it on the defendant's employer. The employer will either confirm or deny that the defendant is earning wages subject to garnishment. If confirmed, it will be up to the employer to withhold the appropriate amount of money, direct the money to you, and report his compliance to the court.

Having the Defendant's Personal Property Sold

What Is "Personal Property"?

The term "personal property" refers to things that can be moved (e.g., cars, furniture, a stamp collection, etc.). Unlike property that can be garnished, like money in a bank account, this option concerns property that the defendant has in his personal possession (unlike the money in his bank accounts, which are in the possession of the bank).

Which Property Can You Sell?

You may sell only property that belongs to the judgment debtor.

- If the debtor co-owns property with his spouse, it cannot be sold to pay a judgment that is only against him. This is because a married couple is recognized by state law as being one unified entity and, therefore, entitled to special protection.

- If the debtor co-owns property with a friend, it CAN be sold, but you will be entitled only to the proceeds from the debtor's share. For example, if Johnny Johnson and Paula Smith are each 50 percent owners of some real estate, the property can be sold, and Johnny Johnson's 50 percent share of the net proceeds can be used to pay your judgment against him. You will not be entitled to reap the benefits of Paula Smith's share of the property.

How to Sell the Defendant's Personal Property

To sell the defendant's personal property to help pay your judgment, you must first record the judgment in the jurisdiction where the defendant is keeping it. You must file a request for property garnishment with the court, identifying not only your case and the amount of the judgment but also specifically identifying the property and its location. This is necessary in view of the fact that it will be the sheriff or constable who actually must take possession of the property. (You didn't think you were going to be allowed to walk into the defendant's home and grab it yourself, did you?)

Note that you will be held responsible for all costs, including sheriff's fees, associated with having the sheriff or constable seize the property. The sheriff will be instructed to pick up the property by the court after consideration of your Request for Garnishment. The property will then be sold and you will become entitled to the net proceeds.

Cars Only

For a car, the costs associated with the seizure and sale can be quite substantial, as they include the costs of towing and storage—for which you will be held liable whether or not you are ever able to realize any money on the car. For this reason, you should have a car seized by the sheriff only if it's been determined that the defendant's interest in the car (how much he owns versus how much the bank owns) is of sufficient value to yield a profit at the sale.

Call the local Department of Motor Vehicles to find out how old the car is. All you need is the tag number. If the car is new, chances are that the bank, not the defendant, owns most of it and a sale will yield nothing. If the car is several years old, the defendant's share of it is usually greater and the sale may be more worthwhile. Note that you should always obtain a copy of the title prior to trying to have the car seized. Copies of the titles are available from each state's Department of Motor Vehicles for a nominal fee.

In addition to having a car physically towed and stored, most states have what they call a "levy and leave" policy whereby the sheriff will post a notice of seizure on the car and leave it in place. This option is much less expensive than actual seizure and scares the defendant just as much.

► THE SCROOGE STRATEGY

I know an attorney who swears that the fastest way to get the debtor to pay is to have the sheriff post a seizure notice on the debtor's car right before Christmas. Sure, you may be turned off by this "scrooge strategy," and I am not necessarily recommending that you use it, but it does have two things going for it:

1. most people somehow find extra cash around the holidays— for presents and celebration; and,
2. it certainly does work.

Selling the Defendant's Real Estate

How far can you go to force the defendant to pay his bill? When it comes right down to it, you can sometimes even sell his house. Of course, it is rare that a creditor actually goes to these lengths, but, as seen in the state chart on pages 114–117, the laws of many states do allow it.

Even if it is a theoretical possibility, I suggest that you exhaust all other alternatives first for a number of reasons:

- First, arranging the sale is expensive. You must advertise the sale, pay the auctioneer, and bear all other costs of selling the house. More important, if the sale of the house does not bring enough to cover the mortgages AND these costs, YOU will be held responsible.

- Second, the whole process can be very time-consuming. Often, the creditor winds up spending more time than the claim was worth in the first place.

- Third, as a practical matter, if the debtor is unable to pay a small-claim judgment, with or without a payment plan, before his house is sold, he probably doesn't have enough equity in his home to make the sale worthwhile.

As I said, before you attempt to sell the defendant's home, you should try the other methods first. Nevertheless, if you decide to force the sale of his house, you should make sure that the defendant told you (either in his Answers to Interrogatories or under oath in his oral examination) about the equity he has in his home. Specifically, you should find out and make him document:

- Who owns the home.
- How much the debtor paid for his home.
- How much the debtor owes on the home (with all mortgages combined, not just the first).

How to Sell the Defendant's Real Estate

To sell the defendant's real estate, you must have your judgment recorded in the jurisdiction where the property is located.

Once you have recorded your judgment in the appropriate location, complete the court form for execution and sale of real estate, usually called a request for writ of execution. Always remember to send a copy to the defendant (by first-class mail is fine) upon filing with the court. Not only is this a requirement, but you may find it gives the defendant that little extra incentive he needs to pay you. (As if ruining his credit, attaching his bank account, garnishing his wages, and selling his car weren't already enough.)

After granting the request, the sheriff will post a notice of sale on the property, usually by taping it to the front door. This is an inexpensive and often effective way of providing the defendant with legal notice that his property will be sold to pay your judgment.

As mentioned previously, you will have to agree to incur all expenses associated with the sale, including the advertisements and auctioneer's fees. Once you reach this point, it would be a good idea to hire an experienced auctioneer. You can look them up in the yellow pages or search for one locally on-line. The auctioneer will walk you through the sale and accounting process in your jurisdiction.

Telling the Court When You Get Paid

As the judgment creditor, you are required to advise the court when/if the judgment has been paid—either in full or partially. This is out of fairness to the debtor, who may rely upon reports that the judgment has been satisfied in Order to redeem his credit. Ask the clerk for the Judgment Creditor's Report or other forms necessary to report payments. File a copy of the completed form with the court and send a copy to the debtor by first-class mail.

After your judgment is paid in full, you have the absolute obligation to advise the court that the judgment has been "satisfied." Although many creditors overlook this step, it is an important one. After all, you may be held responsible for any expenses incurred by the debtor, such as legal fees, resulting from your failure to report the judgment as having been paid in full.

Having gone to court, won your judgment, and collected on it, why take the chance of having to pay the money back to the debtor? Simply file what is known as an Order of satisfaction with the court (available at the clerk's office) and walk away congratulating yourself for taking control of your finances, and for a job well done.

Closing Words

If you have read this far, you deserve my congratulations for overcoming the fear that most people have of the court system. You should also be proud that you are gaining as much control over your finances as one could possibly have in today's business world.

This guide was written out of the firm belief that no one should have to surrender their hard-earned money to unscrupulous or uncaring customers simply because of a lack of understanding of the court system or, worse, because the amount owed was too small to justify the expense of hiring a lawyer. I hope you found this reference to be helpful and will turn to it again and again throughout your business life.

Good luck!

Eliot M. Wagonheim
July 1999

Appendix

How to Locate the Hard-to-Find Defendant

Overview

If you are reading this appendix, I have to assume that your debtor is not where you last left him. Either the home or office address he gave you is no longer valid, or it never was. I shall also assume that you have some basic information about your "subject." After all, if you only know his first name, the problem facing you is beyond the scope of this guide. If, however, you *did* get some information (as I recommended in chapter 1), the fact that the debtor skipped town need only delay and not prevent you from recovering your money.

In this appendix I shall provide you with enough information to locate the vast majority of so-called "disappearing debtors." I shall also show you how to get more sophisticated in your search and, if all else fails, where to turn for help.

In today's society, virtually everything anyone does is documented or recorded by somebody somewhere. Even if your defendant has skipped town in the middle of the night, chances are that by morning he will have established, consciously or unconsciously, some record of his new location.

Consequently, the bulk of your search will consist of sending standardized inquiries to various government agencies or private companies requesting information on your subject. Given enough time and the right addresses and information, odds are you will find your man . . . or woman. I have listed some of the most fruitful areas for your search below.

Using Government Records to Find the Defendant

Few words strike fear into the hearts of businesspeople more than "We're from the government; we're here to help you." In this case, however, those words may just be true. Simply put, the government keeps a record of *everything*. Although I have chosen to discuss

only some of the possibilities here, you should know that the government has literally thousands of record-keeping agencies that
may be helpful to you. In fact, the government may be your most
powerful ally in your search.

The Government Printing Office (GPO)

Every year, the GPO puts out a book called, simply, *The Information Book.* It contains the names, addresses, and telephone numbers
of every government office and agency in the United States. You
can consult a copy at your local library. Chances are one of the
agencies listed can help you.

The Post Office

Don't ignore the obvious. Just because your defendant wants to
avoid you doesn't mean he's willing to give up hearing from his
friends and receiving his favorite magazines. Check with the post
office to see if the defendant has left a forwarding address on record.

If you know the address where your subject was living at some
point during the last twelve months, you can get the address to
which his mail is now being forwarded. Send a card, Attention
Postmaster, with the subject's full name and last known address to
the post office closest to the last known address. The new address
will be provided for a one-dollar fee.

Note: If you want to save the dollar, send a letter to the old
address with the marking "DO NOT FORWARD—Address Correc-
tion Requested" on the envelope. The letter will be returned to you,
along with the new address, free of charge.

Driver's License

In our society, a driver's license comes as close as any document to
being the universal identification. Nondrivers are comparatively
rare, and ever those who choose not to drive often obtain a driver's
license for ease in writing checks, buying alcohol, or use whenever
any form of identification is required.

Every state requires its drivers to update their addresses with the
Motor Vehicle Administration. In most states, you can obtain a copy

286

Get Your Money!

of someone's driving record by providing their full name and date of birth along with a nominal fee.

National Driver's Registration Service

Did you ever wonder how police and state governments prevent people with suspended or revoked driver's licenses from getting a license in another state? For the most part, the answer lies with the National Driver' Registration Service. The NDRS can provide you with an astonishing amount of information on subjects applying for new driver's licenses anywhere in the country.

Write to them at:
National Driver's Registration Service
U.S. Department of Commerce
1717 H Street
Washington, D.C. 20510

Tax Records

It has been said that nothing is inevitable except death and taxes. If that is the case, you might as well use it to your advantage.

Federal Tax Records

The Internal Revenue Service will provide you with the date of the last tax return filed by your subject as well as the address listed on the return. If the subject is a person, all you need is the subject's full name and Social Security number. If the subject is a business, you will also need the federal tax number. Send your inquiry to the nearest IRS office.

State Tax Records

Your state government will also provide you with limited information on a person's state income tax filings. Call your state's Treasury Department and find out current fees, available records, and the location to which your written inquiries should be directed.

Property Tax Records

If the subject owns real estate, he will be listed on the tax rolls. The latest tax bill will provide you with the mailing address, location, and value of the property. If the property has been sold, the tax records will provide you with the new owner's name and address. You may be able to find your subject after a friendly chat with the new owners. Never overlook the personal touch!

Voter Registration

Just because he's a deadbeat doesn't mean he's not a good citizen. If you know the county in which the subject might be living and if he is a registered voter, the board of elections can provide you with a significant amount of information. Although they might require a personal visit, it may be worth the trouble. Check your phone book for the applicable county, parish, or borough board of elections.

Credit Reporting Agencies

Most credit reporting agencies will provide information only to subscribers. If your business does not subscribe to any of these services, your best bet is to find a business that does. If your subject is trying to evade your claim, chances are he has left several other disgruntled creditors in his wake. One of these may be a subscriber.

TRW Consumer Relations

The largest credit service agency in the United States is a division of aerospace giant TRW. Information is obtainable from TRW Consumer Relations as long as you can provide the following information:

- Subject's full name.

- Subject's date of birth.

- Subject's spouse's name.

- Subject's Social Security number.

- Subject's previous address with zip code.

Retrieval of credit records is available by letter only. Send your inquiry and the requisite fee ($8.00 as of the time of this writing) to:

TRW Consumer Relations
P.O. Box 5450
Orange, California 92667
(Don't forget—use a money order, not cash or checks.)

Credit-Card Companies

Every major credit-card company has an investigative unit specializing in tracking down deadbeat creditors. If your subject has credit cards, you should contact the appropriate unit and put their resources to work for you. Try one of the addresses below:

American Express: 1200 Concord Pike, Wilmington, DE 18803

Carte Blanche: 3460 Wilshire Blvd., Los Angeles, CA 90010

Diner's Club: 10 Columbus Circle, New York, NY 10019

Exxon: 1251 Avenue of the Americas, New York, NY 10020

MasterCard: 1 Custom House Square, Wilmington, DE 19899

Private Search Companies

Although most people can be located without the expense of hiring a professional, there are times when private search firms can be helpful and even necessary. You can find many such companies on the Web or in such publications as the business-to-business yellow pages.

The Crisscross Directory

The crisscross directory is simply a telephone book in reverse. You look up the listings by address to find names and telephone numbers. With this directory, you can get the names and numbers of your subject's next-door neighbors. Don't overlook these people (or perhaps a disgruntled landlord) in your search for information on your subject's whereabouts.

The Public Library

Without a doubt, the most effective and extensive resource at your disposal is the public library. First and foremost, there are several excellent books that can provide a much more detailed discussion of search techniques than is possible here. Second, your librarian (yes, the librarian) can be extremely helpful in pointing you to such resources as computer access to reporting agencies, directories of state and federal governmental agencies, and the *Haines Criss-Cross Directory*.

Tip: Go to the main library rather than a branch to find more resources.

Conclusion

People who will give up everything—their friends, their contacts, their jobs, their homes—just to avoid paying their bills are rare. By far, most of the debtors you lose track of moved and forgot or decided not to tell you where they could be reached. Chances are, however, your subject did nor change his name or cut all ties from his former circumstances.

Don't overlook checking with former employers and co-workers, or even the people now living in your debtor's old home. You'd be surprised how much people know and are willing to share.

Bottom line: Your chances of finding your debtor and getting your money increase in direct proportion to your determination to collect what's owed you. The information is out there; it is up to you to find it.

I wish you the best of luck.

Index